How to Interpret Your Dreams
and Discover Your Life Purpose

By

Michael Sheridan

Aisling Dream Interpretation
8 Manor Heath
Rathfarnham
Dublin 16
Republic of Ireland

www.HowToInterpretYourDreams.com

Published by: Aisling Dream Interpretation

Editor: Pat Kerr
Illustrations: Brian Sheridan
Cover: James Coleman, Marion Coleman, Marnie Sheridan

© Copyright 2007 Michael Sheridan

ISBN 978-0-9557295-0-8

Acknowledgements

George Rhatigan for developing and sharing his method of dream analysis, and for his encouragement to teach the subject.

Marnie Sheridan, John Sheridan and Paddy McMahon for encouragement to write this book.

Paddy McMahon for his insightful books.

Pat O'Reilly for pushing me into public speaking.

Neal Keyes for all his help.

Table of Contents

Table of Figures

Forward

You see things; and you say, 'Why?' But I dream things that never were; and I say, "Why not?"

— **George Bernard Shaw**

The word 'dream' in the English language, or its equivalent in other languages, is probably one of the most familiar words in our vocabulary. It tends to have a variety of uses, such as, visionary, as in the above quotation, or wishful, as in hoping to win a lottery or to meet a soul mate or to have a successful career. Such dreams would fall into a category of waking or conscious experiences (mostly!), but the most common form of dreams, I suppose, are the unconscious ones, those that happen to us while our bodies are asleep. In this book Michael helps us to bring the unconscious into the conscious by exploring those dreams and illustrating how interpreting them can help us to free ourselves from restrictive patterns of conditioning.

In the preface Michael outlines the process by which he came to accept that there's more to life than he had previously acknowledged in his scientifically based philosophy. The result to date of this evolution is encapsulated in his book, a significant feature of which is it's deeply spiritual orientation.

A glance at the index shows the comprehensive range of the book. All the issues that feature prominently in people's lives – such as, health, relationships, careers, material challenges, searching for spiritual fulfilment – are covered.

As he has shown in his many public appearances, including radio and television, Michael is an accomplished communicator, who succeeds in bringing simplicity to what are potentially complex and confusing areas of exploration. G.K.Chesterton said, "Angels can fly because they take themselves lightly." Michael, in his angelic mode, invites us to fly with him through our dreams.

Paddy McMahon
(Patrick Francis)

Preface

If anyone had told me before 1990 that I would write this book I would have gotten a hernia from laughing at them. In fact if anyone had tried to talk to me about almost anything in this book I would have immediately branded them as idiot, as my view was that only idiots and scam artists worked in the psychic field. I believed science held the answers. The subjects of God and religion were closed books to me. If God can do anything, can He make a rock so heavy that even He cannot lift it? Whatever answer you give to that question proves the concept of God is fallible. Well it proved it to me anyway! I had also concluded that there was no life after death. I was wrong!

One night as I was waiting for sleep to come, I was suddenly aware there was something in the room. I sat up in the dark and looked around. At the end of my bed were three spirits very close together! They looked just like ordinary people - two men and a woman. They started walking towards me and I screamed in terror. My wife woke up alarmed. I kept shouting and pointing, "right there, right there", but she could not see them. After getting over her initial shock she managed to calm me down!

My scientific world was rocked! I had either gone mad and imagined them, or they were real. The problem was that I knew I had not imagined them. A few weeks later I saw another spirit. Again I became aware of it shortly after going to bed. I sat up in the room and looked around. This one was different. It was like the torso of a man framed with knotted rope with no arms or legs. It came towards me and stopped just inches away. Then I felt unbelievable pain in my chest; like I was being shocked. After about thirty seconds it continued moving and passed through me. With that the pain stopped. This same spirit would return about every 10 days and bring the same excruciating pain. I had to do something about it. I would have to ask the idiots for help!

I sneaked off to a psychic, making sure nobody knew and that no one on the street recognized me as I knocked on his door. The man immediately said my father, who had died eleven years before, was in the room. He described him accurately and among other things told me I had to stop meditating. He did not tell me how to stop seeing the spirits and despite his other good advice I left quite depressed. The local parish priest did not have the answer either. A few weeks later I was at a mind, body and spirit exhibition and someone there told me how to stop the pain. I tried it the next time the spirit came and it worked! He passed right through me and I did not feel any pain.

I was empowered and over time I saw several other types of spirits with differing colors. I noticed their color reflected their ability or intention. I also read voraciously – picking up every book I could find on the subject. Then it happened. My wife called me from my studies, told me to sit down and put a book called *The Grand Design* into my hands, open on the section she had just read. As I read my heart was jumping and I had butterflies in my stomach. It had the answers to my questions. I did not want to stop reading and my wife had to wrestle the book back from me. For the next few days if she was not reading it, I was! We had fantastic debates about what we read and discussed it with anyone who would listen. By my own definition I had graduated to idiot! Life had never made more sense.

I continued to learn about the spiritual field by reading and doing courses. Then a friend phoned me excitedly. "I just had an amazing experience. I was regressed to a former life and YOU were there. We were in Mayan times at the height of their civilization and I was using crystals to defeat armies of people." He knew I was interested in Stone Age structures and the use of crystals. I had to try it. I phoned the therapist to book an appointment but he suspected I only wanted to do it for fun. He was right. In order to be regressed I had to agree to do it as part of working on myself. We settled on a time and he told me to bring along any recent dreams I had.

The night before my appointment I was out with my wife and the same friend. The conversation turned to family karma. I did not believe in it and expressed my view. They both lit on me saying my biggest issues were with my mother and that was my family karma. They did not convince me and I pushed it out of my mind as I went to bed. When I awoke I wrote down the dream I had during the night and headed off to what I knew was going to be a fantastic experience.

I arrived and was greeted by George. I handed him my dream. He only looked at it for a second and said, "Oh, that's about family karma!" I was thinking of the arguments the night before and smirked. He caught my smirk and elaborated, "You see where you wrote on the first line *I was driving the family car towards my mother's house.* Do you normally refer to it as the family car?" "No. Never", I replied. "Then it is clear – family car is a pun on *family karma* and the dream is about family karma with your mother." I had to give up. Forces greater than me were conspiring to get through my thick skull. I decided to listen.

My regression was not the fascinating experience in Mayan times I had hoped for. Instead it brought me to a former life with my mother and to my birth in this one. As part of the session I began a six week process of cutting the ties with her. George suggested I attend his upcoming course on dream interpretation as analyzing my dreams would show my progress with the therapy. Later that day I asked my oldest sister what she remembered about my birth. I told her about the regression and the dream analysis I had received. It impressed her enough to enroll on George's course with me.

We had missed the first week so knew we had to catch up. I brought along a dream and half way through the evening George gave my dream to the group to be analyzed. No one knew it was my dream. The woman he selected to lead the group was amazing. She described my current problems and explained what the dream said to do about them. She even pulled from the dream that I was born through cesarean section. With my jaw hitting the floor I don't know how they did not figure out it was my dream! I was hooked. I could not believe how good you could get in a week. Who needs to go to a psychic when your dreams have all the answers? I threw myself hungrily into learning how to analyze my dreams. Over the next few weeks I attended the classes, poured over all my dreams and when I'd run out I bugged others to tell me theirs. I had finally found something in the spiritual field that I felt connected with.

On the last night of the course I told George I was a software engineer and asked if he was interested in a partnership to develop a computer program to analyze dreams. He immediately agreed to it. I understood why when he later showed me a transcript of a psychic reading he had gotten in the 70s. It told him he would meet a person who would put his dream work onto an electronic device. The PC as we know it today was not invented at the time of his reading!

My wife attended his next course with me and inadvertently submitted a dream on which I had written my analysis on the back. I was mortified when George asked who analyzed it. When I confessed to it he told me I should be teaching my own courses. I jokingly accused him of telling everyone that. He said he had only come across two people in twenty years of teaching his classes and that the other person was a woman years before. I told him there was a woman on my first class that was excellent and clearly better than me. He said she was the other person and had come back after ten years to do a refresher. I was dumbfounded by the coincidence as it was her analysis of my dream that gave me the bug.

With a lot of encouragement from my wife and George I began teaching my own classes. Almost immediately I was interviewed about dream interpretation on national television. Although used to public speaking, I was so terrified I could hardly remember my own name. I do not know how I got through the interview but I did. Shortly after that I was interviewed on radio by Aidan Cooney. He taught me how to relax during the interview and coached me during each ad break. He persuaded me to take calls from listeners and to interpret their dreams live on air. Instead of the intended twenty minutes he kept me on the air for two hours. I knew I would never have a problem accepting an interview again. Over the years I have been interviewed countless times on radio and television and for several years had a regular slot with Aidan and his colleagues on television. I currently have a regular slot back on the radio station he worked for all those years ago and I convert each interview into a pod cast for my website. All these years later, I still get scared and question my ability before each interview. I guess I will never get over that but once the interview starts and I begin talking about dreams it always seems to work out.

Last November, with a little pushing from my wife, I resigned my software engineering job to develop something on my own. Just six days after I resigned I was approached by a publisher and asked to write a book on dream analysis. The coincidence was amazing. For the first time in twenty years I was free from the pressures of work and had the time to undertake such a project. With the support of my wife I dropped my software plans and began writing this book. It is the culmination of my experience to date while working in this field. I also share what I have learned in various other aspects of the spiritual field and include simple but effective techniques on psychic development. I hope you learn something from my journey.

— Michael Sheridan (July 2007)

1. Introduction

They say dreams are the windows of the soul. Take a peek and you can see the inner workings, the nuts and bolts.

— **Henry Bromel**
Northern Exposure, The Big Kiss

Each morning I wake to the sound of my two-year-old daughter singing in the next room. When I pick her up she is full of excitement at the prospect of another beautiful day on the planet. Adults tend to have lost touch with that feeling, but it can be reclaimed. The solution is simply to put back into place the things that are vital to the enjoyment of life that we have dropped over the years. This can take time, but each step taken, literally adds wonders to life ad the only advice needed is your own! It is ironic that at night, when you let go of reality, your dreams try to awaken you to what you are overlooking. The choice is yours to restore the magic to your life by listening to your dreams.

Dreams focus on the most important step at the present time. The focus could be how to restore your health, how to improve your relationship or career, or it could be simply telling you what you need to accept about yourself. The first step, as with any journey, is always about finding out where you are. Dreams show you this and map your journey to where you need to be. The key to unlocking dreams is through understanding the symbols on the map.

Dream interpretation is not new, but in our 'Western' pursuit of science has been forgotten or overlooked by many. As far back as the Old Testament, Joseph showed us that dreams contain important messages. Native American cultures hold dreams in high regard as messages from the spirit world. Saint Patrick was told to come to Ireland in a dream. Einstein admitted to a journalist that his entire scientific career was a meditation on a dream he had as a teenager where he was sledding at the speed of light. Dmitri Mendeleyev dreamed the periodic table in 1869. Friedrich von Kekule revolutionized organic chemistry through determining the structure of the benzene molecule from a dream. The list goes on and on.

The most puzzling thing about dreams for most people is why, if we are meant to understand them, do dreams come to us in symbolic form and why do they appear as a mish mash of seemingly meaningless events? The answer is that dreams are created by you, and because you create them, you can also certainly understand them. With regard to why they are symbolic, recent scientific advancements in brain scanning have taught us much about the two hemispheres of our brain and how they co-operate. The left hemisphere is sequential and deals with one thing at a time. It specializes in analysis. The right hemisphere deals with things simultaneously and specializes in recognizing shapes and connecting isolated events in order to synthesize a bigger picture. The left hemisphere excels at language but the right interprets metaphors, the facial expression of the speaker and how they are speaking. If I were to say it is raining cats and dogs you would understand it even though it logically makes no sense.

Dreams are the big picture. They don't sequentially cover a topic. Lots of things are there at the same time all interacting. Brain scans during dreaming show our visual processing center, our emotional processing center and our long term memory are all active. The symbolism and use of metaphors in dreams is obviously a right hemisphere process. However, when we try to understand our dreams we tend to use our left hemisphere to analyze individual symbols. To be effective at interpreting our dreams, we must engage our right hemisphere and look again at the dream as a metaphor. It does not make sense to the left brain but if we let the right brain in on the task, the dream begins to unfold. The interpretation process requires taking into account all the symbols in the dream at the same time. When you have successfully done so, the interpretation will resonate with you and you will be in no doubt that you understand it.

Take John, for example, who dreamt that Van Morrison was sitting on the floor holding a pint of Guinness in his hand and arguing with his wife. In reality John and his wife were having an ongoing conflict. With the help of dream analysis John learned that he was holding onto a black and white attitude (holding the black and white Guinness) which he had picked up from watching his own parents deal with conflict in his childhood (when John used to sit on the floor).

Amy, who was putting off dealing with childhood issues regarding her mother, dreamt of attending her funeral. At the funeral she noticed the lid on top of the coffin could slide but she was reluctant to open it. She didn't want to see the level of decomposition of her mother's body. In effect, through metaphors her dream is saying, "I am reluctant to open the lid on my mom and look at what I know will be unpleasant".

From the two examples above, it can be seen that taking a symbol in isolation is not the key to interpretation. Context, location and other symbols all come to bear on what a symbol means. In my symbol reference, I explain how the meaning of a symbol can change radically through using examples from real dreams. I will also refer back to topics covered separately and in detail earlier in the book, from which you can get lots of additional information. At the end of some chapters, real dreams covering the relevant topic are fully interpreted by using the information from the reference section. This book covers many topics including health, relationships, career, spirituality, psychic development and your life purpose.

So what are dreams? Dreams are the language of the soul. Through dreams, the soul comments on all aspects of our lives such as health, relationships, career and spirituality.

Health dreams have benefits that cannot be over exaggerated. For example, we know that heart related illness is the leading cause of deaths in the Western world. However, each person who has died in this way had thousands of dreams alerting them of their fatal condition. There is no such thing as a sudden heart attack or stroke. Dreams provide an early warning system for these and other health problems in time for action to be taken, and what is best about dreams is that they also describe the action to take! You will discover that dreams can link physical conditions to events that happened earlier in life. If linked in your dreams these events are the trigger or cause of a condition and need to be dealt with to remove the threat. Appropriate techniques for doing this are also explained.

Relationship advice from a reliable source is always useful and you can't get better advice than from your dreams. Is this relationship *the one*? Are you moving at the right pace? What can you do to keep this one? Are you heading for trouble? If so what do you need to do now to avoid it? If you have previously had a bad relationship are you carrying baggage into this one? All this and more is answered in your dreams.

While it may seem strange, dreams can also tell you what career you should be in. Are you a teacher, a musician, a writer, a counselor? Your dreams help here by telling you what you should be doing and often what your particular slant on it is. When is it right to apply for a promotion and when are others working against you to block your path? If you are in the wrong career your dreams will tell you when it is time to move on and what path to follow.

Spirituality is expression of the soul and includes art, literature, poetry, music, singing and meditation. It also includes spiritual gifts such as channeling, counseling, spiritual healing, absent healing, psychic ability, hypnotism and more. Each of these is explained later. If you already work in the spiritual field your dreams will tell you if you are on the right path and help you sharpen your abilities. If you are considering moving into this field your dreams will tell you exactly what you need to do.

For many, the idea of spiritual gifts seems alien. To understand them you need to discard the idea that you are a body with a soul. You do not have a soul - you *are* a soul and you *have* a body. Literally you are a soul, which temporarily has a body. The body will eventually die but you (the soul or spirit) will live on. This change of perspective will help you enormously to open your mind. The ability to talk with spirits, for example, rather than being supernatural, is natural since that is what you first and foremost are - a spirit. Once explained properly, you'll see the benefits of each particular spiritual gift. You'll learn the difference between gifts, how to recognize them in dreams and how to develop them.

The key to a healthy, happy and successful life is handed to you many times each night. The choice is yours to turn the key and open the door onto a bright new world full of the magic that children see. Nobody can stop dreaming. It is as vital to us as our heartbeat. Tonight, within minutes of falling asleep you'll find yourself back at the door to this mystical world. What will you learn this time on the other side of the threshold?

2. How to Interpret Dreams

He felt that his whole life was some kind of dream and he sometimes wondered whose it was and whether they were enjoying it.

— **Douglas Adams**
The Hitchhiker's Guide to the Galaxy

I am frequently told by people with a novice interest in dream analysis that only the dreamer can interpret their own dream. This is quite untrue. While it is certainly true that any dreamer can get to a level of proficiency with interpreting their dreams, they can not do this without learning how. There are several reasons for this.

A person is quite often too close to the subject matter of their dream to be objective enough to extract the meaning. It takes a lot of honesty, for example, to read from your own dream that you are vindictive. Even if you are honest, you could be completely blind to that part of your nature because you have been that way for most of your life. Think of it this way – we are affected by gravity but it took an apple falling on Newton before anyone became aware of it as an influence in our lives. Dreams are like apples being dropped on you. Dream interpretation gives you hands to catch them – otherwise they just hit you on the head with little lasting effect.

If you have not learned the language of dreams you cannot expect to understand it. You can no more intuitively pick up the language of dreams than you can intuitively pick up Chinese. It is not that either language is difficult but you at least acknowledge you must take lessons to understand Chinese. How many times have you told a friend of your dream in which they featured? I have overheard complete strangers recount their dream to a friend while riding an elevator. They do not have a clue of how much they are telling about themselves! Hopefully from reading this book you will know which dreams to keep to yourself! So here now are some of the basic rules of the language of dream interpretation.

Everything Is You

For the beginner, this is probably the most difficult aspect of dreams to accept. Dreams of family members, friends, and enemies all represent various aspects of your personality such as ideas, emotions, hopes, fears and ideals. These people appear in your dreams, for example, to show you that you are being influenced in some way, have a trait similar to them or need to develop a trait they already posses. If you lack confidence you may dream of a friend who exudes confidence. The dream picks that friend for your dream to symbolically give you confidence.

Solid things such as houses, buildings and cars reflect your physical body. The structure of a house being shown in bad repair indicates poor health in present or future time. When a dream points out a physical health problem that you already have it explains why you have it and what to do about it. If a dream warns of a condition you do not have it is warning you that you could develop it but also tells you how to avoid developing it in the first place.

Symbols of fire, including bombs, electricity, and lightning represent your heart, circulatory system and emotions. For example, a dream in which lightning is striking and causing damage to a house is demonstrating how negative emotions (lightning) are affecting your physical health (structure of house being damaged). As you might suspect from statistics on heart related health problems the heart and emotions are a very common theme in dreams.

Air, atmosphere and the interior of a room show your state of mind with regard to the subject matter of the dream. A dark gloomy room indicates depression while a dirty, dingy room indicates a negative or angry state of mind. Dark clouds overhead also indicate depression.

Water symbols such as the sea, rivers, lakes, and canals reflect your spiritual or cultural life. In this context spirituality has to do with expression of your soul – expression that frees your spirit. It could be music, singing, teaching, leading, counseling, healing, art, poetry, writing and more. A river indicates you need a more natural spiritual flow as rivers follow their own path. Canals and swimming pools are man made structures and indicate that man-made or conventional ideals are restricting your spiritual flow. A lake or pool indicates that you do not have a spiritual outlet as these bodies of water have no outlet. The sea or ocean indicates your spirituality or life is the subject matter. Diving into any body of water is a request for you to get into life.

If you dream of polluted water, it is the condition of your blood that is being highlighted. This indicates a need to cleanse your blood by a change of diet and possibly including improved elimination as toxins are getting into your bloodstream.

Since everything in the dream is an aspect of you, when looking at a dream consider what aspects are represented by objects, location, adults, children, animals, colors, emotions, activities and puns.

Symbols are linked to show cause and effect

All the symbols in a dream are linked to show cause and effect. This is the main problem with just using dream dictionaries to interpret a dream. All symbols in a dream create a context which affects the interpretation of other symbols. For example, if your father appears in a dream about your stomach the dream puts him there to link your current stomach problems to your relationship with him. If you currently do not have stomach problems the dream is pointing out that unless you do something to heal the negative effects of your relationship with him you have the potential to develop a problem there.

In this way, apparently unconnected symbols, people, emotions and events are linked in a chain of cause and effect. Use this to show why you are ill, depressed, cannot get on with your spouse, boss, partner or why your career is not getting off the ground.

Personal Responsibility

Since everything in your dream is an aspect of you it follows that you are always responsible for what happened, is happening, can happen or will happen in the dream. In dreams we find all kinds of apparent accidents and blockages to progress that inhibit movement. On the surface these seem to be outside your control but the reality is that you are responsible for your own progress. For example, an airplane departure symbolizes getting a new project off the ground. However, if in your dream your partner's handbag is stolen along with your passports, you may be inclined to read into the interpretation that your partner is causing problems that are blocking your project from taking off. The reality is, however, that you are using problems in your relationship as an excuse to block your new project. Similarly a delay at an airport means you are reluctant to get a new project off the ground.

Avoidance

Look for what you are trying to avoid in the dream. This is what you need to accept or face up to in waking life. Dreams try to create wholeness or completeness in you by drawing scattered aspects of your personality together. If in real life you suppress your emotions you may still try to avoid them in your dreams. Your dreams, however, will insist that you accept this and all other aspects of your personality. Similarly, dreams ask you to face your fears. In this way you can come to terms with them and heal them.

For example, a woman dreamt she was standing on the roof of the General Post Office in Dublin in a civil war. There is scaffolding around the building. She fears for her life and steps back from the edge of the roof. In reality the woman was in a development circle to learn how to channel (communicate with spirits) and was puzzled as to why her progress seemed stalled. Her dream tells her why. She is *stepping back from the edge* because she fears for her life when it comes to using her channeling ability (indicated by the post office). Not that long ago (civil war in Ireland) people were persecuted and even hanged (scaffolding in the dream) for publicly communicating with the dead. What she must overcome is easily determined from what she avoids in the dream

3. Dreams and Your Health – Introduction

What if nothing exists and we're all in somebody's dream? Or what's worse, what if only that fat guy in the third row exists?

— **Woody Allen**
Without Feathers

Of the hundreds of pages on my website, the health section is the least read and yet the analysis of health dreams is so beneficial for the dreamer. How much would you pay a doctor who could prevent all serious illness by following you throughout your life and observing you? The doctor would observe each and every activity, accurately calculating its effects on your physical and mental health, every morsel of food you eat to determine your tolerance to the food and its effect on your body and mind, every trauma you suffer to determine its impact and establish your psychological state? You would never see the doctor or even be aware of his presence but each night he would send you his report that includes detailed information on all observations with advice on how to improve your situation. You are free to act on his advice or to completely ignore it. Any advice you ignore that is still relevant tomorrow will be repeated in that report. How much would you pay for that service?

The reality is that you do not have to pay anything. You have already engaged this doctor's services and he has been sending you his reports since you were born – wrapped in dreams. All you have to do is unwrap and read the reports. This is the most under utilized aspect of dream analysis. Like most things that are free in life it is often ignored. The beauty of health dreams is that they report on potential future health problems years in advance. Their advice is based on everything about you from the day you were born until now. Nothing else in your life, short of divine communication, can match it.

Each night your body is scanned and dreams are dispatched to report on areas that need attention. They alert like the warning lights in your car – here is a problem that requires your attention now! The dream explains why the warning is there, what needs to be done to

Titles

The main focus of a dream is revealed in the title so always title your dream or get the person telling you their dream to title it. This is excellent for extracting the subject matter, particularly when the dream is very long.

address it and thus remove any health threat. Ignoring the warnings in your dreams is like ignoring the warning lights in your car. It could cost you dearly and it could be your life.

When warnings about health issues are ignored over a long period of time, disease can manifest in your body. Disease in the body is another, albeit stronger, warning light that is a symptom of an imbalance in an aspect of your functioning. While always advancing, Western medicine treats conditions such as cancer, with surgery to remove it. This is analogous to stopping your car, ripping open the dashboard and removing a flashing oil light. Yes it has the immediate effect of stopping the warning light but your car will grind to a halt further down the road. You have removed the symptom but not addressed the real problem. Treating the cause by putting oil in your car will cure the problem and remove the symptom. This is what your dreams ask you to do and the real advantage of dreams is that they warn you years in advance of any physical symptoms, so you have plenty of time to heed their advice and avoid problems.

I am not for one minute advocating that you avoid western medical methods for dealing with health problems. I would be the first in line myself to avail of them! Rather I am saying it is best to complement what your doctor can do by referring to your dreams and following their advice too.

How Dreams Focus on your Body

As you will see, dreams use physical objects to represent your physical body. The most common symbols are houses, buildings and cars. For example, if you find yourself in your kitchen, a place where you prepare and eat food, the dream is about your digestive system. A dream taking place in a restaurant (a building) could be about the same thing. The house in the dream does not have to be your actual house. Sometimes dreams use different dwellings because there is something distinct about them. For example, if you dream of being in a neighbor's house looking at their new kitchen, the dream is attempting to heal problems with your digestive system (kitchen) by symbolically giving you a brand new one.

Different parts of a house represent different parts of your body. The connection is made symbolically to a part of your body that has a similar function. In that way bathrooms represent your elimination system. Bedrooms represent your reproductive system and the need for rest. The attic represents your brain – the top of your body. The back door represents your rectum – the back door to your body. The stairs represents your spine as a stepped object that goes from the base of your body to just below your head (attic). The heating system represents your circulation as it circulates through the house. The electrical wiring represents your nervous system, and so on.

Many of the locations just listed have meanings other than for physical health. To emphasize physical health as the subject matter of a dream, focus is often drawn to physical objects within the location. For example, seeing a crack in the toilet bowl suggests the dream is about your elimination system and the focus on the cracked bowl reinforces this and further refines the attention to your bowel (pun on bowel).

As you will see, dreams point out a physical condition you have, what caused it and what needs to be done to resolve it. If you do not already have the condition, the dream is alerting you to the fact that you are likely to develop it and what the underlying cause is, so you can take steps to prevent it from manifesting.

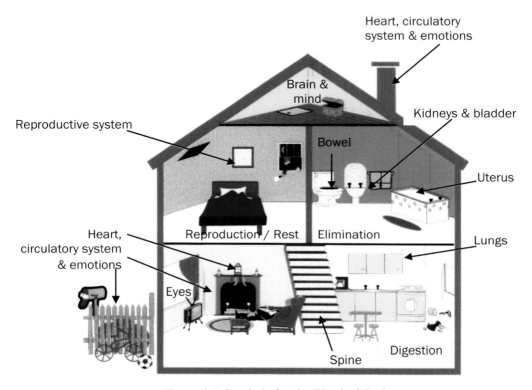

Figure 3-1 Symbols for the Physical Body

4. Heart Matters

We teach people how to remember, we never teach them how to grow.

> — Oscar Wilde
> *Lady Windermere's Fan*

If I say you need to look after your heart what comes to your mind? You probably conjure up an image of the physical organ in your body and then think of other things like diet and exercise. You tick mental boxes beside memories of how often you exercised or ate the *right* food. A quick analysis will deliver a result telling you that you either need to do more or that your heart should be just fine. While it is true the heart needs these things, the way to a healthy heart starts way before you get to either diet or exercise. The way is *balance*.

You are a fusion of male and female energy which ideally should be in balance. The fact that you are a fusion of male and female energy cannot be questioned. The physical you did not come into existence until a male sperm fused with a female egg. Thus your physical form was created; a fusion of male and female energies, both in harmony and balanced. For the rest of your life, each cell in your body and therefore your whole being will continue to be a fusion of that male and female energy. In the West this obvious fact of nature is often overlooked. This is possibly through the confusion of mistaking male and female

Summary

▶ Heart related illness is the biggest cause of death in the Western world. Your dreams warn you years in advance of any action you need to take to keep your heart healthy.

▶ Balanced expression of feelings is as important for your heart as diet and exercise.

▶ Western education biases us towards suppression of feelings. In general only intellectual prowess is measured.

▶ We are a fusion of male and female energy. To move from karma to dharma requires balance and an open heart.

▶ Trauma can cause a wall to be built around your heart to keep from feeling the pain. In adulthood dreams ask that the wall be torn down to restore connection to feelings.

▶ Listening to your heart can become second nature but takes practice.

energies with men and women but that is not the same thing at all. It is perhaps that analogy that causes the concept to be rejected most often. Female energy has nothing to do with being a woman and male energy has nothing to do with being a man. Qualities of either energy can show through in any person regardless of gender.

Knowledge of this fusion of energies is endemic in other cultures. The Chinese concept of Yin and Yang, the symbol for which is shown here, will help illustrate what it means. The outer circle represents you and the black and white shapes within the circle represent the interplay of male and female energy within you. These energies are constantly interacting. Indeed their very interaction is a vital component of life. Neither shape is completely one color, signifying that neither energy can exist without the other and that nothing can be completely just one energy. In Chinese philosophy Yin and Yang extends to everything. You cannot have night without day, light without dark, life without death, positive without negative. Everything is a system of balance.

Figure 4-1 Yin and Yang

In the Hindu chakra system, the heart chakra is the balance point, integrating the world of matter (the lower three chakras) with the world of spirit (the upper three chakras).

Within this balanced system, your heart is governed by female energy and your head by male energy. While this has nothing to do with gender, men in general do tend to display more male energy traits while women show more female energy traits. Women are often accused by men of being too emotional while men are accused by women of being too logical. Emotions come from your heart while logic comes from your head.

A balanced heart is one that is given the opportunity for emotional expression. This is a two way street, a system of give and take. Let your heart feel other people's emotions and allow yourself to express how you feel both to yourself and to others. This sounds so obvious but I can say with certainty that many of us train ourselves not to do it. Indeed we have trained ourselves so well that we are not even aware we are blocking it anymore. Left unchecked, the physical effect of this behavior can be disastrous. An imbalance in your heart can lead to related physical health problems. Indeed heart related illness is responsible for almost half of all deaths in the Western world. Although many people are aware of this staggering statistic they view it merely as a statistic and for some reason people don't relate well to statistics. I encounter this regularly. I am often asked for symbols that indicate cancer but never asked how dreams indicate heart problems! This in itself is indicative of a problem. In my experience, we as a society are not really concerned about our hearts and that leaves the door open for problems to manifest without us even being aware.

We are living in a male energy age - The Piscean Age. We are moving into a female energy age, The Aquarian Age, but we are not there yet. In this male energy age, society has very much adopted male institutions such as the church, the medical profession, schooling, government, etc. These institutions will change in harmony with the female energy of The Aquarian Age or they will be pushed out. Until then we suffer the effects of this male dominance in our society. Again don't confuse male and female energy with men and women. For women to succeed in male energy institutions they must become as male energy oriented as their male counterparts.

You may be surprised to see schooling in my list of male institutions, so let me explain why it is there. Our schools place emphasis on academic achievement (male side of ourselves) and very little on expression of the very feelings within that make us what we are. We are taught in this way from a very young age. The separation of male and female aspects grows as we progress through the school system. Our children are taught to read and answer questions on texts to measure their comprehension (male) - compassion is not encouraged. Children are not given tests that measure their feelings of love, sadness, happiness, anger, joy, etc. or lessons that teach them how to express these feelings. You never see a question on a paper that asks, "*How did you feel when...?*" There is no system in place or training given to mark an answer given to a question like this. It is not that we don't have the ability. Counselors measure and help people to express their feelings all the time. However, it is deemed irrelevant in the pursuit of academic achievement. There are exceptions to this rule but the exceptions are individuals working within a system rather than the system itself.

While the educational system biases us towards suppression of feelings, for many of us the suppression starts at a much younger age. Through hypnotic regression of others I have seen patterns that show typically when separation from feelings begins. A newborn infant expects and needs unconditional love from mother. If this love is not given or not given unconditionally, the newborn feels a great sadness and sense of loss. A newborn cannot rationalize and can only view the world through feelings. This sadness continues for as long as the child is not loved unconditionally. Many parents are guilty of arguing about their newborn or young child in their presence - assuming that a lack of understanding of spoken language prevents the child from picking up on their anguish. This couldn't be further from the truth. The child is more in tune with the parent's feelings than the parent is! They have not yet learned to suppress their sensitivity! They live in this wash of feelings searching for the unconditional love from mother that makes life worth the effort.

Regressions have also shown me that this deep sadness lasts until at most the end of the second year. By then it is replaced with a very deeply rooted anger. If you could visualize it, a wall develops between the sadness and the anger. The sadness was felt continually by the child and in order to prevent this pain a wall was erected so that others cannot get close enough to hurt them in the future. Outside the wall, anger is directed at all who approach. Those close enough to see the anger are unlikely to ever get past the walled defense to see the sadness that is suppressed. The reality is, however, that we cannot just separate ourselves from one feeling (the sadness). In our attempt to separate ourselves from sadness we separate ourselves from all feelings. It is at this point our potential to develop a physical problem to do with the heart is created! From a child's perspective this is not a problem. Their only concern is to suppress the pain. A pain they now associate with living. Anything that will eventually bring them back to the spirit world they just left is not seen as a threat. Many years later, however, when the memory of the spirit world is obscured, the thought of returning there can evoke great fear!

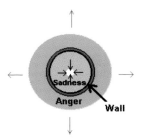

Figure 4-2 Anger as a defense mechanism

As we grow older we lose contact with the fact that we separated from our feelings. That is the whole point of doing it – to train ourselves to forget the pain. So it is unlikely that as adults we will perceive any problem. How can we be aware of a problem with an aspect of ourselves that we have forgotten about? The answer naturally enough is through our dreams.

How to listen to your heart

While it may require work to get to the point where you are tuned into your feelings naturally, there is a simple technique for listening to what your heart says about a decision you are trying to make. For example, say you are thinking of getting back with your boyfriend. Logically you have worked it out or you wouldn't be this far in deciding but what does you heart think? To find out sit comfortably and close your eyes. Now imagine you are back with your boyfriend and a year has gone by. As you imagine this how do you feel? This is the feeling that will enter your life if you choose that road. Now imagine yourself a year from now but this time you did not get back with your boyfriend. How do you feel as you imagine this? Again this is how you will feel now if you choose that option. One option will be a clear winner. When making decisions, you heart cuts through all the logic and reasons you can give for why things should work out or why they will not. It simply tells you how you will feel and you can't argue with that. The truth is, it is telling you all the time but you analyze the feelings away. That is why in this technique you take away the current logical reasoning by imagining yourself a year into the future. You haven't reasoned that far yet so what gets through first is your heart.

Dream Symbols for the Heart

The more common symbols for the heart and emotions are any symbol of fire; these represent the fire in your heart. A fireplace is a common symbol for the heart as *hearth* is an obvious pun for heart. If you dream of a fire needing to be set and lit in the fireplace you are being asked to take the time to rekindle the passion in your heart. If the fire is already lit it still means the same thing, although in one dream you are being shown the current situation and in the other dream you are being shown what is needed. Since a fireplace symbolizes the heart anything connected with it will do the same. So a chimney pot will also be primarily about your heart but there is a tacit connection with smoking – smoking being bad for your heart.

A furnace and heating system are also about the circulatory system. While the furnace is now obvious because it is a symbol of fire, the heating circulation pump and circulation system reinforce the meaning. The heart is the body's pump and the circulation system speaks for itself. So if you dream of a problem with a heating system water pipe, you don't need the other symbols to know it is a warning of a problem with your circulation system. Indeed when focus is drawn to a physical problem such as a cracked chimney pot, a cracked hearth, a broken pipe and so on, the dream is primarily about your physical health and is to be taken more seriously. If there is no reference to a physical problem the dream is about the emotional health of your heart.

Walls are another common symbol for the heart and circulatory system and symbolize the wall built up to protect you from sadness, as explained earlier. To dream of knocking down a wall is very positive and shows that you are actually taking positive steps towards removing the wall and opening up to your feelings. Indeed it is also common to dream of large open plan houses where there are no walls and where the heat from the fireplace can radiate everywhere around the house. The open plan is again asking you to open up and remove the wall you have built around yourself.

The wall does not have to be part of a house. A wall that defines a property line is a perfect symbol of the heart as it emphasizes the levels you have undertaken to separate yourself from others. You have erected a dividing wall between you and your neighbor – literally you and others who are close to you.

Apartments symbolize this division too with the emphasis here being on how you have separated yourself from your own feelings. If this is your experience, do not expect to comprehend this. It is like riding a bike. You only know how to do it when you have experienced doing it. You cannot know what it is like to live with an open heart where you listen to your feelings unless you have experienced it. The big problem is that when you have shut yourself off from such a young age the vague feelings that get through are mistaken as being able to feel. Trust me on this one – you don't know what you are missing until you experience it. For example, your heart can tell you a lot about a person that you never met before. Even just looking at someone from across the road will remind you of someone you do know and their looks have nothing to do with it. You can then safely assume that their character is much the same as the person your heart says they are like.

Dreaming of women can also be about your emotions but this is not always the case. Women can indicate this because the heart is governed by female energy. It is more likely to be the case if there is more than one woman or if they are exercising or dancing. For example, to dream of women in purple leotards exercising in an aerobics class means it is your responsibility (purple) to exercise emotional expression. Emotional expression does not mean outbursts of rage. Remember this is the biggest clue that you are suppressing your feelings. The anger is a childish protection mechanism. You adopted this technique in childhood but never outgrew it. It is time you let the adult take charge of dealing with the painful experience you went through. (Refer to my website for suggestions on how to do this.) Emotional intelligence requires a full understanding of your feelings and where they are coming from. If you find yourself annoyed easily by someone you just met it is likely that they are pushing a button created in your childhood. If the person doing this is a woman then it is a strong clue that the button was created by your mother. Again, mothers are specifically important here because the heart is governed by female energy. It is 99% likely that any issues to do with expression of feelings will link back to your mother. I have dealt with cases where the person felt that all their problems were due to their father and he was the only one they ever talked about and they slam him at every opportunity. The reality often turns out to be that as a child they adopted their mother's hatred or resentment (fill in the negative emotion that fits for you) towards their father and over their childhood years they took it on as their own. These are the most difficult cases to deal with as the person will insist you are looking in the wrong place altogether. The beauty of dreams is that they will reveal the correct place to look for the cause of a problem. Regardless of what a person consciously thinks, dreams will grab the hand of the dreamer and point their finger where it should be pointing.

To dream of a woman at a cash register indicates that mother put a price on her love. Rather than loving unconditionally she loved as a reward or under specific circumstances which the child learned to recognize and eventually adjusted to. In these dreams the woman with the cash register is usually at the exit of a room. To dream of a dead woman would indicate that you are emotionally dead. An exaggeration to help emphasize the point but be effective all the same. A very common dream I come across is where a person dreams of their dead aunt or grandmother coming back to life through something they are doing, perhaps giving them a blood transfusion. This dream is a request for the dreamer to infuse new life into their heart. The connection to the heart is made through the symbol being a woman and the blood is just another link to the circulatory system. These dreams always make the dreamer wake up feeling wonderful.

Bicycles require balance so also symbolize your heart in dreams. Indeed any wheel, whether on a bicycle, car or other device, also symbolizes the circulatory system. Wheels are circular and any circular pattern indicates your circulation system through the pun on circulation. Bicycles are a particularly common symbol because they also imply exercise. In a dream they are symbolically exercising your heart. The number three indicates commitment and people who neglect their hearts often lack commitment to themselves so it is also common in dreams about the heart. The number three and bicycles can be combined into the symbol of a tricycle in dreams.

The number 8 has a unique property. It is the only balanced number in the set of numbers 0 – 9. When turned on its side you can imagine it balanced on the end of your finger. While balance is enough to imply the heart, eight is made up of two circles which themselves would also symbolize it. Lastly eight on its side is the infinity symbol ∞. All put together in dreams, eight symbolizes expansion of the heart without limit. Literally don't put a limit on expanding your heart.

Symbols of sharing are always about the heart. A great symbol for this is a tea pot or jug kettle. When a friend calls over, it is common practice to make them a cup of tea or coffee and share with each other the news and gossip between the last time we saw them and now. Jug kettles and many tea pots also have a half heart shaped handle and this type is common in heart related dreams.

Another less obvious symbol of sharing is a bank. Banks control the flow of money in circulation through sharing deposits with borrowers so a bank is a good symbol for the heart. A bank account is another good symbol as you must take care to keep your bank account in balance. To dream of an overdrawn bank account means you are being asked to address the imbalance in your heart as a matter of importance.

In English slang, the heart is referred to as the ticker. Due to this and the fact that clocks are circular with hands moving in circular paths they too represent the heart in dreams. They commonly feature when dreaming of moving in a particular direction in a location that also symbolizes the heart. For example, the dream of walking in an anti-clockwise direction in a bank would indicate that the path you are following is not wise for your heart, with anti-clockwise translating to 'anti heart wise'.

The balance in the heart can also be indicated by flow of traffic on main roads. Main roads are 'arterial' roads which take the main flow of traffic to and from destinations. This flow and the pun on artery, link the symbolism to the arteries and the heart. An imbalance in traffic flow here indicates that the dreamer either shares too much, not very common or likely, or does not share enough. For example, the lanes on the highway may be divided unevenly - there may be two lanes heading in the direction away from the dreamer and three lanes heading in the other direction. Sharing should be balanced with equal give and take so this symbol indicates that the dreamer chokes the feeling coming from their heart. For sharing to become an issue in a dream the dreamer must have been choking their feelings for some time. They are likely to suppress all the feelings of love, passion, sadness and irritation that try to surface. The feelings are only fleetingly noticed and swiftly pushed back down, but the dreamer could be quite expert at expressing rage or anger in an overbearing way. While rage is a loss of control, anger does have its place. Anger when expressed correctly can help define the boundary between your space and others around you. For example, "Look I've asked you politely but you continue to open my mail. It is beginning to annoy me now to the point that I have to assume that you are deliberately trying to annoy me." In what should be a loving relationship that could be difficult to say, so the feelings around it are suppressed until eventually it comes out in an uncontrollable burst which far exceeds the final straw that triggered it. If this happens to you, it points to an inability to share your feelings in a constructive manner. This comes from not having learned how to do it in childhood.

The two way flow of the heart can also be indicated in dreams by a double door. A double door allows people to enter and exit at the same time. Here again the symbolism is that your heart needs a two way flow of feelings. Let your heart tune into the feelings of others while at the same time allowing you to express your feelings honestly.

Green is the color associated with the heart chakra and therefore can always indicate the heart and circulatory system in dreams. It also indicates sharing, balance and harmony. An inability to share leads to jealousy, rivalry and envy. We are subconsciously aware of green's association with the heart and use the expression, "green with envy." Green is also used in dreams to harmonize opposites. To dream of eating green meat would mean that the dream is attempting to put the meat in harmony with your body by coloring it green. Another example is to dream of opening the fridge and seeing green milk. Always remove foods shown in this way from your diet.

The interpretation of color in dreams comes from their meaning in your aura and to dream of green is like color healing therapy for your heart. In addition to providing healing through color, a dream may symbolically give emotional expression and openness by placing the dreamer in the open green countryside.

Green and red as a color combination is always about the heart, with green being the color of the heart chakra and red the color of passion. The color combination can be achieved in any number of ways, for example, a red car parked in a row of green cabbages. In that dream we also see a reference to the head, as cabbage is referred to as a head of cabbage. It is very common to see references to the head in dreams about the heart. The dream attempts to point out the dreamer's habit of being in their head – in this case parked in the head – and will go on to show that this is at the expense of their heart.

Green also indicates a need for adaptability or reconciliation with regard to the subject matter of the dream. Something is out of harmony and needs healing through balance. This can be aspects of yourself or could be between you and others. For example, to dream of arguing with your partner who is standing on a green rug at the bathroom mirror is pointing out that you need to eliminate (bathroom) the arguments between you and your partner with regard to having children (mirror) (See the chapter on Reproduction).

Pink is the color of unconditional love and in dreams cannot be interpreted in any other way. To see pink in a dream immediately tells us that the dreamer did not bond with their mother and has never learned to be in touch with their feelings and therefore to love themselves. While not always directly about the heart, it is none-the-less significant to the subject matter of the dream as the dreamer will need to learn to open their heart.

Green on its own can indicate you have a counseling ability while green and pink together will always mean this. This is particularly true if a guide appears wearing green in the dream. Counseling works through our female side and as with any female energy ability, it is influenced dramatically by our relationship with mother. A poor relationship with mother can cause us to close our hearts and inhibit the flow of female energy within us. This in turn inhibits abilities associated with our female side.

Engines, when not big and powerful, also indicate the heart because they are the very heart of the propulsion system of any vehicle. Without the engine you wouldn't even get into the vehicle. A propeller, because it is attached to the engine of a plane, ship or submarine also indicates the heart. It is quite common for dreams encouraging expression of your heart to also show the logical side of your nature. A propeller is a case in point, as a totally analytical person is referred to as a propeller head. Most likely then the propeller will be on an airplane which, due to its height, emphasizes being lofty or up in the head. Having problems with an engine in a dream is a health warning about your heart. Remember that dreams warn of health problems many years in advance of a condition manifesting but don't let that put you off doing something about it today.

Since engines represent the heart, oil has to represent the blood stream. Problems with oil pressure or the oil level will therefore be about your blood pressure. A car leaking oil symbolizes you are anemic. Anemia is a loss of red blood cells and a car leaking oil symbolizes this in a dream. Another specific circulatory system health problem that can show up in dreams is stroke. This can be indicated in a number of ways such as a person banging their head off a wall. A wall links the dream to the circulatory system while damage to the head linked with the circulatory system indicates stroke. Any dream that includes symbols for the circulatory system along with blows to the head would indicate the same thing. In much the same way a roof on fire indicates stroke with the roof symbolizing the top of the body or the head and fire representing the heart. A lightening strike damaging the roof of the house would indicate the same thing as lightening is a fire symbol. Heart attack would be indicated by a dream of the fireplace in the living room cracking or crumbling. Indeed any physical problem or defect with a symbol linked to the heart can indicate this.

Dreams do not come to you to scare you with these warnings. Their intention is to alert you to the possible outcome of your continued actions so that your awareness will cause you to change your ways. Think of it this way. If you did not interpret your dreams you would be ignorant of their warnings. Ignorance never prevents an outcome but the difference is that to the uninformed, the health problem will appear to be out of the blue. The point of dreams, and indeed this book, is to hopefully explain to you why so many of us develop problems in this area. Knowing the cause of a problem allows you treat the root rather than the symptoms of a condition. Dreams act as an early warning system to give you plenty of time (years) to change and thereby remove the potential for developing problems in this area.

Now to finish, let's have a look at three dreams that feature the heart as the subject matter. In all three dreams I have shown the text taken exactly as it is from the dictionary reference of this book. Have a look at the dreams and then the extracts from the reference and see if you can put the analysis together. When you've made an attempt look at my analysis underneath to check how you did.

The first two dreams are from the same dreamer. When he had the first dream he was blissfully unaware of any potential health problem regarding his heart. The second dream was just a few weeks later by which stage the dreamer had accepted what his dreams were saying and had begun the process of cutting the ties with his mother. Notice the change shown in the dreams. The process Cutting-the-ties is described separately in this book.

The third dream is from a woman who was questioning her role in the spiritual field and was thinking of changing careers. There are actually two strong veins in this dream but for now I will only focus on what it is saying about her heart.

Quick Symbol Reference for the Heart

The following symbols all indicate the above for various reasons. Complete descriptions are given in the Dream Symbol Reference later.

Numbers 3 and 8	Clockwise	Island	Shell
Activity in open areas	Coat	Italy	Shield
	Country side	Jail	Snow
Apartment	Credit card	Kettle	Sundial
Archway	Cycling	Lightning	Tea pot
Armor	Dancing	Main road	Thermostat
Arterial road	Dirty water	Money	Tricycle
Balcony	Double doors	Oil	Vault
Bank	Engine	Open plan	Wall
Barrier	Fence	Park	Wallet
Battery	Field	Pink	Watch
Boiler	Fire / Fireplace	Polluted water	Water logged lawn
Bonnet (car)	Flame	Prison	Weeds
Breastplate	Furnace	Propeller	Wheels
Cage	Garage	Pump	Women
Central heating	Grass	Purse	
Chimney	Green	Radiator	
Circle	Hearth	Roller coaster	
Clock	Highway	Roundabout	
Clockwork	Hood (car)	Sharing	

Flames like any symbol of fire represent your heart. If something is in **flames** it can indicate a health warning.

A **fighter plane** indicates you are an angry person — ready with a verbal arsenal to win arguments and defend your space.

An **airplane crash** signifies a difficult birth - one that was either emotionally traumatic or life threatening.

To be **hurt** in a dream indicates emotional trauma. While the trauma is likely to be in the past you are dreaming about it because it is still affecting your actions today.

Dream: Fighter Plane

I am watching a news event on the TV. A fighter plane is engulfed in flames and is crashing to the ground. It hits the ground in a forest and the flames go out. The pilot is bruised and hurt but otherwise OK! The news commentator says something like, "notice that even though it was the engines that caused the problem the pilot is taking the time to switch them off." From the angle of the camera you can see a propeller that is already stopped.

Engines represent your heart and circulatory system as they are the heart of a vehicle.

A **news commentator** in a dream represents a counselor and to dream of one means two things. You have a counseling ability that you should develop. You also should take note of what the commentator is pointing out to you in the dream. They are likely indicating something you did in the past that is holding you back in the present day. Their function in the dream is to bring it to your conscious awareness.

A **propeller** is part of an engine and as such symbolizes your heart and in particular means that you are too analytical or logical - a propeller head. Come down from your head and get in touch with your feelings.

To **switch off an engine** indicates you suppress your feelings. The dream is showing you this so that you will switch your feelings back on (get in touch with them).

Having a title, a *pilot* is a guide. It indicates you have a strong intellect and can project your mind onto others. It also indicates you have a counseling / teaching ability where you can work with large groups of people.

Bruises indicate emotional trauma. While the trauma is likely to be in the past you are dreaming about it because it is still affecting your actions today.

Fighter Plane – The Analysis

Remembering that you are everything in the dream the pilot represents the dreamer as a child at birth. The crash landing shows that the child's birth was traumatic and that the child feared for his own survival at the time. The plane being **engulfed in flames** highlights the emotional trauma experienced by the child. We are told that **the engines caused the problem**. This is the best clue we could get as to the reaction of the child to his traumatic birth. The engine is the heart of the plane and symbolizes the child's heart. The child's view is that he was **bruised**, **hurt** and **engulfed in flames** and that this is the fault of the heart (the engines). The solution, from the child's perspective, is to **switch them off**. We are then told that you can already see a **propeller that is already stopped**. A propeller is another strong symbol for the heart. From all this we can see that the dreamer has shut off or closed his heart so that he doesn't experience this emotional trauma again.

In this dream we are not explicitly told what the dreamer must do to 'open' his heart again. This means that he is totally unaware that he has closed his heart off. The first and most important part of any solution to a problem is to accept that you have the problem to begin with. This dreamer must first accept that he has closed himself off from his heart. We can also see that the dreamer is a 'fighter' **fighter plane** or angry person. Again this follows the pattern. Feeling hurt and bruised causes the child to close off the heart and become angry as a defense against being hurt again. To help this person I would suggest talking to older family members and parents to learn about the circumstances of his birth. Parents are unlikely to give the full horrors of the day but siblings can relate it in terms of the anguish they picked up from the parents. If the dreamer had no siblings I would suggest regression back to birth. While this can be traumatic, the purpose is to put him back in touch with his feelings at the time of his birth. After the regression he will again feel the sadness and anger that he felt at the time. He is then at the first stage in dealing with the trauma - acceptance. From there I would suggest the process of *cutting the ties* to clear the trauma and open the heart again (switch the engines back on). Regression without the purpose of healing the trauma afterwards is of no benefit and can in fact damage the person more.

A **bay window**, particularly if it is in your mother's house, represents the womb. The dream is showing you how you are still affected today by something from way back in the past.

A **bonnet** or **hood** being the access to a car engine is about your heart. An **open bonnet** is a request to open up to your feelings or open your heart.

Green is the color of the heart chakra so dreaming about it is healing for your heart. For example, dreams in the countryside where you are surrounded by green are particularly healing and are asking you to open your heart and share your feelings.

Dream: The Bonnet

I am in the front room of my mother's house looking out the bay window. It is raining and my lime green FIAT 127 car is in the driveway. I have the bonnet open as I was having battery trouble. I intended fixing it. My oldest brother is behind me telling me to close the bonnet but I am not concerned about the rain. My other brother comes home from abroad and gives him a birthday present. The funny thing is that it is not his birthday yet.

A **car battery** represents your heart or circulatory system since a battery is an electronic pump and your heart is your body's pump.

A **dead battery** or **battery trouble** means you are not doing what is required to keep your heart engaged and healthy. We easily accept that our heart needs the right diet and exercise but forget that our heart also needs emotional expression for optimum health.

Rain, like any symbol of water, represents life or your spiritual nature. Getting **caught in the rain** in a dream is very positive as it means letting life in. **Sheltering from rain** is about avoiding life or some specific aspect that you need to include in your life.

A **birthday** or **birthday present** is a dream's way of bringing you back to your own birth. This is regardless of whose birthday is being celebrated in the dream.

32

The Bonnet – The Analysis

Green is the color of the heart chakra and by itself is sufficient to symbolize the heart. The bonnet, where we find the engine of the car, has a more obvious connection to the heart as the engine is the heart of the car. The battery is an easy enough one too as batteries are electric pumps. Any symbol indicating a pump represents the heart. Fiat is a little trickier. Fiat is an Italian car manufacturer and Italy as a location indicates the heart (unless you were born in Italy). It would not matter if you missed out on that symbol as we have enough to go on already.

The dreamer says he intended **fixing** the battery problem. This is very positive to see in a dream and means that the dreamer is consciously aware of his heart problem. The cause of the problem is given to us by the location - **mother's bay window**. This symbolizes the womb. Mother's house is mother's body and the dreamer is in the front room bay window, a living space that sticks out on the front of the house / mother's body. So here, while the focus is on fixing the problem, we again see birth being linked to the problem. In case you couldn't get the womb from the symbol of the bay window we see birth being celebrated when one brother brings home a **birthday present** for the other. Since the dreamer is everything in the dream it is his birth and not his brother's that is the focus. What we can determine from this is that the dreamer experienced emotional trauma at the time of his birth. We cannot say why exactly but because the bonnet of the car (body) is open in the dream we know that the dreamer has already closed off his heart and is now in the process of working on himself to 'fix' this. The brother with the present represents a guide (a calling card of guides in dreams is that they often appear bearing gifts) and he is encouraging the dreamer to go forward with the process. A treat, if you will, for work being done. Water, including rain, represents life so the rain getting into the bonnet represents life coming into his heart. The dreamer is correct to ignore the negativity of the brother telling him to close the bonnet (close up the heart again). An older brother in a dream is often a good substitute for a parent when they display the same traits as the parent. So we now know that the dreamer also has problems with dad's negativity that affect his heart.

This dreamer was two weeks into the process of cutting the ties with his mother so my advice would be to continue the process as we can see from the dream that it is reversing the negative effects of his traumatic birth on his heart. Cutting The Ties works by directing the subconscious mind to eliminate the negative influence of an event or person.

Apartments symbolize your heart, circulatory system and emotions. Typically it means that you separate yourself from your feelings. Literally you and your emotions are apart – you are not conscious of them. At least with regard to the subject matter of the dream, you are being too logical and need to involve your heart more in the decision making process.

A *harbor* symbolizes your birth as this is where ships berth with berth being a pun on birth. Dreams about birth will invariably show the spiritual abilities you have as you have these from day one.

Dream: The Man on the Horse

I'm in my apartment, which is at the back of a set of apartments. Next I'm walking along a pier at a harbor and 40 men on horses jump off the end of the pier. I'm surprised that the water was shallow just there. Next a man on a horse is coming towards me. I'm afraid he's going to hit me because he's not looking where he is going. At the last minute he pulls to the side, banging his head off a wall. He gets up and is angry at me for being in his way.

Shallow water indicates that despite what you may think you still have room to deepen your spiritual side.

Watching others *jump into water* is a request to jump into life or develop your spiritual gifts.

To *bang your head off a wall* is a warning of stroke. It signifies this as walls are a common symbol for the heart and circulatory system and the dream is coupling it with damage to the head. Stroke is a circulatory problem that damages your head.

An *angry* man in your dream can indicate your dad was an angry person. Similarly an angry woman indicates your mother was angry.

The Man on the Horse – The Analysis

The location of apartment (being apart from emotions) and the wall (indicating the dreamer has built a wall around her heart) are both classic symbols that indicate the heart. Again, remembering that everything in the dream represents an aspect of the dreamer we know that it is not the man on the horse not looking where he is going but the dreamer herself. She does not see the damage she is causing herself by closing off her heart. The dream again links the problem to birth by introducing a harbor. This is a place where ships berth so indicates the dreamer's own birth. We see the trigger when we see the man on the horse as dad. Through her dream she is reliving the experience at birth that **"dad is angry at me for being in his way."** Because of this the dreamer has developed the pattern of putting herself in second place (at the back of the set of apartments) so as not to be in the way. This is done at the expense of her own feelings and her health! The health problem is given by the man banging his head off a wall and indicates stroke (physical damage to the head that is connected with the circulatory system - the wall). Dreams often show men banging their heads because in an energy sense logic (the head) is male while the heart is female.

To resolve her problem the dreamer must deal with her conflict with dad. This is indicated by the man coming towards her. Dreams often indicate the future by showing something happening further along the path. In her case the man is further along her path and facing her - indicating something she must face in the future. As an incentive the dream shows that she came to this life to deepen her spiritual understanding (indicated by jumping into the shallow water).

In reality this dreamer already works in the spiritual field but also works in a conventional business with her father. Her father does not treat her as an equal and this constant conflict is what is damaging her. She must resolve it. This will heal the root cause of her heart condition.

Note: This dream also has a strong spiritual theme that tells the dreamer that using her spiritual healing ability (horses) is how she can deepen her spirituality (horses jump into shallow water). Healing the issues with her father will improve her gift.

5. Digest This

Last night I dreamed I ate a ten-pound marshmallow, and when I woke up the pillow was gone.

— Tommy Cooper

When it comes to health dreams people tend not to be interested unless they already know they have a problem. Even when problems manifest, depending on where the problem is, many people are reluctant to talk about it. This is particularly true when it comes to bowel and elimination problems – both of which are part of the digestive system. I have on several occasions been the unwitting victim of an audience member who publicly denies the interpretation of their dream because it points to their colon. Afterwards, when the crowd thins out, they invariably approach me with thumbs up confirming the interpretation but stating that they could not own up to it in front of others. On one occasion, during a one to one analysis, a young woman told me of a dream where she was shooting arrows for target practice in the forest. When I told her it was about her colon she confessed that the target she was shooting at was feces but she was extremely embarrassed about it! Some people equate admitting to problems in this area with breaking wind in public.

I titled this chapter *Digest This* because digestion is not just about food. We also digest ideas. Right now you are digesting what you are reading. When something resonates in a positive way, you might feel butterflies in your stomach. When something grates, you may feel your stomach tighten into a knot. You have probably experienced this but may not consciously link assimilation of ideas and emotions with your digestive

Summary

► In addition to food we also digest ideas. Dreams often link problems with assimilation as the cause of your digestive problems.

► Your dreams tell you which foods your system cannot process and why. Dairy products are the most common and this is often linked to issues with mother. Sometimes it is a combination of foods that you need to avoid.

► Dreams of mice, rats and snakes warn of cancer years before it develops physically. They also tell you why and what you need to do to prevent it.

system. However, your dreams will.

The locations most commonly used in dreams to indicate the digestive system are the kitchen, dining room and restaurants. The bathroom, toilet and back garden are most commonly used to indicate the elimination system. Other symbols which indicate the digestive system are a hob, fridge, kitchen table, shopping cart / trolley and items to do with food storage or preparation.

Once the subject matter of the digestive system is established, the dream will reveal more detail. For example, if you or anyone in the dream is boiling milk in the kitchen it means that you have an intolerance to milk and dairy products. In fact it is fair to say that it is not so much the food that you eat that causes you problems but the food you can't excrete. A person with a healthy digestive system will have a bowel movement at least once per day. This natural bodily function means that foods that cannot be broken down are eliminated before any harmful toxins can build up in them.

Food Allergies

Dairy products are probably the most common foods to which people develop allergies. There are several reasons for this. Problems with mother can contribute here, when as infants we not only take our first meal from mother but we also take in everything she feels about us. If an animal is given an electric shock every time it drinks milk it learns to associates milk with something unpleasant and avoids it. In much the same way if a mother resents feeding her newborn he or she will quickly learn to associate milk with an unpleasant situation. In later life, if left untreated, this is likely to show as an intolerance to milk.

▶ After hearing shocking news you can feel your stomach knot up. It is in fact your colon that is knotting. These kinks and knots then restrict the flow of matter along your colon. If you have a blockage your dreams point it out.

▶ If you have ever taken penicillin you have waged war on the natural bacterial flora in your colon. By taking acidophilus it can be easily replaced.

▶ Dreams commonly link anger as a cause of colon problems so always eat in a positive frame of mind. Avoid eating when angry. It programs your food to do you harm.

Holding onto things from the past emotionally also programs your body to do the same. A result often is your body holding onto waste matter that is no longer needed. On a physical level, regardless of what has slowed your digestive system down, once it has, dairy products are likely to cause you trouble. If your digestive system has slowed down to where you have a bowel movement twice per week, when you drink a glass of milk on Monday morning it is still in your digestive system on Thursday evening. Would you drink a glass of milk that has been sitting on the kitchen table for a whole day in the summer? What would that milk be like after three and a half days? In a simplistic sense that is what is in your body! A slow moving colon allows toxins build up on these and other susceptible foods. The toxins pass into your blood stream which must then be cleansed by the liver and lymphatic system. In your dreams, problems with cleansing are shown as dirty water-logged grass or bog land.

A condition which is easy to recognize in dreams is candida albicans. This is a fungus that can grow on waste matter in the colon. In dreams it is symbolized as soggy newspaper in the back garden, mould on the kitchen floor or walls, or moldy hay in a barn. Dreams with these symbols also show what foods contribute to the condition.

It is safe to say that, with rare exception, any food that is depicted in your dream is a food that your body cannot deal with. In cases where a particular ingredient is the culprit you will dream of it. A person with an allergy to wheat can dream of the sun shining beautifully on a field of wheat. Whether the wheat is shown like this or in a poor state it still means you are being asked to change your diet. There are exceptions to this - if you diet too much you can dream of a food banquet to encourage you to eat more. Dreams which show a line of people queuing for an orange drink or even just the color orange are healing for your digestive system. Orange is the color of the sacral chakra which feeds energy to your digestive system.

The Colon

The colon is a very sensitive organ. After hearing shocking news you can feel your stomach knot up. It is in fact your colon that is knotting. These kinks and knots then restrict the flow of matter along your colon. Dr. John Harvey Kellogg M.D. said that of the 22,000 operations performed under his jurisdiction only six percent of colons were normal. Waste matter can cling to the walls of an unhealthy slow moving colon and become cemented there, further restricting the flow. This is shown in dreams as slow moving animals or snails on a cement path in the back garden. This cemented matter can remain in the colon for upwards of twenty years! Dreams often attribute blockages to particular foods. These are usually shown in dreams in a negative light and are often shown to be clogging a toilet preventing it from flushing. In the latter case the foods are usually shown in their containers to indicate that the body cannot break down the food. When the lining of the stomach or intestines is affected dreams show it as wallpaper or plaster falling off the walls in the kitchen or bathroom.

As an infant your digestive system was not fully formed and you relied on your mother's milk to nourish you. After six months or so, acid was produced in your stomach and this allowed you move onto eating solid foods. The acid also protects you against bacterial infection and the level of hygiene

Roles characters play in dreams

Every character in your dream represents an aspect of you, and examination of the characters reveals which aspect. Friends appear in your dreams to display their traits in waking life. You are encouraged to adopt in your life any positive qualities they display in the dream and to eliminate any negative traits. Are they lazy, ambitions, timid, confident, controlling, etc. in waking life or in the dream?

required was subsequently reduced. At this stage something very important has already happened. In the first few months you also ingest bacteria in your mother's milk that is vital to the proper functioning of your developing digestive system. The bacteria passed safely through your stomach, because there was no acid there yet, and accumulated in your large intestine where a slightly acidic condition developed. The bacteria are commonly called acidophilus due to the fact that it requires mildly acidic conditions to live. Acidophilus is essential to keeping your colon in healthy working order. It prevents the spread of toxins from the colon into the small intestine and coats the large intestine, helping the flow of matter.

If you have ever taken a course of penicillin you have waged war on this natural flora. Penicillin fights off harmful bacterial infections but it does not discriminate between harmful bacteria and the helpful bacteria that reside there. In the western world this is probably the single most contributing cause of harm to the colon. Colonic irrigation without subsequently restoring the acidophilus is also harmful.

To dream of an *animal dying* can be about letting your animal nature die. It can also be about your body's immune system fighting off disease. To dream of dead crows, badgers, snakes, worms, or other animals that are either black and white in color or are carrion is good. Here the animals represent a serious health threat such as cancer and them dying or you killing them in a dream shows your immune system is up to the task of fighting off the threat. To dream of these animals laying eggs or with young warns of a disease spreading within your body. The rest of the dream will say what it is that is allowing the spread. The good news is that dreams warn of disease before it manifests so there is plenty of time to take remedial action. It also needs to be pointed out that occasionally dreaming of health threats is fine. It only becomes serious when you consistently dream these symbols.

Cancer

Cancer of the colon is shown as mutated and usually slow moving animals. Often they are shown in a dead forest or forest in fall. Snakes or worms under the cooker in the kitchen or rust eating into a kitchen appliance indicate the same thing. Crows or rats eating into the back door of a house indicate cancer of the rectum (the back door of the body). In these cases it is very important to determine the food being linked to the appearance of the cancer. Quite often the combination of two foods is far worse than the effect of either food on its own. To determine which foods need to be cut out or cut down, eliminate the food for a week or so and then reintroduce it to your diet. If you begin dreaming about it in the next few days you need to cut it out again. Also try the food when purchased from different locations as you may find only particular places

Male characters and the male aspect

This aspect is dominated by your father, career and the outer world. It includes aggression, assertiveness, courage, security, responsibility, drive, sex drive, ambition, creativity, healing, managing and controlling. Problems with the male aspect are shown as males injured, ill, or disabled.

trigger the dreams. I personally had to give up red meat for over two years before my digestive system had healed enough to process it again. This does not mean that red meat is bad for everyone. We are all different and there are many factors that contribute to you becoming unable to process a particular food.

Where your main problem is a slow moving colon your dreams may place you in the drive through of McDonalds or Burger King. Both of these locations symbolize fast food which is the symbolic antidote to the slow moving food in your body.

Interpreting Colors

In dreams yellow and orange are both healing colors for the digestive system. Yellow also stimulates the intellect so can be about digesting a new idea. An unhealthy color combination for the colon is black and white. This indicates you have difficulty letting go of the past and this affects the colon as described earlier. Seeing things as black and white leaves little room for acceptance of new ideas. Often this color combination is shown as black and white tiles on the bathroom or kitchen floor. This indicates you must overcome your black and white attitude. In dreams about the digestive system, references to white on its own point to milk and mother as contributors to the problem.

How Emotions Affect The Digestive System

Anger is commonly linked in dreams to problems with the digestive system. When you sit to eat a meal you charge the food with how you are feeling. Consider your food like a homeopathic remedy which you can program for positive or negative results. If you are feeling angry you are pouring all that negative energy into the food you are about to put into your body. This is programming the food to cause harm. To reverse this trend, put yourself into a positive frame of mind before eating your meals. This charges the food with positive energy and programs it to heal the body. A person who says grace before meals is, in effect, doing this. Dreams will always show the foundation on which anger is built so that you can let it go. Your digestive system is affected by male energy and for this reason problems are often linked to problems with dad or a mother with a male energy approach to life. Healing any rift by letting go of it also heals the digestive system.

When To Be Concerned

Don't worry if you have the odd dream about cancer as we all develop cancers all the time. A healthy body fights off the mutation successfully. Killing snakes, mutated animals, rats, crows, termites or curing rust in dreams all show that the body is successfully fighting off the disease. Also, dreams warn about conditions years before they manifest physically to give you plenty of time to do something to prevent the illness from taking hold in the first place. By the time a doctor diagnoses cancer the person will already have had thousands of dreams telling them what to do to prevent the condition. Cancer is a symptom of a disease in the body. Removing the cancer, while frequently successful, only removes the symptom and leaves the disease behind. View it like the oil warning light in your car. When the light comes on what do you do? You could stop the car, rip open the dashboard and remove the light, or you could replace the oil in the engine. When a warning light comes on in your body what would you rather do? It is best to treat the cause of the symptom so that the warning light stops flashing. Dreams flash the warning light but also show the cause and the solution. Dreams set out to heal by bringing a problem into the light so that something can be done to correct it. The choice is yours to act on their advice.

Dream Symbols for the Digestive System

Kitchens are probably the most common symbol in dreams to indicate the digestive system. Devices in the kitchen also indicate this. For example, a fridge is a place where we temporarily hold food and so indicates the stomach – a place in our bodies where we temporarily hold food. If you live in a country where washing machines are located in your kitchen it also indicates the stomach. The churning nature of the washing machine symbolizes the churning nature of your stomach. The kitchen table also indicates digestion as it is used for both preparing and eating food. A cooker hob is only used for food so again indicates the digestive system. The oven can indicate your stomach but has other meanings to do with the reproductive system so is not enough on its own to indicate your dream is about your digestive system.

The kitchen sink is about your elimination system rather than digestive system. The taps can symbolize the kidneys and the drain symbolizes the bladder. If you are cleaning red meat in soapy water in the sink the dream asks you to cleanse (soapy water) red meat from your system. Bathrooms are more commonly used to indicate elimination and the sink there means the same thing. A bathroom can also symbolize elimination of an influence or trauma so look for specific reference to physical objects in the bathroom to be sure the dream is about the physical elimination. The toilet bowl symbolizes your bowel. If it is blocked up it shows that your system is being blocked with food. The food in question is usually shown in the same dream. For example, dreaming of removing soggy milk cartons from the toilet means your system cannot properly eliminate dairy products. If the toilet has physical damage the dream is more serious and warning you of potential damage to your bowel. A mixing bowl in the kitchen also indicates the bowel.

The bathroom and kitchen floors both symbolize your elimination system. Anything shown on the floor is something you are being asked to eliminate from your diet. The same is true for any food shown in a negative light, such as spilled on the cooker, spilled on the table, exploding or gone off. A garbage disposal, trash can and sewer all indicate the colon and rectum. The back door to the house also indicates the rectum – the back door to your body. The back garden can indicate the past but also can indicate your elimination system. For example, soggy newspapers in the back garden indicate

Female characters and female aspect

This aspect is dominated by the dreamer's mother, emotions and the inner world. It includes caring, nurturing, loving, intuition, and philosophy of life. Problems with this aspect are shown as females who are ill, injured, disabled, drunk, etc.

you have a problem with Candida albicans. Soggy newspapers in the kitchen, mold in the kitchen and moldy hay in a barn also indicate Candida albicans.

Dirt tracks and dirt roads also indicate your colon – the road waste travels in your body. Dark passages with dirt or dust on them also indicate your colon. So too do drain pipes and garden paths. A cement garden path would indicate that food has hardened inside your colon and become cemented to its walls. Dreams of fecal matter are also about your colon. Turf and the color brown also indicate it. Dreams with tubing are also about the colon especially if the tubing is around six feet long. A less common symbol for the colon is the car trunk. It is used to carry food (groceries) and is at the back of the car.

The intestines are indicated in dreams by tights, nylons and hosiery. Lots of people moving along a great many stairs that go up and down and all over the place can also indicate food moving through the intestines. Sausages, because of their association with pig intestines, also indicate it.

A sluggish digestive system is very commonly indicated by a line or queue of people. The line can be anywhere and does not have to be at a location that symbolizes digestion and elimination. Dreams of slow moving animals, such as hedgehogs and snails also indicate your digestive system is slow moving. In all cases the dream is asking you to do something to speed it up.

Trains can be about a stage on your life journey. However, if there is reference to the train track the dream can also be about your digestive tract. Puns on track also indicate this. For example, a tractor or slow moving vehicle that moves on tracks.

Dreams about locations commonly used for eating are also about your digestive system. Dining rooms and restaurants are common symbols. The dream may have more than one thread to it. For example, to dream of seeing movie stars eating in a restaurant points out that your diet (eating) affects your channeling ability (movie stars). Grocery store shopping cart are used to hold food items so also indicate the digestive system.

Sometimes dreams show anger as the trigger for digestive system problems. As discussed earlier, the dream is asking you to not eat with anger. Get yourself into a positive mood before eating and simply do not eat when you are angry or down. All the negative emotion being poured into the food adversely affects your digestive system. Eating in a positive frame of mind programs the food to heal your body.

Quick Symbol Reference for the Digestive System

The following symbols all indicate the above for various reasons. Complete descriptions are given in the Dream Symbol Reference later.

Anger

Back door

Back garden

Back hoe

Badger

Barn

Bathroom / Restroom

Black & White combination

Bowl

Brown

Burial place

Car trunk

Cat

Cemented 'back passage'

Coal

Cooker (hob)

Dark passages

Dirt road

Dirt track

Drain

Drainpipe

Dust bin

Floor

Food items

Forest / Wood

Fridge

Garbage bin

Garbage disposal

Garden path

Grave

Hosiery

Kitchen

Kitchen table

Line of people

Meal time

Mixing bowl

Moldy hay / barn

Moldy room

Mud

Orange

Paper / plaster falling off walls

Queue

Restaurant

Rubbish disposal

Sewer

Shopping trolley

Sink

Slow moving animal

Sludge

Slug

State of floor

Swamp

Tights

Toilet

Tomb

Tractors

Train track

Tubing

Turf

Wash basin

Washing machine

Wood

Dreaming of someone *skinny* is most likely a request for you to eat properly. Are you skipping meals or dieting to lose weight?

Breakfast is a meal time so is about your eating habit or your digestive system. The word itself comes from the two words break and fast so this dream could be a request for you to eat well and avoid dieting or skipping meals.

Cats often indicate your gut or stomach. Cat gut is used for many things and we also have the expression *my stomach is cat*.

A dream including your *father* is likely a comment on your relationship with him and how it is holding you back in some area of your life now. Dreams only focus on problems in your life. Although you may have had a wonderful relationship, there are still often traits or attitudes you copied that you could do without.

Dream: Breakfast

I went to have breakfast at a neighbor's house. Her house was beautiful. She had short blond hair and was very skinny. She was still wearing her nightdress. My dad was there. I don't know where he came from. She had a cat that kept scratching me and climbing up her wallpaper. She told me how wonderful it was to have cats and fed it. It bothered me that the cat was clawing at me but I didn't dare to say a thing. All of a sudden we were in a room, the three of us, with a huge banquet. She sat next to us and started kissing my father's neck. He pushed her away. She started crying. She seemed very upset and manically depressed.

To dream of a *banquet* is a request to be selective about the food you eat, and to eat what is required to keep your body healthy. Do not starve yourself. This is a common symbol for people who are damaging their body through excessive dieting.

To dream of someone with *depression* is about your existing depression or a warning that you are heading towards depression. The same dream is likely to link the depression to a particular parent by featuring them or to a past event through symbolically representing that.

Dreaming of you or someone else *upset* shows that you are hurting with regard to the subject matter of the dream

Crying in a dream is healing as it symbolically gives release to pent up emotions related to the subject matter of the dream.

Wallpaper indicates the lining of your stomach or intestines particularly if in a kitchen, bathroom or dining room.

Breakfast – The Analysis

Several symbols show this dream is about the digestive system (breakfast, cat, wallpaper, feeding and banquet). The cat narrows the area in question to the dreamer's stomach / gut. The specific problem is shown by the cat scratching her and climbing up the wallpaper. Wallpaper represents the lining of the intestines and esophagus and here the dream shows that lining is being damaged by a problem with her stomach (the cat is the rogue element). Her neighbor in this dream is a guide (indicated by her blond hair) and by example is trying to get her to view her digestive system in a positive light. She does this by saying, "*it is wonderful to have cats*" and also by feeding the cat. This along with the title gives the main digestive system problem. The dreamer is not eating enough. Her dream is inviting her to breakfast or in other words to *break* her *fast* – stop dieting. The dream is not focusing on any particular food so she is being asked to eat well in general. Her failure to do this is causing the problem.

As expected the dream links her health problem to something else in life – her father. That is why he appears in the dream. The dreamer is unaware of the link between her health problem and her father. In the dream she says, "I don't know where he came from." This means she does not understand his approach to life. The digestive system is a male energy system in the body and issues with dad can manifest there as physical problems. Later in the dream we see her father pushing the woman away when she begins to kiss his neck. Here again the guide shows an important issue. The dreamer felt that dad pushed her away – just like she did the woman in the dream. At the time this caused upset and tears and is now linked to depression (woman is depressed in the dream).

In summary, for this dreamer the dream links not eating well, the damage to her digestive system and her depression to feelings of rejection from her father. Indeed the issue with dad is underpinning everything and must be dealt with to make effective progress in the other areas. The guide crying in the dream demonstrates that the pent up emotions must be expressed as part of the healing process.

In reality when the dreamer submitted this dream she was already in therapy and recovering from depression. Her therapist had spotted the issues with her father and the dreamer had started cutting-the-ties with him. This is a process that uses symbols of the subconscious to eliminate conditioning. In addition to this she just had a period of dieting behind her where she had lost twelve pounds and still hoped to lose more. She has a tendency to put on weight and this upsets her. For over a year she was also taking medicine to deal with acid reflux / heartburn. This is a condition where stomach acid eats into the walls of the esophagus.

Wood, and anything made from it, symbolizes your colon due to the brown color. Most often a wooden table is the feature of these dreams.

A *bottle* is a common symbol for the kidneys. A *broken bottle* indicates damage to the kidneys. The damage is likely to be indicated by the location where the dream takes place or by food types or drinks being shown specifically in the dream.

Restaurants signify social contact and your digestive system.

A *table for eating at* is about your digestive system. A dining room table indicates the same thing but can also indicate social interaction.

A *waiter* serving food or drink indicates you are a hands-on / spiritual healer. Food is the energy source for the human body and the dream is pointing out that you are a supplier of life sustaining energy.

Dream: Unpleasant Chinese Experience

I am in a wooden building which is a bit like a Chinese restaurant. All of the trimmings are oriental, such as bamboo cane around the doors and chairs. I am sitting at a table with my group. Someone in my group does something to annoy a person in another group. I think he threw something. The other person threw a bottle of water back at him which smashed on the floor.

The head waiter, who was Chinese, went to the first man smiling, but not saying anything, making a gesture as if he knew him. Then he smashed the man in the face with his fist. He then went to the second person and did exactly the same thing.

My group left and I went to the waiter and was telling him he should not have done that. It was completely out of order. I was very aggressive with the waiter.

Anger commonly shows up in dreams to do with patience and the digestive system. Eating while angry is very bad for your digestive system.

To dream of something *out of order* is usually about your physical body and something not functioning correctly within it. The focus is the subject matter of the dream. For example, a toilet out of order would indicate problems with your elimination system.

Floors in kitchens, bathrooms or when the state of the floor is the focus can also symbolize your elimination system. This is particularly the case if the floor is dirty or something has spilled onto it.

Unpleasant Chinese Experience – The Analysis

This wooden building and Chinese restaurant location immediately set the subject matter as the dreamer's digestive system. All the other symbols being interpreted must then be linked back to this. The bamboo cane around the doors and chairs also indicate the digestive system as they are all wooden. Of significance here is they are described as oriental trimmings. We expect to see particular foods mentioned in dreams about the digestive system so it is safe now to accept that Chinese food and oriental spices are the food in question. It is also expected that the food being depicted causes problems for the dreamer and something else in the dream will show how. We immediately see that it annoys the dreamer's body (annoys his person). The area in question is shown as a bottle of water smashing on the floor. The floor symbolizes the elimination system and the bottle narrows it to the dreamer's kidneys. The bottle being smashed dramatizes the problem to show his kidneys are affected very badly. We have to jump to the end of the dream for more of the effects on his kidneys. Here we find that when confronted with Chinese his digestive system goes *completely out of order*. As the dreamer says this himself in the dream it is likely he is aware of his intolerance to this food.

The Chinese head waiter is a guide in the dream and in typical fashion demonstrates by example another of the effects of eating this food. Smashing the two men in the face seems bizarre but the result would be reddened heated skin where contact was made. This shows the dreamer that Chinese (food) hits him in the face or in other words affects his face.

Lastly we see the dreamer himself becoming aggressive. It can be concluded that another reaction to Chinese food is that he becomes irritable and angry.

In reality the dreamer is aware that Chinese food affects him badly. His face sweats and he gets a rash. He is also easily angered for some hours after a meal and it takes his stomach a few days to settle. Despite this he still indulges once or twice a month because he loves the taste.

A *house* represents your physical body in dreams with specific rooms representing different parts of your body.

Dirty walls indicate that your colon needs cleansing. Toxins from your colon are getting into your blood stream

Wallpaper indicates the lining of your stomach or intestines particularly if in a kitchen, bathroom or dining room. Anyone *wallpapering* in a dream is a healing agent. They have the same gender as the parent with which you have issues, with regard to the subject matter of the dream.

Dream: Wallpapering over dirty walls

I dreamed I lived in a huge house. The walls were dusty and dirty. Some people were there putting up the wall paper and they were not doing a very good job because the wallpaper did not go all the way to the baseboards and a male friend said your walls are so dirty. They were really dusty with dust tags hanging from them. In another room they were putting up squares of wall paper. The squares were black and white and she was sticking little things on it that were red with foil sparkle. Outside there was a large pond and my male friend and husband were pumping the water out. At the bottom of the pond there was black sludge mud.

Red is an energizing color used in dreams to give you the energy to be passionate about life. This is especially true when mixed with white.

Sludge at the bottom of the *pond* indicates the state of your colon and that toxins are seeping from your colon into your blood stream.

Black and white together indicates you have a tendency to see life or the subject matter of the dream in black and white terms. This comes across as being intolerant or extremist. You see others are either with you or against you. There is no neutral position allowed. You need to be more tolerant. Another difficulty with being black and white about things is that you judge things as being either in the *right* or *wrong* camp. If presented with a third option it must also fit into the right or wrong camp but only one idea can fit into the *right* one. In order to open your mind to something new you have to first manage to move the current *right* idea into the *wrong* camp and that's a big task to ask. If you allow for more than just right and wrong you can have many shades in-between. Then you can have something that is *almost right*. Not being able to eliminate concepts that are holding you back eventually leads the body into not being able to eliminate waste matter efficiently and manifests as a slow moving colon along with the issues that can go along with that.

Wallpapering over dirty walls – The Analysis

This dream is about the lining of the dreamer's intestines and the state of her colon. Houses represent the physical body and in the context of this dream the walls being relined is an attempt at healing damage to the lining of the intestines. Damage can be caused by a number of reasons. This dream focuses on two reasons, one psychological and one physical. The physical condition is symbolized by dirt and black sludge. This indicates her colon is dirty. The colon is designed to deal with the body's waste and eliminate food that cannot be processed in a timely fashion. When working properly toxins do not have any time to build up on the waste. The mildly acidic condition in the colon also holds the growth of harmful fungus at bay. However, in this dream it is clear that the black sludge and dirt have been there for some time. Black is never a good color in dreams and here it clearly shows the sludge is harmful. The dreamer's colon is full of waste matter that under normal conditions would have been eliminated even years before. This allows toxins to build up which destroys the natural flora of the colon and damages the walls of the colon by eating into them.

The water being pumped from the pool is a very revealing symbol. Water and nutrients are absorbed into the blood stream through the walls of the colon. Now we see why the sludge is colored black in the dream. Every drink the dreamer takes pours over the harmful waste matter before it is absorbed into the bloodstream. Through this, toxins get into the bloodstream and these must cleansed by the liver. An overload of toxins often results in joint pains as they are carried to every part of the body by the bloodstream, while the excessive workload on the liver can result in a severe lack of energy.

The psychological condition is symbolized by black and white squares. This is a common symbol in dreams about the colon and indicates the dreamer holds a black and white view of the world. Things are either right or they are wrong. There is not subtle ground allowed between these extremes and this comes across as an overly critical nature. We see this in the dream too where she is critical of the job being done by the workers. Linking the symbols shows that this is the cause of the physical condition. The dreamer mentally holds onto things too long. Her body copies the psychological programming and holds onto waste matter too long.

My analysis to this point may seem harsh but the dream is not all bad. The red with foil sparkle is healing for a lack of energy and attempts to return a sparkle to life. The dreamer's husband and friend are symbolically healing her condition. When you see help being given in a dream it means there are problems in reality. In the dreamer's case, her husband became impotent due to cancer and a friend has recently been making advances. Since this is on her mind the friend helping in the dream shows the friend could help. Her view of right and wrong being black and white, however, exasperates her problem and is enough to trigger the dream.

6. Reproduction and Children

I'm sick of following my dreams. I'm just going to ask them where they're going and hook up with them later.

— **Mitch Hedberg**

When I started developing my website in 1997 I regularly checked my ranking in each of the major search engines. On one such check I discovered that my site was blocked by cyber patrol for having sexual content. The offending section was the dictionary because it listed symbols that indicated the female reproductive system. Move forward three years and I was writing agony aunt articles on dreams in an attempt to get them published in an American newspaper. The editor returned one article because it included a dream whose analysis included the words uterus and ovaries. I was shocked as reproduction is such an important theme in dreams and is certainly not obscene. To measure my audience I ran a survey on my website asking whether I should include dreams that cover femininity. I was relieved with the result – just over 84% of respondents were in favor of covering the subject.

Summary

► Dreams ask you to not view your gender as a drawback when faced with bias in society. Doing so can lead to health problems.

► Society's portrayal of sex as *dirty* makes it difficult for many people to talk openly about sex or to enjoy it without feelings of guilt.

► If you are having problems conceiving, your dreams point out the specific cause so you can heal it.

► Dreams reflect your anxieties about having or raising children.

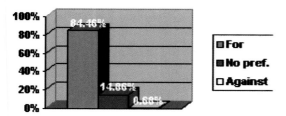

Figure 6-1 Survey Results

The question still has to be asked – why does anyone in our cultures see sex as obscene? The answer is that we are conditioned to think that way! Have you ever left the children with their grandparents and gone off for a 'dirty weekend'? Many who consider themselves liberated would still use that expression. Is sex dirty then? As obvious descendants of a line of people who must have had sex, are we all unclean? It does not help that the most insulting names you can call a person, are slang names for male and female genitals. That context is in the back of people's minds when those words are used. It is rare to come across anyone who can talk openly about sex without either feeling embarrassed or scrutinized. If they talk openly, they fear what others will think of them afterwards – even if the conversation is just with their partner! As you will see, these are some of the main issues raised by dreams on the subject.

Sexual discrimination

In Ireland it is fair to say that many workplaces do not have equal status for women. When I was younger women had to leave their job when they got married! Thinking about that now it seems so outrageous. My own children will grow up oblivious to that ever being part of Irish society. We have moved on but have not let it go fully. In Ireland and in many countries, many women feel that they have to work twice as hard in business just to be given the same breaks as a man doing the same job. Depending on how you are affected you may blame society, blame men, blame government, blame abuse of power or blame your gender. If the latter is true for you, expect dreams asking you to improve your view of your femininity.

During a radio interview a woman who owned two businesses called in with a dream that revealed this very problem. In her dream she found herself decorating a new bedroom she had just designed. The bedroom had two small bedrooms (the ovaries) off a large communal area (the uterus). In her words, "There was nothing exquisite about it." The dream was asking her to improve her view of her femininity and to accept the design of the body she had created. While there may be truth to having difficulty competing in a *man's world,* that is never a reason for blaming your gender. The problem is with society and not with reproductive organs. Left unchecked this negative view of her femininity could lead to health problems in the area being targeted by all the negative thoughts. This would become a self fulfilling prophecy since having a uterus has caused her nothing but problems in the first place!

If this resonates with you consider this to lighten your view. Women are the doorway between the spirit world and the physical world. While there are countless ways to die and leave the planet the only way for a soul to get here in the first place is through a woman's body. As a society we clearly do not give pregnancy and childbirth the respect they deserve. Creating a new human life is the most remarkable gift we have. If bringing a soul onto the planet is worthy of respect, then so too is the act that initiates the process.

Unenlightened view of sex and sexuality

If you have been brought up to believe that sex is dirty you might find yourself in your dreams cleaning a black stain off the carpet in the bedroom. Things underfoot in dreams often represent what we must overcome. The black stain is asking you to overcome your feelings of guilt with regard to the sexual act. Sex being regarded as dirty can also lead to the parts of the body that distinguish gender, being regarded as unclean. Dreams which show an unclean vessel such as a dirty bathtub, dirty bottles or a barrel of unclean water indicate this. You can also adopt a negative view of your gender if your parents were unhappy with your gender at birth. A woman holding up young boy's black briefs in the bedroom indicates that the dreamer picked up a negative attitude (black clothing) towards her gender (boys briefs) at the time of her birth, (indicated in this dream by holding up an object and inspecting it) because her parents were disappointed with her gender. While her parents may quickly move on from their disappointment, it is not so easy for the young child. She will shun the part of herself that her parents found fault with and in later life may develop a problem (psychological or physical) in this area unless something is done to correct the imbalance.

Sexual energy is the most creative energy we have. We can clearly see its ability to create life. Its creative ability, however, is not limited to just this and is used in any creative act. Writing, art, music, poetry, sculpture, etc. are all acts of creation and take on a life of their own once created. As such difficulties working in your creative area can be linked back to the reproductive system in your dreams. When this is the case the dream is pointing out that clearing the issues there will restore the flow of creative energy and thus help in other areas.

Your sexuality is part of your identity and tempers much of your conversation and actions in life. Even without being consciously aware of it you change the words you use, the detail of the conversation, and the manner of your speech depending of the gender of the friends you are talking to. If they are all your gender and age the conversation is least restricted. If the audience is mixed in gender or age certain subjects become taboo. For some people sexual communication is taboo even with their partner. Such a problem can trigger dreams where you are not able to talk on the telephone in a bedroom with your partner.

Problems with conception

Dreams can link problems with conception to the ovaries. One woman who had been trying unsuccessfully to conceive or carry a pregnancy past a few weeks dreamed she was mixing two packets of tomato soup. Red is the color of the base chakra, which feeds energy to the reproductive system, and is healing for it in dreams. It is also the color of passion and indeed tomatoes are known as passion fruit. The red color in her dream links the healing to her reproductive system. The problem being pointed out is that a mucous (soup) is affecting both ovaries (two packets of soup). The mucous attaches to the egg that is released and hinders fertilization and subsequent attachment of the embryo to the

Dream time

Approximately two hours out of eight are spent dreaming. However, we tend to only remember the dreams we have closest to waking. Dream recall is hindered when we do not get enough sleep. That is why we remember our dreams more vividly when on vacation.

uterus wall. In this dreamer's case the link is made to eating (food) and the elimination system (mixed in a bowl). The dream is clearly saying that toxins getting into the blood stream from the colon are causing a mucous to develop in the uterus. Improving diet and elimination are part of the solution to this problem.

Problems raising children

Anguish over raising children is a common theme in dreams and shows up as problems with teeth. We often forget we are animals in the animal world. Animals carry their young around with their teeth so to lose their teeth would inhibit their ability to raise young. Losing teeth in your dream indicates something is blocking your ability to either have children or to raise them. It can be a physical problem, it can be the onset of menopause or it can simply be that you are concerned that you do not have the life skills to raise your child with the attention they need.

These dreams often occur well before you become a parent. They are common with the onset of puberty in girls as the potential to be a mother becomes more real. They are also triggered by worries about being a worthy parent. When you do have children they are triggered when issues cause you to question your ability. For example, if your child becomes ill, your deep concern for their wellbeing can be a trigger. So too can your child getting involved in something life threatening, such as taking drugs. If all avenues for getting your child back on track are exhausted without success you can dream of losing your teeth. It can also be triggered when your child is leaving the nest and they no longer have the supervision you deem they need.

If there is a problem with your parenting you can also have these dreams. For example, if you over indulge in alcohol while around your children or are otherwise influencing them negatively you may dream of your teeth crumbling.

Dream Symbols for the Reproductive System

Red, the color of the base chakra, is linked to the reproductive system and used to heal it in dreams. It is also the color of passion and revitalizes the body. To dream of a thin red border on your partner's dress would indicate your passion is borderline in the relationship. In such dreams you will also be shown why and how to resolve the problem.

Most sexual activity takes place in the bedroom so bedrooms are a common symbol for the reproductive system. One of the most common symbols for reproduction, however, is a mirror. This symbol can appear in any location and still be about reproduction. A mirror reproduces an image of whoever is looking into it so is therefore a reproductive device. Other devices which show up in dreams and all indicate reproduction are cameras, photocopiers and any device with a purpose to

Philosophy of life begins at birth

In the first twenty minutes of your life you decide what type of world you have landed in and what type of person you will be.

53

copy or reproduce things.

Teeth falling out is by far the most common symbol for dreams about reproduction and raising children. As covered earlier this can indicate a physical health problem, the onset of menopause, issues with parenting or concerns over your child's wellbeing.

Water represents life and any vessel used to hold water can indicate the uterus – where new life begins. Mostly in dreams you find the vessel is unclean. Being unclean indicates the dreamer does not respect their reproductive system. Often the cause is they have been conditioned to regard sex as dirty at a young age. Therefore the parts of their body which distinguish gender are regarded as unclean or dirty. Typical examples would be dirty bottles, dirty bath tub, a barrel of unclean water, and so on.

A garden tree (especially in the front garden) is indicative of the family tree. As a symbol it may often appear along with flowers. A harvest field is indicative of the reproductive cycle. Seeds that were planted have now grown. Seeds, seedlings and potted plants are always about new growth.

Animals with young indicate your own young. Rabbits are commonly associated with reproduction and mean that in dreams. A hen house indicates the ovaries as eggs are produced in both locations. Dreams of eggs are about the eggs in the ovaries. For example, to dream of your partner discovering there are only a few good eggs in an egg box indicates coming close to menopause or that there are health issues affecting her ovaries.

The expression *she has a bun in the oven* is synonymous with pregnancy and ovens indicate this in dreams. Quite often the oven is a microwave as the word micro indicates something small. With deliberate care and attention, ingredients are carefully blended and placed in an oven to be transformed into a creation in its own right.

A gate lodge is a good symbol for the womb. A gate lodge is a small lodge in the grounds of a larger house. The larger house indicates yours or your mother's body and the gate lodge indicates a small place where another person can live in your body. You were once a lodger in your mother's body!

The front door of a house can represent the vagina – the front door to the body. The hallway, just inside the front door, indicates the uterus. To dream of being chased down the hallway by a woman with scissors indicates your life was threatened while in the womb. In particular your mother considered abortion (scissors in hallway). A small box room at the end of the hallway can also indicate the uterus. Indeed a box in any location can indicate it.

To dream of a problem with the wing mirror of a Morris Minor car is about potential problems with your reproductive system. The problematic mirror alone tells us this but the car in question is no longer reproduced so this again points to your reproduction stopping. Lastly the pun on minor in the car name *Morris Minor* closes the deal on this dream being about having children – you cannot reproduce minors.

When shown in dreams about relationships or the reproductive system the number thirty six is a pun on 'dirty sex' and indicates you are conditioned to view sex as dirty.

Sexual activity in dreams

Sexual activity in dreams is not about reproduction. Rather it symbolically asks you to get intimately in touch with your male side if you are having sex with a man, or your female side if with a woman. We all have male and female aspects to ourselves which have their own unique traits. For example, compassion, listening, leadership and your philosophy of life work through your female side. Confidence, belief in yourself, feeling worthy of the space you occupy, career and spiritual healing work through your male side. The dream may be triggered due to an imbalance which is affecting your ability to develop or move forward in an aspect of your life related to a particular energy. The dream tries to heal this by representing your male or female side as something desirable.

The dream wants both male and female sides of you to share closeness in an uninhibited way. This sharing restores balance so you can draw on the strength inherent in the aspect of your nature that is being repressed. Many people are shocked to find themselves having sex in a dream with a person of the same sex. This still has the same meaning. A woman having sex with another woman is still a healing device intended to put the dreamer in close contact with her heart / feelings.

Dreams can also include members of the family in sexual roles with the dreamer. Here the intent is to use an existing loving relationship as a pull to seduce the dreamer into have sex, and therefore accept the healing the dream is offering.

Where you are able to be honest to yourself in private but repress your feelings in public, you can dream about having sex in public. Again the purpose of the dream is the same, but here it is also asking you to not be afraid of being honest in front of others.

Another reason for dreaming of having sex is to heal you of a lack of sexual relations with your partner. Here the dream attempts to heal the impact abstinence is having on your relationship.

Quick Symbol Reference for the Reproductive System

The following symbols all indicate the above for various reasons. Complete descriptions are given in the Dream Symbol Reference later.

Animals with young	Gate lodge	Potted plants
Bed	Harvest field	Puns on Gynecological
Bedroom	Hen house	Rabbits
Camera	Loosing teeth	Red
Eggs	Microwave oven	Seedlings
Flower basket	Mirror	Unclean vessel
Fruit	Oven	
Garden trees	Photocopier	

55

A *telephone* can symbolize communication. If you dream about your partner, and there is a telephone in the dream, it is about communication with your partner. The location of the phone can also be significant. For example, a dream of a *broken telephone* in the bedroom means you need to work on sexual communication with your partner.

A *bedroom* symbolizes your reproductive system as sexual activity takes place there.

The most significant place in a *hotel* is the reception and in dreams they symbolize your reception at birth. Due to the normally receptive welcome in a hotel it is healing for your reception at birth. This is the most significant reception of your life and how you were welcomed on your arrival can subconsciously control a lot of your actions and philosophy of life. The birth imprint is so indelible it comes up time and again in your dreams. As with many dreams bringing you back to birth it is likely to also show the spiritual gifts you brought with you for this journey.

Dream: Broken Phone

I was in a hotel, upstairs outside my bedroom. The door was open. A cleaning maid approached with a photocopier that had a silver telephone attached to the top of it. She was wheeling it into my room. I tried to talk to my partner on the phone but couldn't. I discovered the lead connecting the phone to the copier was broken.

The color *silver* always indicates that you have a strong intuition / psychic ability and you are being encouraged by the dream to use it.

A *photocopier* reproduces copies of an original and as such symbolizes your reproductive system. Commonly to reinforce its symbolism the copier is located in the bedroom.

To dream of your *partner* means the dream is primarily about your relationship. The rest of the symbols in the dream will expand on the theme.

A *maid* is a healing agent because she cleans and puts things back into order. Healing agents appear in dreams to heal issues with the parent of the same gender – in this case your mother. Other symbols in the dream may detail the specific issue.

Broken Phone – The Analysis

This dream is about difficulty with sexual communication in the dreamer's relationship. The dream links the current difficulty to the dreamer's reception at birth by locating it in a hotel. The first person he meets in the dream is a maid. She is a healing agent and this means that his problems stem from his relationship with his mother and in particular how she received him when he was born. The maid sets out to heal (clean) the communication problem by bringing a phone onto the scene. The phone is connected to a photocopier. Photocopiers symbolize reproduction and the sexual act so clearly the communication has to do with sexual communication. The open door asks the dreamer to take advantage of an existing opportunity or to create opportunities to deal with the problem.

When the dreamer tries to talk to his partner on the phone he discovers the lead is broken. This again highlights there is no real connection in the relationship when it comes to discussing sexual matters. It is worth pointing out that the maid would not have brought a broken phone into the dream. It is the dreamer's own expectations projected onto the phone that result in the break. Lastly the dreamer has a psychic / intuitive ability which is indicated by the color of the phone. It is common to see spiritual abilities in dreams that reflect the birth imprint as they are so important on our life journey. The dream is encouraging the dreamer to use his intuition (silver) rather than logic (upstairs) to guide him through healing this.

For a boy the first and most important relationship with the opposite sex is with mother. Through that loving, nurturing relationship a boy becomes comfortable with expressing himself. In later life this is built on when it comes to sexual expression with his partner. The more comfortable expression as a child was the more comfortable expression as an adult will be.

In reality the dreamer's mother was sexist, expressing her view openly to her children that all men are only after one thing when it comes to women. As an innocent child with no sexual urges this was taken on by the dreamer. However, when puberty arrived he was thrown into conflict. Has arousal anything to do with love or is he just like the monsters his mother told him about? This results is an inability to talk about sexual desires with his partner as in his mind expressing desire proves he is a monster.

This dream shows the clear connection between conditioning in childhood and problems much later in life. Therapies like cutting-the-ties along with a good experienced counselor are invaluable when dealing with issues like this.

The most significant place in a *hotel* is the reception and in dreams they symbolize your reception at birth. Due to the normally receptive welcome, a hotel is healing for your reception at birth. This is the most significant reception of your life, and how you were welcomed on your arrival can subconsciously control a lot of your actions and philosophy of life.

Dreams of a *baby* or babies can be triggered when you are trying to have one. The dream can also be about influences you picked up as a baby.

A *toddler* can indicate influences you picked up around the age of the toddler in the dream.

A *play pen* indicates the uterus – a place for a child to develop.

A *bed* can symbolize your reproductive system

Diapers indicate your elimination system.

A *screen* can indicate medical screening for health problems.

Dream: Confusion

I walked into what looked like a hotel room and a woman was sitting in an arm chair reading the paper in a robe. There was a young toddler in a play pen on the floor made out of screen material for windows. The child was maybe 9 or 10 months old. On a bed was a young infant wearing a diaper in a basket inside the same type of pen. The pen was covered in screen material with a hole near the feet. Mice with rainbow, blue and spotted light brown and orange colors were running around it. There were paper shreds in the pen and I was afraid the animals would chew on the baby. No one was crying. The baby on the floor in the pen was looking around and the woman was just reading. The baby on the floor was also in paper shredding.

Mice symbolize a serious health threat, such as cancer. If the mice are eating a particular food or it is shown in the same dream, it is likely you are being told your body has a very low tolerance for this food.

Crying in a dream is healing as it symbolically gives release to pent up emotions related to the subject matter of the dream.

Orange is used in dreams to indicate digestive system trouble and to help heal it (The sacral chakra is orange and feeds energy to the stomach and digestive system).

Blue symbolizes philosophy and attitude to life itself. It is one of the most common colors in dreams and is used to show your attitude to the subject matter.

Confusion – The Analysis

A bedroom and bed are the most common symbols for the reproductive system. Play pens and Moses baskets specifically represent the uterus – where babies develop. There is also the pervasive theme of babies throughout the dream so clearly the dream is about the dreamer's reproductive system and having children. The dream shows both symbols for the uterus covered with screen material for windows. This stands out as it is so unusual. It indicates the dreamer is being screened for something to do with reproduction. The window reference is positive in this context as it shows there is light connected with this – light at the end of the tunnel, so to speak.

The dream also links other issues with difficulty having children. The hotel is about her reception at birth and it appears in the dream to show there is a connection there. Since a mother is prominent in the dream the link is with how the dreamer's mother received her at birth. When trauma is involved it is not surprising that similar situations in later life are affected by that event. As a child the dreamer could have looked at her own situation and proclaimed she would never bring a child into the world as she would never want to subject anyone to what she had suffered. The decision is made as a child with child's logic. The dreamer points out that none of the children are crying. This shows that crying is needed to express repressed sadness. Perhaps in her situation crying evoked a negative response from her mother. This conditioning can be removed by cutting the ties with mother or through counseling. The newspaper indicates counseling would be productive. Newspapers, like counselors, provide an unbiased (we hope) account of events as they happened. With informed coverage we can make up our own minds about things. This is what counseling does. It brings you to a space where you can draw your own conclusions and see clearly the ongoing impact of events in your life.

The dream also links in digestive system problems through the symbols of paper shreds, the floor, brown mice and gerbils. The orange color attempts to heal those problems as it is the color of the sacral chakra that feeds energy to that part of her body. The mice indicate a threat of cancer in that area. The link to reproduction is vitally important. The dreamer has bad memories of being in her mother's womb. When we have negative thoughts about part of our body (thinking badly about your mother's womb is the same as thinking badly about your own) we target it with more than just thoughts. In this dreamer's case toxins from the colon target her reproductive system. Correcting her diet and taking necessary steps to restore balance to her digestive system will help resolve her problem.

In reality the dreamer and her partner were trying to have another child and at the time of the dream she was waiting to see if her most recent fertility treatment was successful. As for her own birth, in fits of anger her mother told her she was basically raped by her dad and that she fought delivery. She is also aware of her digestive system problems and monitors her diet.

7. Nightmares

I don't use drugs, my dreams are frightening enough.

— M. C. Escher

Any event during the day can act as a backdrop for your dream that night. However, you usually find that the detail of the dream is subtly different from your waking experience. It is the subtle difference that is often significant. For example, a lady who is an orchestra musician by profession dreamed of playing music. She felt that the standard interpretation for playing music could not hold for her as this is what she does every day. A closer inspection revealed that she was playing a clarinet in her dream whereas in reality she plays violin and cannot play the clarinet. She felt that the difference in instrument was unimportant. Her dream was telling her she is a channel / medium and can communicate with spirits. The dream picked an instrument she cannot play to highlight that her gift is something she has not recognized in herself.

When it comes to nightmares the same is true. A nightmare may be triggered by watching a Frankenstein movie yet you dream of Dracula chasing you rather than Frankenstein. The subtle difference is important. What is most interesting is that just like ordinary dreams, nightmares can comment on any aspect of your life and the message can be something you welcome or something you do not. The only difference is your ability to remember a nightmare is fantastic compared to an ordinary dream. You wake up in a sweat thankful to be awake and away from the horror. Quite often your recall is so good that you try to wake up even more just to be sure you do not enter the same dream again when you lie back down.

In her nightmare, a woman dreamed of

Summary

▶ Just like ordinary dreams, nightmares can comment on any aspect of your life and the message can be something you welcome or something you do not.

▶ There are common themes to nightmares.

▶ Each dream contains a message to effect change in your conscious mind. However, the subconscious mind, like a faithful dog, is always on guard to protect its master. The fears it portrays to reject the change turns some dreams into nightmares.

being chased and caught by a lion. The lion was going to eat her but kept her locked in a cage for later. While the dream itself is horrific the interpretation is very positive. Lions are king of the jungle so represent leadership. Her dream was telling her that she is a leader. Running from the lion shows that she has issues with leadership. In her case the issues stemmed from her teenage years and were something for which she was attending counseling at the time of the dream. We cannot suppress any part of our nature without suppressing some positive aspect at the same time. Her dream showed she was suppressing her leadership ability (running from the lion). The corollary being that dealing with her teenage years was freeing her leadership ability – a fantastic and encouraging message to receive.

There are common themes to nightmares. Being chased is one of the most common. This signifies running away from your past (something behind you). What you are being chased by is important. If a man is chasing you it means you are running away from issues with your father, or the man in the dream. Conversely being chased by a woman means you are running away from issues to do with your mother, or the woman in the dream. It is possible to only be aware of being chased and not know by whom. In these dreams it is clear that there are issues in the past that you are still subconsciously running from. Indeed it is your subconscious mind that asserts itself and turns what would have been an ordinary dream into a nightmare.

Your subconscious mind at work

Dreams come from your soul and are intended to help you progress along your life path. In sleep the focus of the physical world and the body is on hold and during this period your soul has a perfect opportunity to dialogue with your conscious mind...or so it would appear. The problem here is that the subconscious never sleeps. Think of the subconscious like a faithful dog always on guard to protect its master. Your soul asks the conscious mind to make a change to some aspect of functioning in order to avoid a particular undesirable outcome. For example, suppose your soul wants you to be less analytical in your approach to life and to incorporate intuition and feelings into the decision making process. It dispatches a dream for this purpose. Ideally the dream is received well and your conscious mind accepts the direction of your soul and begins a program to change in this direction. The more likely outcome, however, is that your subconscious mind asserts itself in the dream and provides all sorts of reasons why this change should be avoided. Due to this, the dream is effectively spoiled with the message or request discarded. In some cases your subconscious is so effective at giving negative reasons for avoiding a request that your dream becomes a nightmare. The dream can still be interpreted as the message is still there. However, now the symbols indicating fears are stronger.

Negative characters

Negative male and female characters represent negative traits brought out in you by your parents. This does not necessarily reflect how your parents were but rather a trait or traits you adopted as a result of how your parents were.

Why does this happen? What gain does the subconscious make from this? The simple answer is that there is no gain but the subconscious still retains control in the area which was being addressed. The subconscious mind is being helpful as far as it is concerned and sees the reasons it provides for avoiding the change as valid. Drawing on your personal experience as evidence it will tell you "When you are open to your feelings you are open to being hurt, rejected and ignored. You will end up sad and depressed." In this way it appears to protect you from reliving pain from the past.

The price for this protection is very high. Life is about increasing your awareness of yourself. Awareness is gained directly through eliminating the control the subconscious mind has in areas of your life. It cannot be transferred intellectually. You cannot read something and become aware. However, you can read and then be more prepared to accept opportunities to eliminate subconscious control when they present themselves.

In my life I was closed minded to any ideas outside the sphere of science, and I immediately classed as idiot anyone who spoke of things beyond the physical. I was so sure of my conviction that I was unaware that my subconscious mind was in control - protecting me. As long as I continued with that attitude I learned nothing. I was very fortunate to have been put in a position where I faced my fears head on. At the time I did not welcome it and in fact feared for my life. I did not want to see spirit people walking around but there they were! I was so fearful of the very thing that I had proclaimed did not exist. Through my experiences I learned much about spirits and how my fear of them had no basis in fact. From spirits I have learned much about what I am - what we are. From childhood I always had a fear of the dark and slept with some light on in the room - even though I did not believe anything was in the room with me. Ironically, since seeing spirits I now sleep with the light off and am comforted by the fact that they are there. The experience helped me to open my mind.

Most of us allow our subconscious free reign in many areas of our lives. Life shows us where these areas lie and helps us weed out that control. Our dreams support this endeavor by showing the causes and effects of our subconscious conditioning. Typically dreams show what event first caused us to act in a particular way. They let us know how we still re-act today due to the ongoing

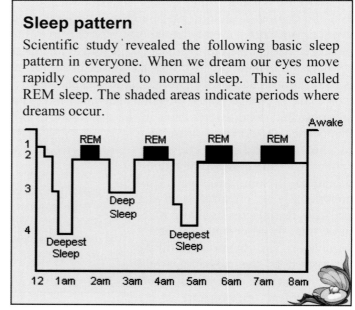

Sleep pattern

Scientific study revealed the following basic sleep pattern in everyone. When we dream our eyes move rapidly compared to normal sleep. This is called REM sleep. The shaded areas indicate periods where dreams occur.

effects of that event and they show us how to change for the better. Dreams often bring us back to childhood as the time of our conditioning. As children we take on board everything about our parents. We see them as infallible and wanting to be so much like them we adopt their ways of behaving - both good and bad. At appropriate times in our lives our dreams select a negative aspect of our conditioning and ask us to eliminate it - thus reducing the control of the subconscious and increasing our awareness. In this way we are helped to achieve our life purpose. This is covered in detail later in the book.

A *cinema* represents expansion of life and is present in dreams where you are being shown how to make your life into the bigger picture that is meant for you. Long before television, cinema was the means for news dispersal and letting the people know what existed in the world.

A *magician* is a guide in a dream and as such his or her advice is infallible. Whatever he or she is trying to get you to do is something you need to do in reality. Magicians are masters of illusion and show you that nothing is impossible.

To dream of your *partner* means the dream is primarily about the nature of your relationship. The rest of the symbols in the dream will expand on the theme.

Dream: The Magician

I am in a cinema theatre with my husband. A magician is in front of the screen. He points at me and I start to lift into the air over the seats towards him. I feel doomed and resist by holding myself down. I manage to move out to the aisle and stay on the ground by digging my heels in as I walk. I am impelled towards him and feel a force on the back of my knees to keep moving. I am terrified.

A *screen* indicates a strong intellect and the ability to project your mind onto others. Along with that comes the ability to perform absent healing and hypnosis – both of which work through mind projection.

To *resist* in a dream means that in waking life you are resisting or stubborn with regard to the subject matter of the dream. The dream is asking you to change this behaviour.

Digging your heels in shows that you are stubborn with regard to the subject matter of the dream.

Strong emotions such as *terror* appear in dreams as a result of your subconscious rejecting the message of the dream. You need to be more accepting of the change your dream is asking you to make.

Dreams evoke a feeling of *doom* when this is how you normally feel with regard to the subject matter of the dream. Other symbols in the dream will tell you how to heal this in reality.

The Magician – The Analysis

The strong sense of fear the dreamer felt from this dream was so overpowering that she had no idea what it could be about. When terror comes into a dream it is hard to accept that the interpretation of the symbols can be the same as for ordinary dreams. However, once we start into it, the analysis becomes clear very early on.

When your partner is in your dream the subject matter is the nature of your relationship. So now we must relate all the other symbols back to that. The cinema theatre tells us the dream is an attempt at expanding her relationship – always a good symbol. The magician, having both a title and a position of authority, is a guide and as such we expect him to show her how to expand and bring her relationship to a new level. He does this firstly by appearing as a magician. Magicians make the impossible happen with incredible ease right before your eyes. So if he did nothing else his presence tells the dreamer that she can achieve what she currently thinks is impossible. However, he goes a step further and tries to help her.

By trying to lift her into the air he is symbolically removing all obstacles from her path to bring her quickly to where she needs to be. The location is the front of the stage or the limelight. This gives a clue as to the problems in the relationship. The dreamer does not feel she is important to her partner – he's not giving her the spotlight. Rising into the air is symbolic of mentally rising above her problems. Many times we amplify our problems by replaying them on a loop in our heads. Each time around the loop they somehow become stronger. The screen in the dream shows this dreamer has a strong intellect. We would expect this as she needs it to mentally rise above her problems. However, it also reminds her that her negative thoughts are powerful too. The solution to her relationship issues is to accept help where it's offered (accept help from the guide) and to tap into her enlightened intellect to gain a bigger perspective on life.

Instead we see the dreamer's reaction to her current problems. She feels a sense of doom in the relationship and allows this give her permission to 'hold myself down' or in other words indulge depression. Her resistance to change is repeated several times in the dream (resist, hold myself down, digging my heels in). She must overcome this to improve her relationship. A dream will not tell you what your partner must do for things to get better. Dreams only focus on your part in the picture. If she wants her partner to treat her differently she must change. Once changed she may no longer want her partner to be any different than he currently is!

The terror shows up as a result of her massive subconscious resistance to her having to do the work to improve the relationship. The magician shows her, however, that even if she takes the long and slow route to the front, her guides will keep putting pressure on her to move forward.

8. The Power of Lucid Dreams

In forming a bridge between body and mind, dreams may be used as a springboard from which man can leap to new realms of experience lying outside his normal state of consciousness.

— Ann Faraday

A lucid dream is one in which you are aware you are dreaming while in the dream. Everyone has them from time to time. What do you do in your lucid dreams? Many people tell me that when they become aware they are dreaming they fly or do something else they know they can only do in a dream. For the duration of the dream, and their awareness of it, they enjoy the exhilarating freedom this brings. However, there is an untapped power available to you in lucid dreams. Consider why you dream in the first place - each dream sets out to heal you or to guide you in order to bring you one step closer to achieving your life purpose. Then also consider that you frequently reject the messages of your dreams by projecting your own negativity and fears into them. Lucid dreams give you a powerful opportunity to change this by consciously accepting the healing and guidance of your dreams.

For example, one person dreamed of an open field beside a shopping centre. In the field a man was building a grey brick wall. This dream was telling the dreamer it is his responsibility (shopping centre) to open his heart (open field) and let others get to know him – to openly share his feelings. His rejection of the message is symbolized by the man building a grey wall in the field. Grey represents mental denial of emotion and the wall symbolizes keeping others away from his heart. So even at this very early point in the dream we have the dream's request and the dreamer's rejection of that request. The dream continued with the dreamer walking down the hill to the shopping centre. At some point on his trek he became aware he was dreaming and then realizing that the wall was a negative symbol

Summary

▶ In a lucid dream you are aware you are dreaming. Since it is a dream you need not fear anything you encounter.

▶ You can train yourself to become lucid in your dreams.

▶ You can ask questions of characters in your lucid dreams. They can tell you what they represent in your dream.

he ran back to it and knocked it down. The man building it was gone when he got back to it. Being lucid allowed the dreamer take control over his subconscious and assert his acceptance of the dream's message. Even though he was not consciously aware of why the wall was a negative symbol, his actions effectively told his subconscious to tear down the walls he has erected in a misguided attempt to protect himself from ings of rejection.

This dreamer did not remember what the wall symbolized in his dream but did remember that it was negative. However, there is another power you can use in lucid dreams even if you have never attended any dream classes. You can ask any living characters in the dream what aspect of you they represent and they will answer honestly. The dreamer above could have asked the man building the wall why he was building it or simply asked him what the wall represented or what he represented in the dream. The man would have given a meaningful answer as he knows his purpose in the dream. It is important to realize that while the man knows his purpose in the dream he does not necessarily know anything else about you. If you were to ask him whether you should change your job he may answer but it would not be accurate as he has nothing to do with your career. Staying focused on the dream is important but sometimes hard to do if you have a question that is pressing on your mind. You are more likely to ask your pressing question when you become aware you are dreaming rather than questions about the dream itself. When you do this the opportunity is lost. It is best to remember to ask, "What aspect of me do you represent?" This will lead into dialogue where the character can advise you correctly.

Another power available in lucid dreams is to face your fears. For example, if you are being chased through your house, when you realize it is a dream you know that you cannot be hurt or physically killed – it is only a dream. Whatever is in pursuit of you is an aspect of you that is crying to be understood. Stop running from it and face it. It may take courage to do this initially, but when you have frequent lucid dreams, you learn that you can remove the threat from fearsome characters. After all, it is your mind that projects them into the dream in the first place. For example, one man had recurring dreams of being chased by a gang of youths intent on harming him. While running away he had to step over the mutilated bodies of others they had caught. In one such dream he became aware he was dreaming and mustering up courage turned to face his attackers. To his amazement he discovered the leader of the gang was someone he went to high school with. They acknowledged each other and the leader told the others, "This guy is okay. I know him." He never had the dream again. By consciously facing his fears in a lucid dream he effectively diffused them.

When it comes to health, lucid dreams are again very powerful. One man dreamed he was in a forest and culling black and white animals that had mu-

Are dreams in your head?

When you ponder an issue it is obvious your thoughts are occurring inside your head. An interesting aspect of lucid dreams is, that even when you are aware you are in a dream, you never feel that the dream itself is taking place inside your head.

tated into new breeds. He decided to keep two of the young from each of the different kinds of animals in a cardboard box so they could continue breeding and he culled the rest. When he became aware he was dreaming he realized what the animals represented and immediately went back to the box and killed the young he had kept. While this seems gruesome, the mutated animals breeding represent cancer (mutation) multiplying in his colon (forest). Culling them was positive and showed his immune system at work destroying the cancer cells. However, his reluctance to cull all of them showed that his own actions were blocking the effectiveness of his immune system and keeping the cancer alive in his body. Through lucid dreaming he changed that.

How to trigger lucid dreams

The difficulty with realizing you are in a dream is that they appear to be reality in the dream state and so seem normal at the time. One aspect of dreams is that they always change and you can use this to detect when you are dreaming. If you look at a clock in a dream and then look at it again the time will be different. If you are reading a newspaper and look away for a moment the newspaper will have changed when you look back. The same is true of everything in dreams. Armed with this knowledge you can practice testing whether you are dreaming when you are awake. When you read a clock, look away and then read the clock again to ensure the time remains the same. Similarly when reading a newspaper, look away for a moment and then look back at what you were reading to ensure the page has not changed. Obviously the time will read the same and so will your newspaper. However, once you have developed the habit of testing whether you are dreaming you will automatically use it in your dreams and switch easily into lucid dreaming. It is a wonderful feeling. The moment you look back at the clock in your dream and see the time changed you immediately become aware you are in a dream. It is amusing that a simple time change on a clock can trigger your awareness of being in a dream yet having tea with a talking elephant will not! What you do from that point forward is under your control. To get the most benefit remember to

- ► Ask characters what aspect of you they represent. Only ask questions relevant to what they are doing. They may answer other questions but the answer is meaningless.

- ► Ask for advice from guides. A guide is a person bearing a gift, with a title or in a position of authority. Ask in a general way, such as, "What advice do you wish to give?" or "What is the message of this dream?" Guides can answer questions outside the message of the dream but they may not want to. The dream obviously has an important message of its own and they will want to impart that.

- ► Eliminate negative symbols. You may have to interrogate them first to find out if they are negative.

- ► Face your fears while realizing it is a dream as you cannot be physically hurt regardless of how the dream turns out.

9. Colors in Dreams

We don't have an eternity to realize our dreams, only the time we are here.

— **Susan Taylor**

It is remarkable that light, which travels as a photon, is the only atomic particle that you can detect with your senses directly. Your eyes are so sensitive that you can see a single photon of light! You also detect the wavelength of that particle as color. You have a natural association with colors whether you are consciously aware of it or not. They permeate your aura and can be subconsciously picked up on by others around you. Have you ever been red with anger or green with envy? Have you been down with the blues? Ever called anyone a yellow belly? Do you have a friend who sees things as black and white? Have you described things you are not clear on as a grey area? Do you associate pink with love? Perfection and innocence are associated with white and specific occasions demand that color. Our association with colors is also precise when it comes to their meaning in dreams. The colors listed have those exact meanings and more in your dreams.

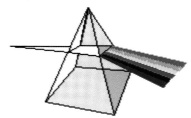

Figure 9-1 White light split into a rainbow of colors with a prism

There is a myth that people only dream in black and white. When I am asked, it

Summary

► Colors are used in your dreams to heal you, to guide you or as a symbolic expression of your normal reaction to the subject matter of the dream.

► If you have not dreamed in color or cannot remember doing so it simply means just that. It does not mean that others do not.

► The interpretation of colors in dreams comes from their meaning in the human aura.

► Each chakra has a specific color and purpose associated with it. To dream of a chakra's color helps with that purpose and heals the areas of your body connected to the chakra.

always reminds me of an argument between my mother and eldest brother. She was arguing that cats can only see in black and white but he was having none of it. Voices got raised and my sister came in to see what the commotion was. "Oh, Jimmy was here in his last life as a cat", smirked my mother with victory in her eyes. Quick as a flash Jimmy replied, "And mother was here as a color blind one!"

If you have not dreamed in color or cannot remember doing so it simply means just that. It does not mean that others do not. When I first hear a dream I zero in on any colors that are mentioned because they are so easy to interpret. I then look for symbols to support the interpretation they give. After I cover this aspect on my courses, people subsequently detail lots of colors in dreams they submit. Until that point they do not put any significance on colors in dreams and that is why they are not recalled.

The interpretation of colors in dreams comes from their interpretation in the human aura. As with anything else in your dreams each color is there to heal you, to guide your or to indicate your normal reaction to the subject matter of the dream. Positive colors, usually bright shades or pastels, are in your dreams as a form of healing or guidance. Dark colors and combinations with dark colors are a reflection of your fears and reservations about such healing and guidance. Unlike other symbols your personal association with color can not change the meaning of that color for you. For example, you may like black as a color but it will never have a positive interpretation if you see it in your dream. Each color has a specific purpose in your aura just like oxygen does in your lungs. Some clairvoyants give readings by looking at the colors in your aura and tuning into them. The detail obtained can be amazing.

In your dreams the position of the color is important. Colors underfoot or where you must walk show what you must eliminate or overcome in yourself. Back and white tiles show that your standpoint on the subject matter of the dream is that it is black and white. By pointing it out the dream is asking you to overcome this extremism. Colors above eye level indicate something to strive for because you have to look up to see them. We will see some examples of this later.

Colors worn or brought by a healing agent, a positive, helpful or supportive character, indicate what emotions you need to develop in yourself to ensure good health. Colors worn or brought by a guide, a positive character in a position of authority, indicate what spiritual gifts you need to develop and use.

Negative shades of color worn by negative male characters indicate what negative attributes you picked up from dad. For example, a black coat indicates that you copied his fear or he made you afraid. Similarly, negative shades of color worn by negative female characters indicate the negative effect your mother had on you. For example, a red and black dress indicates you picked up her anger.

For example, if you find yourself in a pink room, a green field, a yellow toilet, driving a brown car, watching an orange sun the dream is trying to heal you with love (pink), harmony (green), letting go (yellow), practicality (brown), ambition (orange) and so on.

The meaning of colors in dreams

The main colors and color combinations that you find in dreams are listed here. Where appropriate, the keyword or phrase for the color is in italics. This is the most common interpretation for the color but it could be any of the other listed meanings. If the color is associated with a chakra that information is also listed. If a particular color is not listed then combine the meanings of the colors that constitute it. If the dream is about physical health refer to the meaning in the *Color Healing Chart* later.

| **Black** | | Fear |

Meaning: Negativity, fear, anxiety, hatred, resentment, guilt, depression (no hope / faith).

Black is never a positive color to see in any dream. For example, a man in black behind you would indicate fears picked up from dad. A black stain on the bedroom floor would indicate you have guilt issues with regard to sex. A dark cloud or black crow flying over your head would indicate depression. When black is mixed or associated with other colors it adulterates their meaning. For example, red indicates passion but when mixed with black it indicates anger.

Black and white as a combination indicates that you view the subject matter of the dream in black and white terms. The dream is asking you to overcome your intolerance or simplistic extremism. Allow for subtle shades between your point of view and the other end of the spectrum. Drop the attitude that if something is not good it must be evil. For example, sitting on the floor holding a pint of Guinness while watching your parents argue would indicate that you have a black and white attitude (color of Guinness) when dealing with conflict in relationships (parents arguing in their relationship) that you picked up in childhood (sitting on the floor).

| **Blue** | Philosophy of life | Throat Chakra |

Meaning: Spirituality, religion, art, culture, philosophy, attitude to life itself.

Blue is probably the most common color to see in dreams. When you see other positive colors with it you are being asked to add their meaning to your philosophy of life. For example, if you dream of blue and gold you are being asked to accept that you are a spiritual healer as part of your philosophy. Another common combination to see is blue, red and white. This may be in the dream as a flag, such as the French, English or American flags, or simply as the colors themselves, a blue sea with white waves and a beautiful red tinted sky. Here the dream asks you to add joy and hope (red and white) to your philosophy of life.

When you see negative colors with blue you are being asked to remove these from your philosophy. A common example is navy, which is a mixture of blue and black or blue and black as a combination. Both mean that you have a negative philosophy or attitude towards the subject matter of the dream. If this philosophy is pervasive throughout your life then it may very well be the subject matter of the dream itself. It could be superstition or a negative form of religion where you feel you will be punished eternally or are being judged by God now. Whatever the cause you are being asked to lighten up and adopt a more positive attitude.

Brown   Practicality

Meaning: Earthy, practical, of the earth.

People who have not bonded well with the earth, are not happy with their body, or constantly think that life in spirit is so much better than life here, can often dream of brown. Dreaming of a brown door on a church asks the dreamer to be practical (earthly) when considering their spiritual development. In other words don't give up on this life in the hope that the next one will solve everything.

Dark or dull brown indicates an unenlightened or depressing earthiness such as a materialistic viewpoint that includes denial of spirit. For example, to be met at a train station by a man wearing a dark brown coat means you were influenced by dad's materialistic view of the world from birth (arrival at train station).

Cream   Acceptance

Meaning: Acceptance, tolerance, a growing maturity or a need for tolerance.

Quite often cream appears in dreams as an antidote to white. It asks the dreamer to be less critical of themselves and others. A woman wearing a cream blouse in a dream asks you to accept your mother as she is. Through doing this you are developing tolerance and growing through it. Parents are always the most difficult to deal with. Life is designed to be that way. I will accept my mother / father if they will just …. fill in the blank yourself. That intolerance will cause you to dream of cream. If a person tells lies about you do you set out to correct your image in their eyes of everyone they spoke to? That will cause you to dream of cream. Don't focus on controlling others. Rather, focus on being the person you know you are.

Green   Sharing / Balance   Heart Chakra

Meaning: Need for healing, harmony, balance, reconciliation (within yourself or between you and others).

Green, another common color for dreams, asks the dreamer to restore balance and healing for the heart, circulatory systems and emotions by becoming more giving, generous and emotionally open.

Green is the color of the heart chakra so dreaming about it is healing for the heart. Dreams in the countryside where you are surrounded by green are asking you to open your heart and share your feelings. In most cases the sharing must first begin with you. Learn how to listen to your feelings and acknowledge them. Many people have learned to suppress their feelings from a young age and started so long ago that they are now doing it subconsciously.

Green also attempts to harmonize opposites. For example, dreaming of green pork meat means your body cannot digest pork. The dream tries to put the food in harmony with your body by making it green. Always stop eating foods shown in this way.

If a guide is wearing green in your dream, especially if combined with pink, it means you have the potential to be a counselor (having empathy and harmony).

Dark green or green and black show difficulty with sharing and indicate jealousy, envy or rivalry. Indeed envy is referred to as the green eyed monster! Dark green shows disharmony and indicates a need to balance male and female aspects within.

Green and red as a color combination always symbolize your heart and circulatory system.

Grey — Uncommitted

Meaning: uncommitted, uncertain - 'grey area'. Mental denial of emotion, depression.

A common color for relationship dreams. In these cases the dreamer is not usually aware that they suppress their feelings. They tend to say things like, "I know she loves me - she wants to marry me", rather than, "I know she loves me because I can feel it." Dreaming of your fiancé wearing a grey wedding dress shows you are not in touch with your feelings. Is your marriage an acquisition, for status or have you found a trophy wife? The problem here is that when you are not in touch with your feelings you are unlikely to be aware of it. Only when you do a therapy to restore that connection will you have a frame of reference to know what the difference *feels* like.

Grey clouds can indicate depression, either present or imminent. A grey fog indicates you cannot see your way from where you are now to where you need to go with regard to the subject matter of the dream.

Gold — Spiritual Healing

Meaning: Spiritual healing, creativity.

This color asks the dreamer to develop their spiritual healing ability. Spiritual healing is done through placing your hands on your target and channeling energy through your body and out from your hands into the client. If you could see clairvoyantly you would see a spirit healer standing in your aura and partially overlaying your body. This spirit directs the energy and uses it to trigger the healing process.

People with this ability often use it to heal themselves in their own dreams. For example, when you are run down you could dream of lying on a beach with the sun beaming down on you. Here the golden sun is the healing symbol and is restoring your body to health.

Orange — Drive / Ambition — Sacral Chakra

Meaning: Drive, ambition (mix of yellow and red). Energizing color, especially in career dreams.

Orange has to do with assimilation of new ideas and can indicate a profound change in perspective is being attempted or required. The sacral chakra, which is located close to the stomach, is energized by this color and helps with assimilation. When given good news we can feel it here as butterflies in our stomach. When given overwhelmingly bad news we feel it as if our stomach is in knots.

The sacral chakra also feeds energy to the stomach and digestive system. Orange is used in dreams to indicate digestive system trouble and to help heal it. A common theme is to dream of standing in line for orange drink. The slow moving line indicates that your digestive system is slow moving and the orange drink symbolically heals this.

Black and orange as a color combination in dreams indicates ambition driven out of fear and always indicates career. Tigers have this color combination so often symbolize career in dreams.

Peach   Empathy

Meaning: Empathy.

Empathy is the trademark of a skilled counselor. If a guide wears or brings peach it means that the dreamer has the potential to be a counselor. It is common to have other gifts that complement your counseling ability. For example, to dream of peach lamp shades means that your intuition (lamp) helps you when counseling.

Pink   Unconditional Love

Meaning: Love, need for unconditional love, usually mother love or love for mother.

Pink, a mix of red (passion) and white (perfection), indicates love. To dream of this color is enough to show that you did not bond well with your mother or that she did not love unconditionally. The most significant bond is at birth so it is likely the dream brings you right back to the start of childhood. A poor bond affects the flow of female energy within and negatively impacts on spiritual gifts that require a female energy flow such as intuition, counseling, and teaching.

Cutting-the-ties with mother is a very effective way of healing this poor bond.

Purple   Spiritual Leader / Teacher   Crown Chakra

Meaning: Nobility of purpose, spiritual leadership, spiritual teaching, regal, power, authority in spiritual matters (bishops wear purple)

Purple is the color of the crown chakra which is associated with spiritual understanding. Purple has long been associated with leadership, royalty and religious dress. In Roman times only leaders and boys under 17 years old (potential future leaders) were allowed wear the color purple. In dreams it signifies you are a spiritual leader / teacher. Spiritual leadership works through empowering other to be able to face their own challenges and works through female energy.

The shade of purple is important. Mauve indicates endurance while lilac indicates responsibility. To dream of women exercising in lilac leotards tells you it is your responsibility (lilac) to develop your emotional expression (women exercising). Indigo is another shade of purple and is the color of the brow chakra. This chakra is often depicted as the third eye and in dreams indicates you are clairvoyant.

Red   Passion   Base Chakra

Meaning: Joy, sexuality, aggression, animal passion, fun.

Red is the color associated with your base chakra which connects you with the earth and points directly downwards. It is responsible for keeping you grounded.

Red in dreams has to do with passion and joy. In a negative context it symbolizes anger. For example, to dream of your fiancé in a dress with a red border would indicate that your passion is borderline in the relationship.

Red is an energizing color in dreams and is often used to give you the energy to be passionate about life. This is especially true when mixed with white. For example, to dream of your deceased son greeting you wearing a red and white shirt attempts to restore your lost joy and hope in life after his death. It is common after such dreams to wake up feeling like you can once again get on with your life.

When mixed with black the meaning is negative. For example, to dream of following a woman wearing a black and red dress would indicate that you copied (followed) your mother's anger (black and red). The dream is identifying the source of your anger so you can do something about it.

Silver   Intuition

Meaning: Intuition.

Silver is always a positive color in dreams and indicates that you are psychic / intuitive. This is where you have a strong connection with your higher self and through that connection can get wisdom on events and issues around you. It comes as a feeling where you just know something, although there does not appear to be any logical reason for knowing it.

Dreaming of silver is a request for you to value your psychic ability and develop it. For example, to dream of the moon lighting your way in the dark tells you that your intuition (silver moon) will help you in times of trouble (when you are in the dark).

White   Perfection

Meaning: Hope, faith, purity, perfection, confidence, enlightenment.

While the keyword for this color is perfection, to dream of white alone can indicate you strive for perfection to such an extent that you are rarely impressed with your own efforts. It is almost impossible to reach the exceptionally high standard you set for yourself. You could never achieve the level of perfection you aspire to in the short while you give yourself to achieve it. For example, if you were to begin painting you would be overly critical of your first attempts because they are not good enough to hang in a museum. White in this context indicates a proud, rigid, judgmental immaturity - a 'should be', controlling attitude. While you are hard on yourself you would also be hard on others as it is unlikely they will reach your standard either. Dreams point this out in an effort to get you to realize your controlling nature so that you go easier on yourself. Do not start by trying to be easier on others as when you slip at this you will be even more critical of yourself because you did not reach that goal on your first attempt either. When you ease up on yourself and become more tolerant, that will eventually spill over onto others and they will benefit. The dream invariably shows you where this part of your nature began.

Striving for perfection reminds me of a friend who takes great pride in his meticulously manicured garden. While sitting on the porch with his wife, passers by would stop to comment on the beauty of the garden, or even ask for a slip from one of the many plants. Due to a recent illness, he could only sit uncomfortably in his chair and while his wife went to talk to each of the people who stopped, he eyed with distain a dandelion that had come up in a section of the grass. Unwilling to suffer the pain of moving to crop it, he mused over the fact that others enjoyed the beauty of the whole garden and yet his eyes were only drawn to the weed. When his wife next sat beside him, he shared his observation with her. She asked why he would choose to only see the dandelion. Having had time to discover his flaw he explained, "It is because I'm a perfectionist." He did not have to suffer his curse for long. Looking at him in disbelief she said, "I don't think you're perfect!"

White, when mixed or associated with other colors, purifies and refines their meaning. To dream of navy with white is an attempt to heal your negative philosophy of life (navy) by giving you faith and confidence in the future.

The soft or pearl white associated with a crystal ball indicates the gift of prophesy. This is not a very common gift so look for other symbols to confirm this.

Yellow	Intellect	Solar Plexus

Meaning: Mental activity, intellect.

Yellow may represent your usual reaction to the subject matter of the dream showing that you rationalize at the expense of your feelings. This is the meaning for normal yellow color.

If brought by a healing agent, a supportive, helpful character in the dream, it means you have difficulty rationalizing or are timid with regard to the subject matter of the dream. The healing agent brings yellow to help you rationalize your fears. An irrational fear, like a fear of spiders, has no basis and never helps you in life. Muddy or mustard yellow also indicates that you have a difficulty rationalizing with regard to the subject matter of the dream.

If a guide wears or brings pure bright yellow then you have an intuitive or enlightened intellect - yellow (intellect) plus white (enlightenment). You are being asked to use this to gain an enlightened perspective on the subject matter of the dream. To dream of pure bright yellow on its own is also sufficient to indicate you have this ability.

Interpretation in practice

Here are a few short dream segments from the same person. In her first dream she is given a gift of a grey cashmere dress. This reveals that she denies her emotions as a means of protecting herself from being hurt. This trait was copied from her mother if a woman gave her the dress, otherwise it is from her father. The fact that it is a gift means she sees this as a positive thing in life. It is common to see our security mechanisms in a positive light.

In another dream she is sheltering from the pouring rain with a large black umbrella. In dreams rain represents life, so here the umbrella is symbolically protecting her from life. The color black reveals that the protection is done out of fear.

In yet another she is given a black silk banner which will help her get through the traffic. Traffic represents career so in this case the black banner would have to do with title or recognition being perceived as necessary for succeeding in career. Again the black shows this is fear based indicating that the dreamer questions her own self worth – without a title she may feel inadequate in some way. The black color always means that what it is associated with in the dream is negative. So the dream is not telling her to get a qualification but rather telling her she is only doing this for negative reasons.

In other dreams she sees supportive male characters wearing dark blue usually mixed with a lighter blue. This tells she picked up a negative philosophy of life from her father. From that we can collude that the negative symbols in her other dreams are connected with issues around her father. The supportive male character is a healing agent and they always do the opposite of the parent of the same gender in reality. From that we can say with regard to the subject matter of the dream her father was not supportive and this is why she feels the need to compensate. A good counselor along with cutting-the-ties with her father would be one means to deal with her issues.

A man who lets his head rule his heart dreamt of parking his red car in a row of green cabbages. The red and green combination show that the dream is attempting healing for his heart. The pun in head of cabbage is a little derogatory and telling him he is a cabbage for letting his head rule his heart.

Sitting on a floor in a dream brings you back to your childhood as that is when you used to sit on the floor.

To dream of a *book on a specific subject* means you have knowledge of that subject area. This is particularly the case when you have the book in your hands in the dream and even more so when it is not a book that you are familiar with or is not available in reality.

Pink: To dream of this color is enough to show that you did not bond well with your mother or that she did not love unconditionally. The most significant bond is at birth so it is likely the dream brings you right back to the start of childhood. A poor bond affects the flow of female energy within and negatively impacts on spiritual gifts that require a female energy flow such as intuition, counseling, and teaching.

Dream: The Book

I was sitting on the floor in the living room on a pink carpet. There were a few women in the room but I don't think they had anything to do with me. I was reading a new book on teaching a specialist subject. I was aware that the book had not yet been published but somehow I had it in my hands. The cover was bright yellow on the top and bottom with a normal shade of yellow in the middle. There were a few other women sitting in the room.

Pure *bright yellow* indicates you have an intuitive or enlightened. You are being asked to use this to gain an enlightened perspective on the subject matter of the dream. Ordinary yellow represents you normally rationalize with regard to the subject matter of the dream.

Women can represent expression of feelings, as your heart is governed by female energy. In fact difficulty with emotional expression is often connected to issues with your mother as it is through her unconditional love that we learn to love ourselves and stay in touch with our hearts. If this was lacking from your mother it will show up in your dreams.

The Book – The Analysis

From just looking at the three colors, bright yellow, normal yellow, and pink we can get ninety percent of what this dream is asking of the dreamer. It is asking him to overcome the poor bond with mother (pink on the floor) in order to move away from rationalizing (normal yellow) and towards using his intuition (bright yellow). So from the colors alone and using just the first paragraph of the dream we have discovered its message. We could also interpret the dream without relying on the colors but the simplicity colors bring to dream interpretation is worth the effort of getting to know their meanings. Naturally enough everything else in the dream can be explained. So let's interpret the rest of the dream.

The subject matter is indicated by the book. Whatever the book's specialist subject is, the dreamer already has a grasp of it. This is given by the fact that he has the book in his hands and also because he has it before the book is published. So the dream is encouraging him to use intuition when it comes to practicing the books subject rather than using purely intellectual methods.

It should be no surprise to realize that the dream is pushing for using intuition. This is always the case as dreams encourage you to develop your spiritual gifts. The dreamer's reluctance to use intuition comes from a poor bond with mother at birth. While the pink tells us this we can also see it from the women who have nothing to do with him. This indicates that from the dreamer's perspective his mother had nothing to do with him. All the women in the dream represent both his mother and his female side. The large number of women in the dream gives symbolic expression to a female side that does not get much expression in reality. Early childhood is when we mostly sit on the floor and the dream places the dreamer there to link the problem to his childhood. Intuition is a female energy gift and requires a healthy flow and connection to female energy within. A poor bond with mother inhibits this flow and blocks the ability.

In reality the dreamer was born through caesarean section. His mother, not being fully conscious at the time, could not hold him when he first came into the world. This was partially responsible for the poor bond. He knew he was intuitive but always feared not reading his intuition correctly. The pain in childhood caused him to close off from his feelings and rationalize almost everything in life. It is difficult to listen to your heart when all your concentration is in your head. To arrive at a result he heavily relied on intellectual box ticking when it came to his specialist subject. He subsequently worked on his issues with mother through cutting-the-ties and that helped him move from purely logical analysis to intuitive reasoning.

Color Healing Chart

Color therapy uses the healing effects of colors to heal the body. The diagram below shows the location of the seven main chakras and the color and purpose associated with each. These colors are especially therapeutic and they may also appear in your dreams in their healing capacity. If you determine your dream is health related use the meaning of the color listed here.

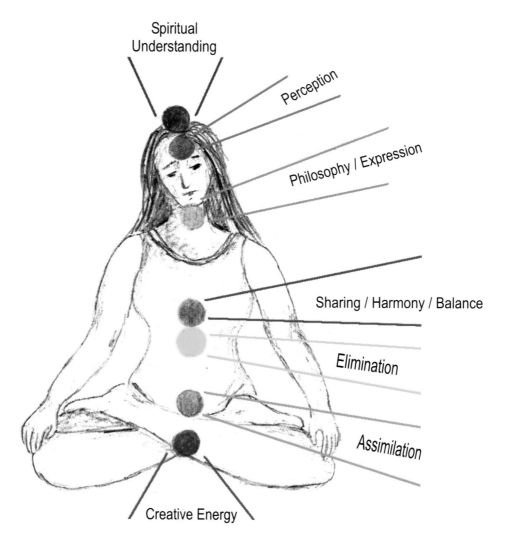

Figure 9-2 Color & Function of Human Chakras

Color	Healing Effect
Violet	Brings spiritual peace. Heals insomnia, tumors of the brain. Calms highly-strung, excitable people.
Indigo	Develops psychic perception, intuition, Heals eyes, ears, nose and mental problems.
Blue	Fights infections. Heals throat, fevers, etc.. Gives peace of mind.
Green	Creates balance of energy. Heals the heart, circulatory system. Helps you overcome fear of giving, sharing, adaptability.
Yellow	Heals nervous system, elimination, liver, intestines, pancreas. Balances adrenal glands, heals skin troubles, diabetes. Stimulates intellect.
Orange	Help digestion, assimilation of new ideas, removes repression and inhibitions. Broadens the mind, helps you cope with life and career.
Red	Heals the creative, reproductive systems. Stimulates circulation of blood and flow of adrenaline. Energizes, gives confidence and courage.

10. Numbers in Dreams

One can always be kind to people about whom one cares nothing.

— Oscar Wilde

Numbers are used for several purposes in dreams but it is easy to determine their purpose. A common use of numbers is to indicate you at a particular age. This may be obvious because the dream has, for example, a 3 year old child in it. The gender of the child does not matter as far as indicating age is concerned. Dreams can use a boy to indicate issues with dad or your male side and a girl to indicate issues with mother or your female side. A less obvious example for age would be use of a number of people. A dream with 2 women behind you is introducing an issue with mother when you were 2 years old. A dream with 7 children playing together brings you back to the age 7, and so on.

Individual numbers can also be combined, as in 35, 47, 50 etc, and when this is the case, you look at the meaning of the individual numbers and put their meanings together. A common use of numbers in this way, is to put a price on something through the use of money. Being offered a job in the music industry at $600,000 per year tells you the payback for developing your channeling ability (music) is enormous. This is not a financial payback – it allows you achieve your goals (zeros) and is part of your karmic path (5 zeros). Being offered a fountain pen for $3 asks you to commit (3) to developing your writing gift. Not purchasing it in your dream would mean that you have no intention of developing your ability.

Catching a bus is also a common place where numbers are used in dreams. Busses themselves are usually about your life journey or stages on your life journey. Usually in these dreams there is a choice of which bus to catch. You may have a choice between the 37, which asks for commitment (3) to your spiritual development (7), and the 47, which tells you your choices are limiting (4) your

Summary

► Numbers in dreams are generally interpreted one digit at a time. They can however, also indicate a specific age.

► The price tag on an item can show the commitment required to attain what it symbolically represents.

spiritual development (7).

Let's now have a look at single digit numbers and what they mean. In general, just like above, when you see numbers combined you look at the meaning of the individual numbers and put their meanings together.

One is a male number and indicates individuality and creativity. These are two sides of the same coin. The more individual you remain the more creative you are as you do your own thing rather than follow the crowd. This number can also indicate that you are being selfish with regard to the subject matter of the dream. This number will almost always be shown with other numbers and is usually first. For example, catching the 17 bus tells you that your spiritual journey (7) is unique (1). One can also indicate commitment – being at one with yourself.

Two is a female number and indicates balance, sharing, give and take and two way communication. Two way communication is important for channels (mediums) and as such they will often have dreams littered with the number two, such as, the number 2 itself, weddings, twins or two of anything. Dreaming of the number 2 is not enough in itself to indicate that the dreamer is a channel but it is a very good indicator. The balance indicated by this number can be about communication in your relationship or anything else that is unbalanced in your life. Highways are often used to indicate balance in dreams with emphasis being given to the two way flow on the road. This refers to balance in your heart. Do you share your feelings honestly? Do you always take or do you give too much of yourself?

Three has to do with commitment to the subject matter of the dream. It stands for mind, body and soul and is a request to commit mind body and soul to improving yourself in the direction indicated in the dream. Three will often appear in dreams about the heart as people who have suppressed their feelings often lack passion and commitment for new things in life. It is also similar to a broken 8 in appearance and 8 always symbolizes the heart. A triangle or pyramid also indicate commitment and request the dreamer to meditate on the subject matter of the dream.

Four indicates limitation. For example, catching the number 4 bus would indicate the dreamer is limiting their life journey through their actions or thoughts. A box or square also indicate limitation. This number is very common in dreams and is usually linked with other numbers. A choice between the 23 and 24 buses to Parnell Square reminds you that you have a choice between committing (3) to keeping balance (2) in your life or limiting (4) that balance (2). The rest of the dream indicates where the balance is required. In the previous example it is between work and the dreamer's relationship (as symbolized by the Irish patriot Parnell).

Five is another male number and indicates sensuality as we have five human senses. It is very common in dreams as it also indicates the karmic path and that is such an important topic for dreams. It symbolizes the karmic path because karma is where you learn your life lessons only through your five senses.

Six is another female number and indicates Dharma, Christ Consciousness, Grace, love, forgiveness, and compassion. In dreams it is a request to go beyond the five senses and karma and develop compassion within yourself. In the example earlier the $600,000 for music tells the dreamer that channeling (music) is his way off the karmic path and onto the path of dharma.

Seven always indicates spiritual enlightenment. Your spiritual center is your seventh chakra which is located at the very top of your head.. A dream where you catch the number 37 bus to church is a request to commit (3) to developing your spiritual side (7 and church). Paying $47 for something indicates that the dreamer is limiting (4) their spiritual nature (7) by not putting enough energy (paying for something) into developing it.

Eight, is the only balanced number and indicates expansion through balance of the heart. If you turn 8 on its side you get ∞. You can easily imagine balancing that shape on the end of your finger. It is also the symbol for infinity which indicates limitless expansion. Eight features in dreams about the heart and circulatory system. The symbol itself is made of two circles and anything circular in a dream symbolizes your circulatory system.

Nine is not very common in dreams and indicates that you are spiritually advanced. It is a reminder to follow your life purpose because within this lifetime you have the potential to repay all your karma and make this your last necessary earth life. It does not mean you cannot come back for another earth experience – rather that you do not have to. If you dream of 9 you would find yourself naturally drawn to learning about spiritual matters.

Zero is the perfect symbol with no beginning or end and as such in dreams it indicates God, ideals and goals. For example, 70 would indicate Spiritual ideals and 30 would indicate commitment to your goals.

Some combined numbers that have specific meanings are *ten* which indicates completion as it is at the end of the set of individual numbers. *Twelve* indicates being judgmental as there are twelve people on a jury. Lastly *thirty six*, while not common, can be a pun on 'dirty sex'. This is a common hang-up in western culture where young adults are told that sexual activity is dirty – even talking about it is taboo.

11. Spirituality & Life Purpose

The aim of life is self-development. To realize one's nature perfectly - that is what each of us is here for.

— Oscar Wilde

Dreams comment on our spiritual path and how true we are to that path. This is hardly surprising since dreams come from a spiritual source. What does surprise many people though is the diversity of paths in the spiritual field. When I first began to explore this realm I went to a "Mind, Body and Spirit Exhibition" expecting to find a lot of eccentric people peddling their cause. Instead I was almost shocked to find normal people, and lots of them, who had found something that they wanted to share with others. The one thing that stood out, however, was that most of these people claimed that their answer was the only answer and path to take in life. With so many people saying they have the answer how do you know which person, if any, actually does? Years later I discovered through working with dreams that they all do! There are many paths to awareness and the path for you is detailed in your dreams. It is as unique to you as any other aspect of your personality. When you have found it you will know it. The mistake to avoid is to assume that because a particular path is right for you, that it is right for everyone. As you will see in dreams, following the wrong path can be damaging.

Spirituality is expression of the soul. People often think it refers only to things of a psychic nature but spirituality is anything within you that allows you to shine and free your spirit. It could be a writing ability, counseling skills, a

Summary

▶ Dreams comment on your spiritual path and how true you are to that path.

▶ Everyone has at least one spiritual ability. Your dreams relentlessly remind you of that and why you need to develop it.

▶ Do you see yourself as a body with a spirit or a spirit with a body?

▶ Are Guardian Angels real or are they symbolic in dreams?

▶ You have a specific life purpose. Your dreams remind you of it and ask you to be true to that purpose.

▶ Does reincarnation make sense?

▶ What are the karmic and dharmic paths?

specialty for teaching, a musical ability, a love for dance and yes of course, things of a psychic nature too. Each one of us has at least one spiritual ability. Our dreams relentlessly remind us of that and why we need to develop it. People who feel drawn to work in the spiritual field usually do so out of a desire to help others. Most soon learn, however, that in order to become good at what they do, they must first help themselves by clearing any baggage they are carrying from childhood, relationships or other negatively conditioning environments they were subjected to. If you work in the spiritual field and have not cleared your baggage, your dreams show how the negative conditioning inhibits your ability in some way. Dreams also show under what circumstances you should use particular abilities.

If the idea that we have spiritual abilities seems alien to you, just consider for a moment that you are first and foremost a spirit or soul. You temporarily have a body that you know someday will die but you, the spirit, will live on. When you accept that you are a spirit, the concept of having a spiritual ability is natural. You talking with a spirit is simply one spirit talking to another; spiritual healing is one spirit healing another. Many people refer to these abilities as gifts. A gift implies something that has been given but these gifts can neither be given to you nor taken away. They are simply part of your nature. For this reason I sometimes use the terms spiritual power or spiritual ability.

Dreams that reflect the spiritual dimension invariably take place in locations that indicate spirituality. The most obvious locations are churches, synagogues, mosques, and other places of worship. Whether we believe in a God or not, we still associate these locations with receiving direction from the spiritual realm. Other locations and symbols may not be so obvious. In a dream, unpolluted water represents spirituality, so a river indicates a request to let your spiritual side flow more freely. Just like the river, find your own path and overcome any obstacles in your way. A canal is a body of water where the flow is controlled by man made structures, so in dreams this means your spirituality is restricted by man made structures or conventional ideals. A swimming pool has a somewhat similar meaning. A lake is a body of water with no outlet, so symbolically asks you to develop an outlet for your spirituality. A beach is the approach to the sea and since the sea represents spirituality the beach indicates your spiritual approach, while a road running alongside a canal or river, indicates striving towards your spiritual path.

Dreams taking place on a high location, such as on the roof of a high-rise building, can also be about your higher purpose. Dreams in university, college, high-school or other places of higher learning also indicate this. Taking exams is a particularly common dream. We are given the opportunity to take exams when we have completed the required course of learning. Passing the exam opens the door for us to move on to a higher level of learning or gives us the qualification to use what we learned in the real world. Exams in dreams are always a good symbol. It means that you have completed one phase of your learning or life and are now ready to move from this phase to the next phase. This indicates that your state of consciousness is ready to change with the ground work already done. The dream will show what needs to be developed in order to pass to the next phase of your spiritual evolution. Dreams that take place at a border, customs post, check-point or interview room have the same meaning.

Spiritual abilities are the most precious part of our nature, so will often feature in dreams that take place in jewelry shops or locations where precious items are displayed. Guardian angels often appear in these dreams and hand a 'gift' to the dreamer where the gift symbolizes a particular ability. If the item has to be paid for, the price indicates what is required to attain the ability. For example, a price tag of $3 indicates commitment is required while $370 indicates commitment to spiritual goals is required.

When we are born we are aware of our life purpose and our spiritual abilities. Dreams that symbolically reflect birth often remind you of your life purpose and show your abilities in symbolic form. For example, a newborn able to talk would indicate you have a special communication ability.

Guardian Angels

The subject of guides or guardian angels tends to be black and white in people's minds. People are either fully accepting of the concept or don't believe in it at all. However, even people who are aware of their guides can be surprised at how much they limit their guidance. As you might expect, you can see just how much you do limit their guidance and what causes you to do this from your dreams.

I find that the best way to open somebody's mind to the idea of guardian angels is to show them how to see them and I regularly do this on my courses. It generally only takes about ten minutes for everyone in the class to be able to see them. After this point it is easier to discuss them and explain how and why they help with our lives. I am not asking you, the reader, to believe me that guides exist. However, just because the concept may be new to you does not mean that they do not. Fortunately they do not need you to believe in them for them to exist and still help you in your life!

We live in a world where we expect to 'see' something if it is real. However, we believe in a lot of things that we ourselves may never have seen and never will. I cannot see radio waves, x-rays, microwaves or radiation other than light and yet they exist. They existed since the creation of our universe but until someone on earth relatively recently invented devices to detect and use them they could not be proven to exist. It is possible that somebody will invent a device to see into the spirit world and just like radio waves the spirit world will not spring into existence when this device is created. It is already there - just as gravity was before the apple fell on Newton's head.

I am saying this so that you find it easier to keep an open mind. An open mind does not mean that you must believe. Don't believe me! Look for corroborative evidence to support or refute what you read. We all have different paths so it does not reflect badly on either of us if you decide to hold to a different truth

Guides in your dreams

As you develop you attract higher guides. They make their presence known in your dreams.

than me. That being said I will now outline briefly how and why guides come into our lives. Oh and if you are interested in how to see guardian angels refer to the exercises later in this book.

Life Purpose

Guardian angels appear in our dreams with messages to remind us to be true to our life purpose, to get in touch with our soul and to create outlets for expression of our soul in our life. It is such an important message in dreams because it is that lost connection that has us here in the first place! Life is about restoring this connection so that when we move back to the spirit world we have learned more about who we are and continue to build on our experiences when there. There is no miraculous transformation to enlightened being when we die. We can still be much the same as while on earth. If we are closed minded and intolerant on earth we can remain that way in spirit. If the blindness of our conditioning could just be lifted at the moment of death there would be no need to go through the earth experience in the first place. In the spirit world you would just take an enlightenment pill and 'hey presto' your awareness would be restored. This cannot happen because awareness cannot be lost in the first place. We started spiritual existence with full awareness but through various actions on our part it has been obscured from our view over time. To restore awareness we must clear away the beliefs that obscure it. For this reason growth towards awareness is an experiential process where we unearth truths about ourselves. This is the case in both the physical and spirit worlds but there are good reasons why we take on a physical body to move ourselves forward.

While in the spirit world your journey into expanded awareness is facilitated by eliminating negative thoughts and conditioning you are holding onto. In some cases, however, the conditioning is so ingrained that it forms your reality and you have severe difficulty in reshaping it. While in the spirit world nothing can force you to deal with it. Pain can be avoided and often is when you hit a limitation you have difficulty dealing with. So if, for example, your three biggest blocks are vindictiveness, intolerance and a controlling nature, how do you eliminate them? Firstly you have to decide you want to eliminate them and that a new earth experience would be the best way to deal with it. Once you make that decision, help is at hand. Certain spirits specialize in helping others plan and tailor new earth experiences based on what they need to work on. They are the first to engage in the process of designing your upcoming earth life. The earth life is planned in fantastic detail with the express purpose of helping you to eliminate the chosen conditioning. The planning includes choosing an environment and parents that are suitable for your purpose. You also plan events to help you pick up your spirit world conditioning on the earth plane. In most cases you may also plan other events and people to help you eliminate it later in your life once it has been absorbed into your personality.

Parents are the most instrumental in the early establishment of your problems on the earth plane. They quite often have the task of passing on to you the very nature that you already exhibit on the spirit plane. Your mother might be very vindictive herself and through mimicking her behavior you are able to manifest in the physical world a problem that you already have on the spirit plane. The strong separation between the physical and spirit worlds allows you to focus on just one or a few negative traits in a life time. If you had full memory of past earth experiences or brought all of your difficulties with you at once, your chance of success is diminished. The separation also allows you to protect previous advances you made in expanding your awareness as you are not putting everything at risk. Each life is like a quest to obtain a precious jewel and you have to run the gauntlet of life to get it. If you brought all the previous jewels you collected with you through the gauntlet each time, you risk dropping the pouch and losing them.

It is entirely possible that you end up not having progressed at all in a particular lifetime. You may have picked up the conditioning you needed to but you may deepen your conditioning by missing the opportunities life presented for purging it. You are a free soul with free will and that allows you to deviate from your planned path whenever you want. However, your likelihood to deviate is already taken into account in the planning process. To help you stay on track while on earth, you engage the help of spirits who specialize in that task. These spirits are your guardian angels and they remain with you throughout your life, always nudging you in the direction you need to be going. They have a very strong connection with you and can greatly influence your feelings towards others and feelings around decisions you make. At the same time another person's guides can greatly influence their feelings about you and in this way you find yourself in the company of other people who are meant to be in your path.

From a human perspective, help does not always appear to be what it is. From the human perspective an abusive childhood, whether physical or psychological, appears to have no value whatsoever. Also from the human perspective alone, it is impossible to tell whether a particular act is part of a planned life, so it is not correct to look at everything as though it has a purpose. What you can be certain of, is that your guides will make every effort to help you get maximum spiritual value from all events in your life. You are a spirit and cannot take anything from the earth plane except its effect on you. Earth is a school for spirits. Just like in your childhood school, your participation in this school determines the course of your life afterwards, and the ease with which you can further your goals when back in the spirit world.

Guides do not judge you or

Reincarnation

For over thirty years, Dr. Ian Stevenson, a professor of psychiatry at the University of Virginia Medical School has interviewed young children who have spontaneously remembered previous existences. Frequently their memories are so detailed Stevenson has been able to track down the identity of their previous personality and verify virtually everything they have said. The prestigious *Journal of the American Medical Association* stated that he has "painstakingly and unemotionally collected a detailed series of cases in which the evidence for reincarnation is difficult to understand on any other grounds."
— Michael Talbot
The Holographic Universe

try to control your free will in any way. It would be inconsistent with their level of awareness to do so. This also precludes them from helping unless asked by you. So remember to ask! They seek to help by empowering you to find your answers. This may be a difficult concept to grasp as most of us do not do this. Guides arrange all sorts of coincidences by which you find yourself in the right place at the right time. However, guides do not control the choices you make and you can find yourself letting an opportunity pass you by. Organizing these coincidences is not interfering with your life as this has already been arranged between you and them by prior agreement.

When you get a flash of inspiration or a feeling and go with it you are following guidance. However, if instead you rationalize what you have received and let negative emotion take over, you block or limit the guidance. The more you follow your feelings the more open you become to guidance.

It is useful to always keep in mind a guide's method of helping. The next time you are asked for help by a fellow soul, seek to empower them by openly sharing what you know. A person is empowered if they can deal with the situation without your help should they find themselves facing the same issue again. Make it your intention to empower others and opportunities to do so will unfold.

Guides in Dreams

Guides appear in dreams in a number of ways and it is worth learning how to spot them as their advice in a dream is infallible. The easiest way to tell this, is to note if the person in the dream has a title such as a doctor, president or bus driver. In this case the profession of the person indicates one of your spiritual abilities. In the list above, a doctor indicates you are a healer, president indicates you are a spiritual teacher or leader and bus driver indicates you are a counselor that works with groups of people to take them from where they are to where they need to be. These are covered in detail later.

It is very common for guides to offer a gift in your dream. In this case the guide is indicated by this action and they do not need to have a title. What is of great interest here, is that if you recognize a person you already know as a guide in your dream, it means they are a guide in reality too even though they are on the earth plane.

Use a pendulum

If you are familiar with the use of a pendulum you can use it to check that you have the correct meaning of a symbol or of the whole dream. Simply ask the pendulum *yes* and *no* questions.

Note: How to use a pendulum is described in the Psychic Development section of this book.

If a person speaks with authority in a dream they are also a guide. For example, a person in a hostile mob speaking up and taking charge of the situation to calm their rage indicates that you are a spiritual leader. A guide may also speak with authority to give you direction on either what you are doing wrong or what way you should change. A disembodied voice is also indicative of a guide in dreams.

It has been proven psychologically that we subconsciously grant authority to people occupying a position slightly above us and to our right. Guides will almost always assume this position in your dreams. It is also common for there to be a source of light near them, such as a window.

Dreams of aliens or spacecraft can also indicate guides. Aliens, like guides, are from another world. If they appear this way in your dream it is likely that you still see the whole concept as alien and have not reconciled the fact that both you and your guides are the same. The only difference is that they have regained more of their former awareness.

Karma

In spiritual terms we have two choices as to how we will live our lives. The first and predominantly most common choice made today is to live on a karmic path. Karma is neither positive nor negative. It is simply a method by which you are repeatedly presented with opportunities to overcome the limiting conditioning that blocks your awareness. From a human perspective this is usually seen as negative since you can find yourself having to deal with the same difficulties over and over. However, from a spiritual perspective it is a healthy ingredient for growth in awareness, where you come face to face with your limitations, while at the same time you are being helped and supported by your guides to overcome them. If two of your life tasks are to overcome anger and the abuse of power, it may be as simple as repeatedly finding yourself in situations where you find your anger boiling over and you take it out on others, such as your employees, your spouse or your children. As each opportunity presents itself and you waste it, your guides will set up another one. They know that eventually you will grow tired of being angry and will question your motives and yourself. Change can only come from within and with great patience and love they will persist with you, waiting for that moment of enlightenment.

People who are unaware of the spiritual dimension of life, may judge you harshly and pity your wife and children. The life task of these people may be to learn how to love unconditionally rather than sit in judgment. In being the angry man you are, you are also helping them by bringing out in them their own limitations. As for your wife and children, their persistence with you may be in payment for help you provided to them in previous lives where they wronged you. They feel they owe you a debt and were delighted with the opportunity presented in this life time to repay you by being the main targets for your anger and abuse of power in this life time. They agreed to it be-

The Grand Design

If you wish to explore more about Guardian Angels and life purpose I highly recommend the five book series *The Grand Design* by Patrick Francis.

cause they know the design of your life and it is their greatest hope that you will shine through this time around. Either way their debt will be repaid but that does not stop them from taking what seems to humans as a victim position in this role with you.

While on this karmic path your own energy draws to you events that allow you to clear your karma. Indeed karmic fields in your aura can be read by clairvoyants and they can tell from these fields what your life purpose is. When you refuse the learning opportunity of an event and repeat your limiting conditioning, you draw more karma to yourself. In energy terms, at the moment of the event, the karmic field connected to that limiting trait collapses. Your reaction to the event, however, determines whether the field is restored again and to what strength. Your awareness at the time of the event is of major significance. The level to which you know your action is inappropriate, is proportional to the karmic debt incurred by that action. A person who really knows no better incurs the least karmic debt while a person who is aware incurs the most for the very same actions.

A good analogy is that we are all waking around with multiple karmic magnets stuck to our bodies. Instead of just north and south poles, however, there are many polarities on the magnets. The magnets attract appropriate people and events to us that will allow us to overcome the limitations we hold onto. The people attracted are wearing the opposite magnet on their body. The opposite polarity means they are skilled in pushing the buttons that trigger our faults. On earth most are blissfully unaware of the fantastic design of the karmic system. The angry man on earth is pulling his hair out, wondering how despite his best efforts he managed to land himself in more of the same. At the same time his guides are thrilled for him as he has yet again come face to face with his problem and maybe this is the time he will grow past it.

souls chose the karmic path because it is an easy way to grow spiritually. All the major events in your life are going to happen to you, rather than you choosing to experience them. In this way you can learn lots about yourself, based on how you react to and cope with the experiences life throws at you. Essentially by choosing karma, you are forcing yourself to learn about yourself and hopefully advance in the process. Time is what makes karma work. Time does not exist in the Spirit sense and you instantly feel the effects of your own actions towards yourself and others. Karma and the physical plane allows there to be a delay between your actions and the feeling of the effect. The intention is that within this period of time, due to advances you make in your own understanding, you have opportunities to subtract from your karmic debt and so incur either positive effects or less negative ones. To help further, karma can span lifetimes. Due to this, karma is the most chosen path in life. From a human perspective it is not the easiest but from a spiritual perspective it is a blessing.

The term karmic debt comes from how we feel when we fully understand the effect of our actions on others. When we die our guides help us review the human life we just lived in great detail. When reviewing an event we don't just feel how we felt at the time. We also get to completely feel how everyone affected by our action felt at the time and how it subsequently affected them. This is feeling with deep understanding. If you caused somebody great pain you feel that pain as they did and with the full understanding that you caused it. If on the other hand you caused great joy you have one tremendously uplifting experience to look forward to. It is during this life review process that a soul decides they owe a karmic debt and they let it be known to their victims and guides. The guides will then engineer opportunities in further lifetimes for the aggressor to repay the debt they feel they owe. It may be through suffering as a victim or it may be through using their talents to help others to grow on the earth plane.

It is worth noting that there is no spiritual law that says an aggressor owes a karmic debt. To have such a law would negate free will. Growth in awareness is an individual path. If on the spirit plane you can forgive yourself for all the wrongs you have caused you are free of any debt. However, your deep understanding of the effects of your wrong doing makes that very difficult. On the earth plane it is almost impossible to correctly categorize your actions as wrong or right. Actions that appear negative from a human perspective can have a far reaching positive spiritual impact. A spouse leaving a partner may well be a spiritual requirement in their partner's life plan, and may allow for growth in their feelings of self worth, confidence and independence. The partner may never take the steps to receive the counseling they require without the apparent selfish act of their spouse.

Dharma

The second path we can choose to follow in life is Dharma. While karma allows a focus on outer events, people, possessions and society to trigger inner growth, the dharma path is achieved by focusing directly on your inner being and choosing to live a life that is directly inline with your life purpose. The dharma path achieves the maximum spiritual growth and is at the heart of many eastern philosophies and religions. It is known as a state of grace by the Christian Church and the Christ Consciousness in New Age literature. For comparison, the Old Testament is karma, espousing the philosophy of an eye for an eye while the New Testament is dharma encouraging you to turn the other cheek and forgive your enemies.

On this path you choose your avenues in life because you are consciously aware of what is best from your soul's perspective. The choices made are not always logical or understandable by those on the karmic path. Both paths will ultimately lead to the same place but dharma is by far the quickest. It is not chosen as much by souls entering the planet because it requires a compassionate heart combined with a state of spiritual awareness and forgiveness.

Through work on balancing your male and female energies you can switch from karma to dharma during your lifetime. This balance is achieved through consciously working on issues that form part of your limiting conditioning. This likely involves a deep look at your childhood and cutting the ties with mum, dad or possibly both. The technique for cutting the ties is described on my website. Sometimes the conditioning comes from a former life and so is trickier to pinpoint. Even in these cases the former conditioning is often linked to a particular parent and a rigorous cutting the ties will still heal it. No matter where you live there are plenty of therapies out there that are effective, such as counseling from a competent therapist.

Once on the dharma path you will know it. Your happiness comes from within and is infectious to those around you. You develop a strong compassionate understanding of others and this gives you a great tolerance. Of most importance is your feeling of unconditional love for yourself. Through this you can work through your problems more effectively as you do not criticize yourself for failing to achieve. Instead you love yourself for coming through to the point you are now at and for each step further you achieve.

A person on the dharma path can seem selfish to a person still on the karmic path as they choose what they want to do in life rather than letting circumstance and others dictate it. This spiritual freedom can be perceived as rejection to the person on the karmic path who still has conditioning they need to break free from. For example, it may be that they throw guilt to exert control over others but a person on the dharma path does not catch it.

Karma and Dharma in Dreams

In dreams karma and dharma are usually shown as a choice. Karma is learning about yourself through the five physical senses so is most commonly represented in dreams by the number 5. Karma is a male energy approach to life. A perfect symbol for karma is to dream of looking into a black mirror. In a symbolic sense this represents negativity (black) reflecting back onto itself. A more common symbol for karma is to dream of a car. Driving a *car* to *ma*'s house is a pun but a car on its own is sometimes sufficient to indicate this path. A rocky terrain or steep hill in your path also indicates karma where life is seen as an uphill struggle. Other common symbols are revolving doors, Ferris wheels (big wheels), and being on an endless road. As we come to the end of what we can learn from having earth incarnations, we include in our life purpose the repayment of karmic debts to others. It is common, however, to get here and decide all this spiritual stuff is mumbo jumbo and so not develop our spiritual abilities. If we do not develop them we can not use them as planned to help the very souls we owe debts to. Through not developing them we cannot repay our debts as planned before coming here. When we pass back into spirit we clearly see the missed opportunities and the debts still owed. We plan another life to repay them. If this has happened a number of times, we can have dreams reminding us to not procrastinate this time around.

Dharma is a female energy approach to life and is represented in dreams by the number 6. This indicates having gone beyond the 5 senses. Dreams about short journeys with illogical connections also indicate dharma. Crazy rides in carnivals indicate moving from karma to dharma, for example, a ride where you are heading towards a missing piece of the road and what seems like a cliff like drop, when suddenly a platform swings out carrying you safely to the next segment of the road and then disappears. This emphasizes the need for trust that your spiritual path will connect up with where you need be.

Dreams often show that you have a choice between karma and dharma. Common techniques are choices between getting the number 5 or number 6 bus to go home.

94

Taking the right-hand turn at a Y-junction or T-junction on a road chooses karma - the left turn chooses dharma. This is because the male side is often indicated by movement to the right while the female side is indicated by movement to the left and karma is male while dharma is female. Dreams will always encourage you to develop your female side through expression of the heart so that you can switch to a dharma path and so return 'home' more quickly.

Quick Symbol Reference for Spiritual Dreams

The following symbols all indicate your dream is about the above for various reasons. Complete descriptions are given in the Dream Symbol Reference later.

Any symbol indicating a spiritual ability

Beach

Border

Buried treasure

Canals

Check-point

Church

College

Customs post

Examination hall

Gold

High location

High rise building

Interview room

Jewelry

Lakes

Mosque

Place of worship

Rivers

School

Silver

Synagogue

University

Your **son** can indicate your male side or that you had issues with your father when you were the age of the boy in the dream. We each have both male and female aspects to ourselves. Dreams always encourage you to restore balance to this energy mix. In fact that is one of the main purposes of your life.

An **endless road** indicates you are on the karmic path and more particularly being caught on a karmic cycle. A **dark road** means you cannot see where you are going. This invariable means that you are unaware of the direction your actions are taking you. Other symbols in the dream will show why this is the case.

A **club** is a male symbol and indicates that you have a male energy approach to life or the subject matter of the dream.

Dream: Endless Road

I am on a dark endless road at night with my 3 year old son. A man in black comes towards me wielding a club tying to hit my 3 year old. I am crouched down trying to protect him.

Crouching in a dream indicates you are protecting yourself in some way. This protection comes at a price and the dream is asking you to deal with whatever caused you to be this way.

Wielding indicates a strong male approach to life. You act without listening to your heart. You need to restore the balance between male and female aspects of yourself. Female energy allows you to forgive, listen, lead, have two-way communication, and more.

Protecting yourself in a dream is pointing out that the effect of a negative situation is causing you to protect yourself in some way. This protection comes at a price and the dream is asking you to deal with whatever caused you to be this way.

It is very common for a **man** to stand in for your father. In this case he is likely to be either healing an issue with your father or to demonstrate a trait that you adopted as a result of the way he was. Usually the dream is asking you to eliminate this trait as it is affecting you negatively with regard to the subject matter of the dream. For example, a **man in black** indicates that you picked up fears (black) from your father (the man).

Endless Road – The Analysis

This dream is about being caught in a karmic cycle. Spiritually this is where you live a life with the intention of repaying all your karmic debts. However, something does not work out right for you and when you review your life on your return to the spirit world you discover that you either have not paid all your debts or that you have incurred others. The result is you need to plan another life to repay your new debts! This dream shows this happened to the dreamer at least once. The big question is how many times? The purpose of pointing this out is so she does not make similar mistakes this time around.

The dreamer is unaware of this consciously. She cannot see (dark, at night) that she has a male approach to life (wielding, club). She adopted this attitude to life as a result of issues with her father (man) at age 3. The 3 year old son shows the age in question but it also symbolically shows at that age she adopted a male approach to life. The man represents her father but the fact that she points out he is wearing black symbolizes fears (black) picked up from her relationship with him. In reality her father was an alcoholic and violent. Her mother divorced him when she was 3. The dream is addressing the lack of a loving supportive father in her life at that age. Children that young can not see who has the problem and blame themselves for the behavior of their parent. In her eyes dad's behavior and his departure from the family must have been because she did something wrong. In her case the pain caused her to separate from her feelings and live life in her head. In addition she lashes out (club) at anyone who would try to get close to her. The man not only symbolizes her father but also any man who would attempt to get close. This started at age 3 but was reinforced when she was later abused as a teenager.

The dream is asking her to cut-the-ties with her father and free the 3 year old she is still trying to protect. Her childhood allowed her to carry through some amazing spiritual abilities that she was already aware of at the time of this dream. Some years after the dream she had developed them to such a level that she works full time in the spiritual field helping others. Her spiritual gifts allow her to repay her karma and break the karmic cycle. However, she no longer needs to carry the negative effects of that childhood.

A *cinema* represents expansion of life and is present in dreams where you are being shown how to make your life into the bigger picture that is meant for you. Long before television, cinema was the means for news dispersal and letting the people know what existed in the world.

The number *five* indicates the karma path in dreams. Literally you are experiencing your world through the five physical senses alone. Dreams with the number five quite often show what you are obliged to develop on this path so look for other symbols to indicate this in the dream.

To be at the *top of the queue* means you are further along than you think with regard to the subject matter of the dream.

Peter, being the name of one of the apostles and bible writers, can indicate a spiritual leadership ability. Look for other apostle names in your dreams to confirm this.

To be *entitled* to something in a dream means you need to accept your entitlement with regard to the subject matter of the dream.

Dream: The Cinema

I am at the cinema with my son and daughter. I'm near the top of the queue. I am wondering if I have enough money in $5 to pay for the three of us. Peter, a friend from work, comes along and comes up to us. I go with him towards the exit for some reason. We go back to the queue. I think that we'll go to the end of the queue again but he walks right up to where we were. I think that he has a neck because he was not with us but he is the one who feels entitled to go back to that position! When I get to the counter a guy on my left gets served ahead of me. I point out to the cashier that I'm next. Then my friend tells me that he already bought all the tickets. I'm relieved because I didn't think that $5 was enough.

A *ticket* indicates a karmic debt to be paid. If the ticket is already paid for in your dream you are being asked to realise that your karma is paid already.

To feel *relieved* in a dream asks you to relax with regard to the subject matter of the dream.

The Cinema – The Analysis

The cinema location indicates an expansion of life so we expect the rest of the dream to say how. You are with your son and daughter so this indicates using your male and female side in harmony as you go forward. You are at the top of the queue – this means you do not realize how far along your path you actually are! You are concerned with being able to pay for the three of you with just $5. Three asks for commitment – to put your mind, body and soul behind your purpose. 5 indicates karma so the real concern is will you be able to fulfill your karma or pay your karmic debts in this life.

Very interestingly Peter enters the dream at this point. Peter is the name of the first apostle and his entry now shows you what you now must do. He takes you to the exit. He is a guide and is clearly asking you to bring your awareness outside to help others. You obviously don't feel ready to do this as you go back to the queue.

The guide adapts to your response and shows you that you have earned your position with regard to teaching spirituality by showing you are entitled to return to your position. Despite this demonstration you still feel you have karma to pay (indicated by jockeying for position with others). In a final attempt he tells you that your karma (the ticket) is already paid. You are relieved to know this in the dream so in reality it will be quite a relief to you.

This dreamer had done many courses in the spiritual field over a number of years and in the eyes of all who knew him was ready to run his own classes. However, he kept his spiritual understanding to himself and in a way led a double life. Only a select few of his family and friends knew of his training. Even when situations were blatantly presented to him he refused to acknowledge it. Like many about to enter the field his view was that by sharing his understanding with others he could incur karma by inadvertently causing them to stray from their path.

The number *six* indicates the dharmic path. Six symbolizes going beyond the five senses and karma and experiencing life as a spiritual journey in a state of Grace. Choices are made through the heart and the path in life you follow is the path you know is of most benefit to you spiritually. This way of living has a strong connection to life, the spirit world and a great sense of purpose. To others it can appear irrational and crazy at times but that is because they are still experiencing life through karma.

Graceland symbolizes the dharmic path. This is where you live in a state of grace - living your life in accordance with your spiritual path. Depending on your age you may dream of the album Graceland by Paul Simon or Elvis Presley's mansion. In both cases your dharmic path includes channeling as this is what music indicates in dreams.

A *locker* represents keeping things hidden or locked away. *Opening a locker* indicates dealing with something hidden.

A *music album*, when full length, indicates you are on the karmic path.

Dream: Crazy Train

I open my locker door to look in there. I notice some tapes near the front of the shelf and I start handing them to my wife, who is in bed. She is putting on a walkman. Two of the albums were *Graceland* and *Hall and Oats*, but there were about 6 of them. I gave them all to her. She put on one and the song that started playing was *Stay With Me 'till Dawn* by Jude Tzuke. It was playing out over loudspeakers and was really beautiful. The words were, "It's a crazy situation. I don't really know what's going on." In reality I know this song from a long time ago but my wife does not. In the dream she recognized it.

I am now putting away the album cover. It is an LP now and not a tape. I discarded the plastic covering from the album. It was a very large clear plastic bag. Now the album is a train set and I show it to my wife. A small engine is racing around the track. When it reaches a part where the track ends abruptly, it is transported at speed by a harness to the next part of the track. It's crazy. I decide to put some of the bigger trains on the track.

Plastic wrapping often indicates a man made obstacle to spiritual understanding. Literally the spiritual goal you are trying to reach is obscured by conventional views Discarding plastic wrapping indicates you are clearing through this.

A *train set* symbolizes your life journey.

An *engine* represents your heart and circulatory system as an engine is the heart of a vehicle.

Crazy Train – The Analysis

This dream is from someone close to completing the transition to the dharmic path. Opening the door to the locker at the start of the dream represents dealing with something hidden. Bringing things into the open is always good in a dream. The music albums in the locker represent the karmic path. This is the path most of us choose when we undertake an earth journey. Music albums are long play and indeed were call long plays (LPs) before the advent of compact discs. While the karmic path increases self awareness, it takes a much longer period of time compared to the dharmic path. However, things are now changing as the dreamer specifically selects *Graceland* and *Hall and Oats*. The dharmic path is living in a state of grace and is clearly signified by Graceland. The dharmic path also connects an individual with the spirit Halls of Learning so that he or she may choose the avenues in life specifically suited for their spiritual goals. The Hall and Oats album is a pun on this. Lastly, there are 6 albums and that number alone indicates dharma.

The dharmic path is achieved through a connection with our female energy and in the dream his wife represents his female side. She uses a walkman, signifying that it is his individual goal but that it is achieved through his female side. The song that plays tells the dreamer that he is unfamiliar with what is going on and needs female support (stay with me) until he reaches enlightenment (dawn) as he is not used to listening to his heart. If this support does not come from his wife he must seek it someplace else, such as counseling.

Discarding the plastic bag is doing away with the conventional (plastic is man made) and is good in the context of moving to dharma. The crazy train is a perfect symbol for the dharmic path. This path is not mapped out the same way as karma and indeed the path seems crazy or illogical to people still on that path. A person looking at the choices this dreamer is making can clearly see they are heading to a dead end. However, the person on the dharmic path trusts, however illogical it may look to others, that they will somehow find themselves brought to the correct place they need to be. How they get there will often seem crazy or just pure luck to others.

Putting larger trains onto the track shows that the dreamer is now accepting responsibility for what he has to deal with – an essential trait on the dharmic path..

For those interested the ingredients for this dreamer to achieve the dharmic path were a voracious appetite for information on spiritual matters and life purpose, coupled with cutting the ties with his mother to free himself from the necessary conditioning he picked up in childhood.

12. Communication with Angels

We are all in the gutter, but some of us are looking at the stars.

— Oscar Wilde
Lady Windermere's Fan

In today's usage the terms psychic, medium, channel, clairvoyant and clairaudient are often used interchangeably but they mean very different abilities. All however, have one thing in common. Each allows the person with the ability to communicate with the Spirit world. I am always impressed by anyone who has developed any of these abilities. I think it is from being taught as a child to say prayers but never to listen for the answer. So when I first met a person who could hear answers I was shocked that it was even possible! I thought I would have to wait until I was dead.

Since then I have come to realize that an ability to communicate with spirits and hear their answers is a natural thing. We would easily accept that two spirits can communicate with each other but we tend to be skeptical when a human being claims they can communicate with spirits. Due to Western upbringing we judge this to be impossible. Then I realized we can and we do it all the time. I can communicate with you without any difficulty and we are both spirits – we just happen to be incarnated into physical bodies at this moment in time! That was the breakthrough for me. From my new perspective I see all communication as communication with spirit whether it is the living with the living or the living with the dead. Some spirits just happen to be incarnated in physical bodies while others are not. When considering if a human can communicate with a spirit, first remind yourself of what a human being is. A human is a spirit who has taken on a physical body. A human communicating

Summary

► There are many ways to communicate with Angels. As expected your dreams show you exactly how it works for you.

► The terms psychic, medium, channel, clairvoyant and clairaudient are often used incorrectly. The difference in meaning is explained here.

► Belief in the ability to communicate is a key to making it a reality.

► You are first and foremost a spirit. Communication with other spirits, whether incarnate or not, is a totally natural thing.

with a spirit can be more correctly phrased as *A Spirit in a human body communicating with another Spirit*. Now that does not sound nearly as miraculous!

Many people block their spiritual abilities, such as communication with spirits, because they believe it to be beyond their reach. What we believe forms the basis of our reality, so we must clear these blocks to clear the way for our communication ability to work. We accept, or hope, that when we die our Spirit lives on. But our attachment to the body in the short time we have been here, usually means our consciousness has been dragged down to thinking that we are the body. Several things such as pain and our senses converge to make us believe this. It is best for everything you do in life, to remember that you are a spirit with a body rather than a body with a spirit. This will elevate your consciousness and help you to make choices that are more in line with why you took this spiritual journey in the first place.

As you might expect, our dreams tell us exactly how we each individually communicate with spirit and what, if anything, is preventing us from working that ability. I firmly believe that everyone can communicate with spirits. However, not everyone is here to pass on messages from spirit. Communication is a natural ability we are born with. Children can communicate well before they can use a language. By coincidence as I am writing this, my 10 year old son is teaching my 4 year old daughter how to say the word 'binoculars' and laughing at the word she is coming up with. It brings home the effort we each put into learning to speak in the human world. This is a lot more complex than communicating with spirits!

So as you approach communication with spirits, come from the perspective that you are first and foremost a spirit, and that communication with other spirits, whether incarnate or not, is a totally natural thing. Now let's look at the different styles of communication.

Psychic / Intuitive

The word psychic is often used to describe anybody with a spiritual gift, so let me explain the true meaning of being psychic. We all have a higher self or soul. It is termed higher self because it is the part of us that never lost awareness and is therefore at a higher state of awareness than our physical self. All souls are connected through love. Therefore our higher self is in tune with all other souls. A psychic has a special connection with their higher self while on the earth plane. Through this connection they can tap into their own higher wisdom, but since this is already connected to all souls, they have the wisdom of all souls at their disposal. A psychic has no need to communicate with other spirits because all their information comes through the special link they have with their higher self.

There is no restriction on the information that can be received over a psychic connection compared to other types of connections. However, one important advantage is that no other soul in the physical or spirit world can interfere with this connection. It is a connection that is tamper proof! The psychic, however, still has their own bias to deal with so their ability to receive information clearly is improved by being as objective as possible about what is being received and what it will be used for. If receiving particular information might upset the psychic, this would affect their ability to pick it up correctly in the first place.

An intuitive is the same as a psychic. They are really just two words for the one ability which works through feelings. Most of us would be aware of following our intuition / feelings on at least one occasion, where despite all logic our gut pointed us in a particular direction which we knew would work out. There is no arguing with a feeling. It just is. When developed we can receive an enormous amount of information through this connection and at phenomenal speed. It is like we receive a flash and everything is contained in that flash. It could take hours to expand it all as it is so comprehensive. A challenge for psychics is to discern their own feelings from the information they are tuning into. An inexperienced psychic could be convinced they are picking up something when in fact they are tuning into their own hopes or expectations about the subject in question. Learning to tell the difference requires practice.

Dream Symbols for Psychic / Intuitive

In dreams a psychic ability is indicated by symbols such as glass doors or unusually large windows on a house or building. It is quite common for psychics to dream of walls in a building being made out of glass, particularly the top half. These all symbolize their special ability to see through things. To the rest of us it appears like they have a special vision to see through our problems and pluck the solution or cause out of thin air. Another common symbol is the moon or anything that illuminates the dark such as a candle or lamp. Again these represent their ability to shine a light in the dark.

A psychic is often referred to as having a sixth sense. You will often see an eye, which represents the third eye at the sixth chakra, on their business cards. Therefore dreaming about somebody with a sixth sense or even dreaming of visiting a psychic, means that you have the ability yourself. Dreaming about the color indigo, the color of the sixth chakra (at the brow), or silver, the color

Improve dream recall

Our mind works through association and suggestion. You can use this fact to help you remember your dreams. Here's what to do.

- ▶ When going to bed pour yourself a glass of water and put it on your night stand.
- ▶ Sitting in bed, cup your hands around the glass without touching it. Do not let either hand touch the other.
- ▶ Imagine invisible energy flowing from one hand, through the glass and water, to your other hand. The direction does not matter.
- ▶ Now mentally say to yourself, "*I am going to have a dream tonight and I will remember it in the morning.*" You can even suggest what the dream will be about.
- ▶ Drink half the water and put the glass back on your nightstand. Cover the top of the glass.
- ▶ When you wake up reach for the glass and drink the remainder of the water.
- ▶ As you feel the water go through your body try to recall your dreams.

of the moon also indicates you have this ability.

Psychic abilities work through our female energy so it is important for a budding psychic to deal with any unresolved issues they have with mother. For this reason you will often see dreams about this ability also asking you to cut the ties with your mother. Doing this clears the blocks you are carrying and opens up the pathways for your special power to flow freely.

Channel / Medium

A channel is a person who specifically talks with discarnate spirits. When giving you a reading they will tell you who is giving them the message. Mostly we go to a channel in the hope that our deceased father, mother or a loved one that we miss will come through. Often we are surprised at who does actually show up. People who have wronged us while living often appear in our readings to apologize for their behavior. Many people are initially unreceptive to these apologies. However, the fact that they happen is very revealing. To me it shows that the spirit world does indeed have a view of the bigger picture. When a soul passes over and sees things from this higher perspective they can clearly see the damage they have caused their victim.

A channel is not limited to communicating with souls who have crossed over. They can also communicate with other spirits. Anyone who knows about their involvement in our lives wants to hear from their Angels or Guides. Almost everyone has had the sense in childhood that they were being watched over. The souls helping us in this way are our guides. At least one of our guides will remain with us from birth right through until death. At various points along the way our guides will organize other guides to help us in areas that require expertise best provided by other souls. Quite often guides will use a departed loved one to communicate with us. This is for three main reasons. The first is that we will accept more easily a message from someone we loved dearly while on earth as we already have a trusting connection with them. The second is that it adds a touch of earthiness to what can often appear to be a cold message from a spirit who has long since evolved past the level we are at on earth. Lastly it is much easier for a channel to communicate with a soul who recently shared the same plane as the channel. Communicating with a guide requires the channel to elevate their vibration to quite a high level. This takes a lot of energy. Communicating with any soul takes energy and the higher the vibration of the soul being connected with the more energy it takes. Conversely it is far easier to connect with souls who are at a lower level of awareness.

A channel has a particular guide working with them specifically controlling the channeling gateway from the spirit side. This is very important to realize as it is best to allow this guide to control who can gain a connection to the channel. After all they can clearly see the level of each spirit who comes along. It takes time to develop trust with this guide but it is well worth the effort. Start by asking your guides to never allow anyone come through who would harm you. This is very easy for guides to do and you only need to ask them once. Once you ask, trust that they know what they are doing. Don't ask them and then continue to worry about it as you are then keeping control and blocking their help. It is like you keep a foot in the door when they want to close it! It is your body and your connection after all so you have the ultimate say.

As a channel begins to develop their ability, they are likely to first connect with earth bound souls. These are the easiest to connect with as they have not really left the vibration we exist in. It is best to be aware of how to help these souls before you begin. Explaining to them that they have guides and all they need to do is ask them for assistance is quite often sufficient. However, you can come across souls who have been stuck for a long time and it can take longer to help them move on. Usually it will take at most twenty minutes to help someone who is fairly stuck. Others can be helped in a lot less time. Remember to ask your guides to keep souls away from you that can cause you difficulties before doing this for the first time. Always trust that your guides will keep undesirables out. They are the ultimate bouncers – after all they can see who is knocking at the door. In time you can learn to be the bouncer but there is no need to give yourself that extra task in the beginning.

This brings me on to a point that is very important for channels. There are souls whose level of awareness is so low that they amuse themselves by interfering with a budding channel. This interference can be in many ways. It can be pestering you constantly so you can't think straight or sleep properly. It can be pretending to be your Guide and giving you false direction or it can be downright malicious, prophesizing the death of those close to you or claiming that it will bring that about. Even before a person realizes that they are a channel, souls in the spirit world can see their ability shining like a beacon. This can draw these undesirable souls into their life and many channels experience this problem. Part of developing as a channel is learning how to protect yourself from this. Protection is quite easy and like most things awareness is the key. First you must realize the level of awareness held by any soul who would intend to do you harm

The Aquarian Age

The vibration of the earth is increasing and this is creating more opportunities for increasing awareness for its occupants. You will probably have noticed how much more accepted it is today to talk about 'awareness' and guides or guardian angels. Not too long ago people were persecuted for believing in such things. This is often at the heart of our fears about developing our own spiritual gifts. Today more and more people see and talk to their guides.

We are experiencing a shift from the age of Pisces to the age of Aquarius. The difference we will see between the two ages is much the same as the difference we see between male and female energy. So what does this mean for our evolution?

We can see the male institutions around us losing their control. In Pisces societies we have institutions 'outside' of ourselves, to which we are told to go for help for separate aspects of our functioning. We go to the doctor to heal us of disease in the body. We go to church for spiritual guidance and salvation. We turn to the psychologist for emotional and mental problems and scientists for explanations about our reality, etc. All the time we are told that we are not expert on these subjects and is akin to that of a child. If a three year old child picked up a knife with the intention of hurting you, you would realize that the child is more likely to hurt himself than you. With considerable ease you can remove the knife from the child. You will also realize that the child needs love and nurturing and has obviously been influenced in the wrong direction. So too it is with souls who would intend to harm you. They do not have any real power, despite their claims, and the best thing you can do for them is to send them love. This problem only happens with channels. A psychic is not open to the influence of other spirits unless they are also a channel. So a psychic can happily wade into getting information for any client that comes to them whereas a channel must first test the energy the client brings with them. Once they tune into that, they will know whether to only connect with their own guides for information or whether they are safe to allow souls around the client to come through. In some cases it is best to just send the client on their way and explain that the connection is not working. Never put yourself through an ordeal that you do not need. As your experience grows you can take on more complex situations with ease.

None of this has to happen to a channel. The key to developing yourself is getting into the right circle and only connecting when the energy is conducive to development. On my courses I briefly touch on how to do this, and also how to tell whether a psychic or channel who is doing a reading for you, is actually connecting with the spirit world or not. My wife, who is a channel by profession, runs courses on how to communicate with Angels, and at least the first half of the course is taken up by learning how to tune into the energy around you to determine whether it is a good space for connecting with the spirit world. This is learned as a series of simple exercises. Ensure that any course you take covers this. While it not essential that you are shown how to do this, it is important that the facilitator creates a 'safe place' for the participants. Many facilitators

---

must look outside of ourselves for solutions to our problems. These institutions condition us to disassociate ourselves from our problems. However, this 'not owning' our problems prevents us from finding their cause and solving them, as we tell ourselves we are incapable of solving them ourselves.

With the dawning of Aquarius we are realizing that all aspects of our functioning are interconnected and that we are responsible for our reality. That cannot be over stated. Once we accept this basic premise we can then accept that we are responsible for everything in our lives. We can change our reality by changing how we think. This may sound incredible to somebody suffering from an illness, but health is free should we choose (at a soul level) to be healthy. We need to look to the aspect of our functioning, which we have ignored or separated from, which causes the disease.

We hold the keys to our reality and are directors and stars in a play where we draw the complete cast of characters to ourselves based on how we think. Each event in our lives is designed for and by us as an opportunity to evolve. There is no such thing as bad luck. Every moment is an opportunity to be grasped.

do this for you without pointing it out. They tune into the energy of souls around and even the energy of the participants. All who would drag the energy down are excluded from the session through various techniques employed by the facilitator. For example, if a participant is depressed over something, their energy must not be tied in with the rest of the group for that session, as their negative energy will draw souls with negative energy.

Dream Symbols for Channeling

A person is either born a channel or they are not a channel at all. Channeling requires both male and female energy working in balance, and as such is often indicated in dreams by weddings or attention being drawn to the aisle in a church. A church or other place of worship is obviously a spiritual location so indicates the dream is about the dreamer's spiritual dimension. The aisle is a channel between the seats which usually separates the left side from the right. The left and right indicate male and female sides and the channel is a pun on the word itself. In fact any pun on the word channel will do in a dream. For instance, the Channel Isles or the English Channel would also indicate the ability. A symbol which is perhaps more common than any other is a post office or a mailman. A post office is where messages are sent for sorting and delivering. A mailman is the agent who carries out this function. A channel does the same thing with spiritual messages. It is their job to pick up messages and deliver them to the correct recipient! A common symbol which always amuses people is a whale or dolphin. They symbolize a channel with their special ability to live in the sea (the spirit world) despite the fact that they are air breathing mammals like us. I find it amusing that it is almost always an orca or killer whale that shows up in dreams. The word *killer* highlights the fear people have with regard to getting into channeling and the black and white colors show how much it goes against the grain of what they have been taught to believe in life.

Flying with a Guide in a dream also indicates that the dreamer is a channel through the ability to rise up to the level of the spirit world. Music is part of the spirit world so also indicates channeling in dreams. People with near death experiences (NDE) report hearing the most beautiful music while in the other world. Others report that each soul has it own frequencies of colors and sound. As you pass by or touch them you hear their musical notes join and harmonize with your own. Film stars are a common symbol as they don't say their own lines - they say what they are told to say. Again this is what a channel does. Symbols which are not as common are tubes or cylinders especially if they are open at both ends. A channel is open at both ends with one end being the physical world and the other being the spirit world. Usually some trauma around the time of a person's birth is what makes them a channel. Life being threatening, either through physical danger such as a premature delivery, or through emotional trauma such as not being wanted, causes the soul to step back from the earth plane rather than come into it fully. This action causes them to have one foot in the spirit world and one foot in the physical world. This is maintained throughout their life. While it is indeed a trauma it is something that is most likely planned to happen well in advance. There is almost always more than just maintaining the connection with the spirit world that is the reason for this being part of their life.

Lastly if you dream of a medium or channel then you clearly have that ability.

Clairvoyant

This is the term that is popularly used to refer to anyone with a psychic or channeling gift. However, clairvoyant literally means to see clearly. A clairvoyant receives messages from the spirit world through images or symbols. As with any of the other communication abilities you can develop your clairvoyance just for your exclusive use or you can use it to help others. It is always best for the clairvoyant to interpret the images themselves rather than to just pass a description of them on to their client. If this is how communication works for you, push yourself to make sense of the images. Give yourself time as quite often a clairvoyant needs to think about what they have received to decipher it. Then say what comes to you. Remember the words do not need to make sense to you - it is the person you are reading for that can best make sense of the message.

I have found that clairvoyants can also see the aura and spirits very clearly. On my courses I find that one person in twenty five or more has this ability. While others describe the aura they are seeing as something with a touch of color here and there, the clairvoyant comes out with such detail that everyone else in the group stops to listen to what they get. This happens spontaneously even if the person is unaware until that moment that they are clairvoyant. Invariably clairvoyants are also good artists and can draw what they are seeing. They can also explain the meaning of the colors and energy they see when looking at a person's aura. When we move on to seeing spirits they shine again. They can see the clothes a spirit is appearing in and describe the features with amazing detail. All very interesting to others who are straining to see just a haze!

Dream Symbols for Clairvoyance

In dreams a strong focus on eyes would indicate you have clairvoyant sight. While clairvoyance does not work through your physical eyes, (or we all would have it) most clairvoyants leave their eyes open and use them to focus on their area of interest. When reading for others, clairvoyants tend to initially focus on the aura reading the detail there. Once they have read enough from the aura to get the story of what is currently going on for their client, they launch into the reading. The reading is usually heavily backed up with further clairvoyant images that the reader may close their eyes to get. It is a matter of personal choice for the clairvoyant.

Another dream symbol that indicates you are clairvoyant is a television receiver. It is important to note that a television station does not mean the same thing. A television set receives encoded images from a distant source, decodes and displays them to the viewer. That's exactly what a clairvoyant does!

Here's an example of how clairvoyance works. John had been thinking of moving house for nearly five years and out of the blue saw a house come available in an area he liked. Not sure if he should make an offer he decided to ask his guides for a message on it. To start the process he lay down to completely relax. He closed his eyes and imagined the front of the house as if looking at it from the street. The image faded and was replaced with an image of two frosted ring doughnuts sprinkled with hundreds and thousands. The top doughnut had slipped to the side and was now leaning against the bottom one.

John knows his clairvoyance is working when he gets an image like this as it is nothing he was thinking about. Also he doesn't immediately know what it means but within minutes he deciphered it as, "Do not (pun on doughnut) buy the house as the money you put into it (hundreds and thousands) will not stack up (doughnut stack had fallen over)." The significance of the image is aimed purely at the receiver – John in this case. It has happened that John gets images he cannot decipher but he simply asks for another. In this case the doughnut image was the second attempt at the message as he could not make sense of the first image he got. It is important to realize that you can simply ask the question again. To get another image John reset the question by imagining the house again.

The image John got does not explain to him specifically why it would be a bad move except that it would be a financial drain. While that information would be interesting it is not necessarily important. The most important message is, "Do not go for this house". Maybe in time he will find out why but it will not be at his expense.

Clairaudient

Channeling works mainly through three methods; feelings (similar to a psychic connection), clairvoyance and clairaudience. Clairaudient means to hear clearly and a clairaudient hears messages from the spirit world. The beauty of getting communication this way is that you don't have to decipher it. You hear the words and you repeat them!

This gift is in more of us than you'd think. When we are off guard our guides can pass us a message by giving us the line of a song. You could wake up with it on your mind or it could just pop into your head when you're walking down the street. Take note of this and see if it is an answer to a question you were pondering. Then wait to see what else you get. You find that the line or song stays with you until you acknowledge it. Then it just stops. Wait to see if another song or line pops into your head. Don't try to force one. It will come spontaneously. Putting all the lines together will make a message that requires little to decipher.

For the true clairaudient, however, the words they hear are just like they are talking to another person in the room. Many report that they hear the words in their own voice while others hear it differently. Whatever way it works for you just take the time to become familiar with it so that you can be sure that you are being given a message rather than putting words into your own head!

Many channels start off with getting messages one way but it changes as they become more experienced. My wife, for example, used to hear her guides. Now she gets all her communication through feelings. Ironically the depth of information she now gets is much greater now than when it worked through hearing. As you progress allow that your communication techniques may be varied and change over time.

Dream Symbols for Clairaudience

The symbols that indicate this in dreams are ears and radio sets. Clairaudience is always connected with the channeling gift so you would usually see other symbols in the same dream indicating channeling is a gift of the dreamer.

Quick Symbol Reference for Communication with Angels

The following symbols all indicate the above for various reasons. Complete descriptions are given in the Dream Symbol Reference later.

Psychic

Babies born developed or with sixth sense

Candle

Chandeliers

Indigo color

Lamp

Light

Light switch

Lighthouse

Moon

Psychic as guide.

Silver

Silver coins

Silver color

Third eye

Unusual large windows or glass doors on house

Medium / Channel

Actor

Aisles

Cylinder

Dolphins

Film star

Flying with guide

Medium as guide

Music

Post office

Postman

Puns on the word channel

Reference to twins

Singer

Tube

Two of anything

Whales

Clairvoyant

Eyes

Television Set

Clairvoyant as a guide

Clairaudient

Ears, Earrings

Radio

Telephone

A *swimming pool* is about your spiritual side. These dreams normally focus on specific spiritual abilities which are indicated by other symbols in the dream. The significance of the swimming pool is that it is a contained body of water with no outlet. The dream is asking you to remove any tendency you have to contain or limit your ability and to create an outlet for it in your life.

A *dolphin* symbolizes channeling in a dream. A channel is someone who can communicate directly with spirits and Angels. Dolphins are mammals like us but live in the ocean. In dreams the ocean represents spirituality so here it is an air breathing mammal that has adapted to travel into the spirit world.

Swimming - getting in touch with your spiritual nature.

Dream: Swimming with Dolphins

I'm in a large swimming pool, trying to get out but there are about 6 large dolphins in the water and they keep nudging me back into the pool, it is a beautiful dream they are swimming under me and pushing me under the belly up out of the water it keeps happening then I wake up.

The *belly* is the location for digestion and in dreams indications assimilation or digestion of new ideas. Normally it means that you are having difficulty assimilating a new concept that affects your philosophy of life.

Water can symbolize your spiritual side or life itself. It has no shape of its own and can assume the shape of anything into which it is placed. How the water is depicted in the dream says something about your spiritual side. Our spiritual side is quite often the most neglected aspect of our nature. Spirituality is expression of the soul and not to be confused with religion. Expression of the soul connects you with life and is your true essence.

The number *six* indicates the dharma path in dreams. Six symbolizes going beyond the five senses and karma and experiencing life as a spiritual journey in a state of Grace. Choices are made through the heart and the path in life you follow is the path you know is of most benefit to you spiritually. This way of living has a strong connection to life, the spirit world and a great sense of purpose.

Swimming with Dolphins – The Analysis

This dream is clearly encouraging the dreamer to get in touch with her spiritual channeling ability (dolphins). Water indicates spirituality / life. The fact that a swimming pool is a contained body of water with no outlet is sufficient to say that the dreamer is containing or limiting her spiritual side and is being asked to create an outlet for it in her life. The dolphins keep nudging her back into the pool so the dream is clearly encouraging her to immerse herself in her spiritual nature and stay with it.

Dolphins represent channeling as they are air breathing mammals that live in the sea. This indicates that although you are air breathing on the earth plane you can venture into the spirit world (the sea) to communicate with spirits. The size of the dolphins emphasizes that this ability cannot be denied – it is meant to be large in the dreamer's life. In this dream the dolphins are also guides as they have command in the water. Swimming with the dolphins is then similar to flying with a guide so is another strong symbol for channeling for the dreamer.

The dolphins push her under her belly to encourage her to open up to the concept of channeling or of using her channeling ability in life. Since they are doing this in the dream is a clue that the dreamer has not taken her gift on board and while she may be aware of it she has pushed it to the back of her mind with regard to importance. The pushing shows that her guides will persist with pushing her into using her ability until she does open up to it.

The last part of significance is the fact that there are six dolphins. Six represent the dharma path where life is lived in a state of spiritual acceptance. This tells the dreamer that to way to living on the dharma path is through developing her channeling ability. The dharma path is a much quicker route to restoring former awareness as on it we chose avenues that we know are best for achieving our life purpose.

A *whale* symbolizes channeling in a dream. A channel is someone who can communicate directly with spirits and Angels. Whales mean this because they are mammals, like us humans, but live in the ocean. In dreams the ocean represents spirituality so whales represent air breathing mammals that are adapted enough to travel into the spirit world. The type of whale involved is not important although it is almost always *killer whales* that show up in dreams. In this context the killer portion of the name shows the fear the dreamer has with regard to talking with *the dead*. Also their strong black and white color would indicate a difficulty the dreamer has with regard to accepting spiritual communication. In essence they must overcome their black and white attitude that tells them things are either good or evil. When you have this attitude it is difficult to open your mind to something new. This could be due to religious doctrine.

A *beach* represents your spiritual approach or your approach to life itself. The sea represents life since that is where life on earth began. The beach is the approach to the sea so symbolically represents your approach to life.

Dream: Whale Rider

I was on a sunny, sandy beach. A black and white killer whale surfaced and I climbed on his back. We went for a ride below the water, which was so crystal clear that it seemed light as air. I could clearly see the sun shining down from the sky and the colors around me. The whale surfaced and returned me to the beach. The whole event was peaceful and pleasant.

The *sun* is the life giver for planet earth. Without it life here would not exist and if it were to stop shining tomorrow life on this planet would disappear almost instantly. In dreams the sun represents healing energy and it means you have a hands-on healing ability just like Jesus uses in the bible. Hands-on healing involves channeling energy through your body and projecting that life energy into your client

Water symbolizes your spiritual side or life itself. It has no shape of its own and can assume the shape of anything into which it is placed. How the water is depicted in the dream says something about your spiritual side. Our spiritual side is quite often the most neglected aspect of our nature. Spirituality is expression of the soul and not to be confused with religion. Expression of the soul connects you with life and is your true essence.

Whale Rider – The Analysis

The whale represents the dreamer's chandelling ability. That means she has the ability to communicate with spirits / angels. Like the whale this ability is surfacing for her now and again just like in the dream she is being asked to climb on board and go with it. The thought of communicating with *dead people* evokes fear initially and this manifests in the dream as the whale being a *killer* whale. The black and white colors of the whale also show that this does not fit snugly into the dreamer's spiritual approach (the beach). It is along the lines of - if this is correct then something else I have learned must be wrong!

The sun indicates she also has a hands-on healing ability. Just like Jesus did, she can place her hands on someone who is ill and heal them. This idea of this can be a source of conflict with religious upbringing despite the fact that in the bible Jesus says anyone who believes is capable of performing the miracles he performed and can even do greater ones than he did (John 14:12).

The dream starting and ending on the beach asks the dreamer to find her unique approach to spirituality. That is the purpose of her life. Good news in the dream is that the water is *crystal* clear. Crystals have long been used in the spiritual field, and more recently in electronics, to tune into specific energy frequencies. Here the dream tells the dreamer that she can tune clearly into the messages and healing energy being transmitted to her.

In reality the dreamer was raised a traditional Protestant and has found it difficult to merge what she was taught as a child with what she has learned as an adult. She is aware of times when, as she puts it, "silent words were placed in my thoughts while awake. It was unsettling. The messages were brief but brought me comfort." In her case the messages were from her late husband and recently deceased mother. She is not sure where her fear comes from. A common source is fear of persecution for delving into other worldly activity. Persecution by those who claim to know better than you is still common. Who will shun you? What friends and family will turn their backs on you? It is not long since we stopped burning witches at the stake! Despite living in a more open society it is entirely possible the subconscious memory of this happening in a former life evokes fear this time around.

A *guide* symbolizes one of your guardian angels. They are often silent in dreams and indicate their message by what they are doing, wearing, or have with them. For example, if he or she is ignoring you it means you are ignoring your guide in reality. When a guide speaks in a dream they are infallible. Always take their message as it is.

A *radio* indicates that you are a clairaudient channel. Clairaudience is a gift where you literally hear messages from the spirit world. Mostly the messages are heard as lines from songs popping into your head. The segment of the song will repeat over and over making you wonder why you can't get it out of your head. Once you accept it is a message it immediately changes to a line from another song or stops if it is the end of the message. It can also work through hearing lines from movies.

Dream: The Radio

My dream features a radio, with no details about it. Then our guide told us that we should get up early in the morning in order to help people. He woke us up at 5 AM, even though we went to sleep very late.

To *help others* in a dream is indicative that you are a spiritual teacher / leader. Spiritual leaders empower others to be able deal with their challenges themselves.

Being *late* in a dream is a reminder that you are on the karmic path and have not developed yourself to the degree you agreed and had planned before being born.

The number *five* indicates the karmic path in dreams. Literally you are experiencing your world through the five physical senses alone. Dreams with the number 5 quite often show what you are obliged to develop on this path so look for other symbols to indicate this in the dream.

The Radio – The Analysis

This dreamer is a clairaudient channel (he hears messages). The guide in the dream is one of his guides in reality. As a guide what he says is infallible. Telling the dreamer to awaken early is asking him to get in touch with the spiritual purpose of his life. He specifically tells him he is to help others so he is to use his clairaudient ability to do this. Five is a reminder to the dreamer of his karmic obligation to help others. This is in his best interest. References to being late or time in dreams are also about being on the karmic path. On this path various milestones have to be achieved. When we fall behind on these we can dream about being late and that is why it shows up in this dream. The reference to having no detail on the radio tells the dreamer that he does not need to know how this channeling works. Simply use it as you would a radio – you do not need to know how it works to tune in and listen to it.

In reality the dreamer was unaware that he was a channel but in his own words says, "For many years I noticed that songs are popping into my head with their meaning reflecting a state of mind or an insight on a particular situation." This agrees with the dream saying he does not need to know the details of how clairaudience works.

13. Counseling

I have spread my dreams under your feet. Tread softly because you tread on my dreams.

— **William Butler Yeats**

Counseling is a carefully controlled field in most western countries and rightfully so. To become qualified usually takes three years of training. During the training you must attend counseling yourself to clear up any baggage you may be carrying, so that you remain objective with prospective clients. Your first clients are taken on while still in training and your interactions are heavily monitored by experienced counselors. All this is done to both ensure the client is getting the help they need and that you are supported in dealing with your first cases. The support includes ensuring you are not traumatized by the reality of these cases. Once qualified you remain within a hierarchical system while working in the field. You are assigned a supervising counselor with whom you meet on a regular basis – perhaps once every two weeks in the beginning. The supervising counselor will know if you are being adversely affected by any of your cases and appropriate measures can be taken.

With the work I do, I frequently refer people to counseling. Over the years I have met some extraordinary counselors and others who are in the wrong vocation. Despite the hard work it takes to get it, a counseling qualification on its own it does not make you a good counselor. Counseling is a spiritual ability and comes from within. The best counselors make a huge sacrifice before being born. If it applies to you your sacrifice is to choose a life where you feel like you don't fit in. It is this feeling of isolation that begins your training. You may try lots of things in life but while you can clearly see how things work for others you always end up, from your perspective, looking on from the sidelines, even when in the middle of a crowd. You simply can not switch off your ability to see the uniqueness in everyone, including yourself. It is this life of observing individuals that trains you for a

Summary

► If you have a counseling ability your dreams tell you how to use it.

► Like any other spiritual ability, counselors are born prepared for that vocation rather than trained.

► Throughout childhood and often adult life they have a pervasive feeling of isolation.

later role in counseling. You look at everyone around you and see how they interact with and are affected by others. You don't see a crowd. You see a lot of individuals standing together.

This feeling of isolation carries from childhood right through your adult life. As adults the feeling of isolation can be addressed through Cutting-the-Ties or another appropriate therapy. Counseling works through your female side requiring a great deal of compassion with an open and non-judgmental heart. As with any female energy gift, a counseling ability is influenced dramatically by your relationship with your mother. A poor bond with her can cause you to close your heart and thus inhibit the flow of female energy within you. This in turn inhibits abilities associated with your female side which includes counseling. Cutting-the-ties can heal this and it also improves your counseling ability because it enhances the flow of female energy within you. Sadly, I have met many middle-aged people who still feel this isolation and never realized before that it could be healed.

As a counselor you draw to you people who need your help and you can be counseling without even realizing it. Your friends seek you out for help with their problems. When you think about it you realize that this has always been the case. Strangely enough, that is the one time that you feel you belong. While counseling you know it is your part in the big picture.

Dream Symbols for Counseling

In dreams the color combination green and pink together always indicates this gift. Green is the color of the heart chakra and pink is associated with unconditional love, both of which are required to counsel effectively. The color peach is sufficient on its own to indicate you are a counselor.

The feeling of isolation in life is so pervasive it can often show up in dreams of counselors. Look for other counseling symbols in the same dream when you see it.

Books and libraries represent knowledge and wisdom. A counselor does not seek to change you. They seek to educate you about yourself so you understand why you are the way you are. This awareness is key and books and libraries in dreams, represent you have the ability to do this. Pearls are also associated with wisdom and also indicate you are a counselor. Newspapers indicate it too as their purpose is to open your mind to what is going on around you.

Therapy

Any therapy that effectively deals with difficult issues will trigger symbolic representation of those issues in your dreams. Under normal analysis this would be interpreted as issues that need to be dealt with. However, when already in therapy, these dreams show what issues the therapy is working on and the progress being made. It is common during therapy to have frightening dreams of being chased and others with blood and gore. This all changes when the therapy is coming to a successful conclusion.

118

Counseling bridges the gap between where you are and where you need to be. As such, bridges in dreams indicate you have the ability. A taxi takes you from where you are to where you need to be so it too indicates you are a counselor and can work with people on an individual basis. A bus does the same thing with more than one person at a time, so indicates you can work with groups of people. According to Chinese astrology, people born in the year of the snake, poses wisdom. For this reason, snakes can indicate counseling in dreams but that interpretation is uncommon.

Snakes due to the Chinese astrological connection, can also indicate you are a counselor but it is very rarely that they do indicate this in dreams.

Guides often appear in dreams to show us our abilities. Whatever ability they have in the dream we have in reality. A guide is anyone who has a title, appears bearing a gift or speaks with authority on a subject. So if you dream of a counselor, a person with a title, you know they are a guide and that you therefore have a counseling ability. To dream of a county councilor would indicate the same thing. A barrister also indicates it because they are senior counsel in court.

Quick Symbol Reference for Counseling Dreams

The following symbols all indicate your dream is about the above for various reasons. Complete descriptions are given in the Dream Symbol Reference later.

A history of isolation in the family

Ability to harmonize opposites

Barrister

Books

Bridge

Color green with pink

Color peach

Counselor as guide

Libraries

Newspapers

Pearls

Puns on the word council

Snakes

Taxi driver

A *salesman* is a guide in a dream. Guides are often silent in dreams and indicate their message by what they are doing, wearing, or have with them. For example, if the salesman is ignoring you it means you are ignoring your guides in reality.

Car can be a pun on Karma and indicate that you are on a karmic path. The dream will show you what is holding you on this path and what you need to do to move past it.

A *telephone* can symbolize communication.

A *sports car* indicates you have a great power in your body (cars represent your body) and this manifests as a spiritual healing ability in your hands. Spiritual healing is what Jesus uses in the bible when he places his hands on people to cure them.

Dream: Trading Cars

I was in a car salesman's office. He was sitting behind his desk talking on the phone. I went in to ask him if I could trade my car in for the red sports car in the forecourt. He was annoyed at me for interrupting him and was pointing to the telephone. I walked closer to his desk. There were magazines and books spread across his desk. He was wearing an army type uniform.

A *forecourt* is a pun on court and symbolizes that you are judgmental with regard to the subject matter of the dream.

Books on a table mean you have a counseling ability. However, in this case you are being told that you are responsible for developing this ability to a level where you can formally practice it.

Magazines indicate you have a counseling ability. You have a depth of knowledge which can be used to help others see where they are in their life and what they need to do to get to where they need to be.

Army uniforms indicate you have a regimented way of thinking that needs to change. In the army troops are trained through boot camp to not question the orders of their superior regardless of the threat to their own life. Green army uniforms ask you to listen to your heart rather than your head.

120

Trading Cars – The Analysis

This dreamer has a counseling ability (magazines and books) but wants to trade that gift for spiritual healing (the sports car). It is her judgment (the forecourt) that she needs to do this in order to make a living. She has the ability to channel (salesman talking on the phone) and is annoyed at what she is being told by her guides (salesman is annoyed on the phone). Her karma is to develop her counseling ability and use it to help others. However, she wants to change her karma (trade cars). The guide shows that this is not possible. Working in the counseling field is what is on the table for her (magazines and books on the table). The guide is telling her to listen to the guidance she has received (pointing to the phone).

In reality this woman is an excellent trance channel. She has easy communication with her guides but at the time of this dream was stressed with other worries and this can block her connection. She knows she is meant to work in the counseling field but does not see how she could make a living at that. At the time of the dream she had gone as far a quitting her job and opening and renovating a spiritual centre. The costs were high and she wanted to learn how to do spiritual healing to help cover costs. The problem was that this would be at the expense of getting a qualification in counseling. The dream is clearly telling her to listen to the guidance she has already received and stick with the counseling. Also because the guide is wearing an army uniform she is being shown that her thinking is limited due to conditioning she picked up from her dad. Cutting the ties with him would help put her heart in the leading position (green uniform) it needs to have in order to allow her counseling gift flourish.

14. Spiritual Healing

What is a cynic? A man who knows the price of everything and the value of nothing.

— **Oscar Wilde**
Lady Windermere's Fan

The spiritual dimension of dreams reminds us that we are more than just physical beings and more specifically it reminds us of our life purpose. The difficulty with this aspect for us is that there is quite often no frame of reference from which to start. When talking about health and relationships we can all relate to the subject. However, if I start talking about a special ability to heal by channeling energy through your hands, it is less likely that any person taken at random has a practical connection with this. As already discussed, our society is not as open to these things as we like to believe. We can connect with physical things such as cars, clothes and houses and accept that somebody with a special skill developed the necessary components for their manufacture. We are also likely to connect with non physical things such as writing, story telling, public speaking and counseling even though they are not physical skills. Most people when presented with a list of spiritual abilities are unlikely to be accepting of the full list. We know this of others, but usually do not see it in ourselves because we may be accepting of one or two of the abilities. Only accepting one or two from a list is better than none, but it is still being closed to many things in the spiritual field.

I met a remarkable English man in Sligo, Ireland when I was visiting one of the many Stone Age structures there. He was a spiritual healer and claimed he had used his healing gift many times to cure serious illnesses such as cancer. In my innocence I assumed that once one person was cured of cancer he must have had a line of people outside his door waiting for treatment. He told me, however, that everyone in the neighborhood stayed away from him because he had let everyone know he was a healer. Even though he had treated and cured some of them, they would never tell anyone they had even been to him! It was a real cloak and dagger operation for somebody to visit him for

Summary

► Your dreams tell you if you have a Spiritual healing ability.

► Spiritual Healing is what Jesus uses in the bible by channeling healing energy through his hands.

treatment in a rural community like that. People were happy to steal away to get treatment and then sit silent lipped when others sat in judgment of him. The irony of the whole situation was that he got most of his work from farmers who hired him to heal their animals. To their credit the farmers did tell other farmers about their success with him, but it was kept secret from the general public lest anyone would avoid buying their "possessed" meat. In ways like this we help keep society closed to some of the most wonderful gifts mankind has.

With hands-on healing the therapist channels healing energy into the client but does not focus the energy with an intention. Their focus is simply on being an open channel for the healing energy. If you could see what is happening clairvoyantly, you would see a spirit standing beside the healer and in fact probably taking up some of the same physical space as the healer. This spirit is the one guiding the healing energy to its target and working with this energy to heal the client. Many healers are aware of this and many are not but it does not affect the healing in any way. The spirit guides them to where they want energy channeled and the way to place their hands. For some techniques only one hand is on the client while the other acts as a sink for energy being earthed. This is a joint effort between the healer and the spirit and over time their connection improves to where they are completely in harmony with each other.

You do not have to know how spiritual healing works for it to be effective. If your dreams tell you that this is one of your abilities then you have it and it will work for you. Just like driving a car, your ability will improve with experience without having to know how a car engine works. If you also have the ability to communicate with spirits you can ask for guidance as you are working. Some therapists channel messages for clients while they are working on them as they are already in that connected space. This too can be very effective at opening the client's mind to accepting the healing energy they are receiving.

It is possible to force energy into a person but it is not advisable to do so, unless your connection is good enough to know your spirit helper wants you to do it. Normally you act as an open channel for the energy and let the spirit guide the flow. To force healing without awareness can incur karma. It is also not advisable to do spiritual healing on anyone unless you have confirmed that you have the ability from your dreams or from another reputable source. There are many schools that teach you how to perform spiritual healing without regard to whether it is part of your life purpose. Just because you can learn to do it doesn't mean you should do it. I have noticed that some of the best healers and longest working in the field had several years experience in the martial arts field before they got into healing. It is not by coincidence that they practiced a system for grounding themselves for years before tackling illnesses. Martial arts, Qigong (pronounced Chi Gung) and Tai Chi are all methods that control the flow of energy through the body. Practice of any of these techniques clears the energy pathways in the body and in particular results in a deep grounding where there is a very strong connection with the energy of the earth. When working on a client, this connection is used to dissipate the energy blockages in the client and most healers will not begin working until they feel this connection. If it is not open the energy drawn away from the client remains in the healer's energy field and can immediately start creating health issues for the healer.

This is what happens if being a spiritual healer is not in your life plan. You can end up channeling your own life energy into your client and you may pick up their physical problems because you don't have the pathways to keep your energy space clean and clear. I have seen people who are not healers but who work in this profession become ill in this way. Their illness can be seen as karma in operation. It causes them to stop working in the field so that they can then get back onto their intended path. To continue to work in this field while ill can have serious life threatening consequences.

To the uninitiated, it can seem like nothing is happening, but the therapist will feel the energy flowing from their hands and into the client. In 99% of cases the client will also feel the energy flowing into them. In very strong healing sessions, the therapist will feel like a pair of hands is working under the skin of the client. The client will also feel this.

Hands-on healing uses male energy and as such is strongly influenced by the relationship with dad. A poor relationship can cause us to inhibit the flow of male energy within us and thus block our healing ability. This can be resolved by Cutting-the-Ties with dad to remove the issues causing the blocks and thus enhance your healing ability.

There are many types of healing that are different from hands-on healing described here. Therapies such as western medicine, bio-energy healing, reflexology, acupuncture, reiki, secheim and more fit this bill. These are invasive therapies where the human healer is directing the healing energy or scalpel with intent. Their intention is always to heal the client. The difference between these therapies and spiritual healing is that in the former the therapist controls the flow and intention of the energy while with the latter the healer's intent is to be an open channel for energy and spirits control the flow and healing intent. Spiritual healing will not heal you of your physical problem if your life purpose requires you to keep it at that stage in your life. Invasive therapies should be used in combination with a strong connection with your spirit guides. You still do the healing but accept guidance on what should be dealt with.

Airport Departure / Pregnancy

Dreams about being pregnant usually indicate a new project is around the corner in your life. Giving birth is the most creative act you can ever do and in a dream means something new is brewing. When it arrives in your life you will become more creative if you take it on. It is always a good dream to have.

A departure at an airport indicates the same thing. You are being asked to depart on a new project. Obstacles to the departure, such as missing passport or tickets indicate reluctance on your part to get going on the new project

Symbols in dreams that indicate a Spiritual Healing ability

All symbols of energy sources such as the sun, power generators, electricity generation stations, gas stations and oil tankers indicate the dreamer is a healer. Gold or gold coins also indicate it because they have the color of the sun. Powerful horses, powerful motorbikes or cars indicate it because of their emphasis on power. You are a healer if your dreams refer to hands or feature a spiritual healer as a guide. Rheumatic healing is indicated by copper or copper coins. A crystal healer is indicated by dreams of diamonds and other crystals.

Psychic Surgery

Psychic surgery is an astounding ability which people rarely ever believe when they first hear of it. It comes in two parts. Firstly it is where a person can simply look at another person's body and detect illnesses within them directly. It is akin to having x-ray vision but rather than seeing an x-ray image they simply see where the physical problems are. The illness highlights itself in an unquestionable way like someone drew a dotted line around it.

The second part of this gift is where a person can literally put their hands inside a person's body and work on the organs under the skin. It is like the skin is a soft jelly membrane that can be easily breached without cutting it. The healer can remove cancers by simply pulling the affected tissue out of the body.

In Western culture psychic surgery is probably the rarest of all spiritual gifts and complements the spiritual healing gift. It is possible to only have recognized and developed the first or second part of this ability. It is also possible to develop a toned down version of the second part. In this case if someone is using this gift on you it will feel like there are many hands inside your body. The practitioner does not physically have their hands inside you but yet you feel other hands working in there under the skin. It is a strange feeling but is not unpleasant and the healer can feel it too. It is the practitioner's spirit guides who are working on the inside.

Psychic Surgery symbols in dreams

The most common symbols for this are x-ray machines, having x-ray vision or having the ability to look inside a person's body in your dream.

Clairsentient

Clairsentient means clear feeling and as expected works through feeling. This includes your sense of touch being triggered even though you are not actually touching anything. I most commonly see this ability active in hands-on healers who use techniques that involve putting their hands into a person's aura but not physically touching them. Sensations such as tingling, static, cold, heat, numbness, etc. are perceived in detail with their hands and fingers while scanning a client. Lessons from experienced healers teach them what each sensation signifies. It is a most amusing technique to witness when performed on a skeptical client. Their jaw drops when without ever touching them the therapist tells them where their physical problem is. This can be quite beneficial for the healing process as it opens the clients mind to the potential for healing from sources other than medical practitioners.

Clairsentience is not normally seen as the main method of communication from spirit except in scanning as just described. Even in that case, the scanning is not sufficient on its own to perform healing - the healer must also have a healing ability.

Another form of clairsentience that is popularized by Hollywood is where a reader feels in their body the signature of the illness or impact that caused the communicating spirit to leave their physical body. While unpleasant for the clairsentient it can serve as a speedy and practical confirmation for a skeptical client.

Dream Symbols for Healing

If you have a hands-on healing ability you are likely to have Clairsentience also.

Quick Symbol Reference for Healing Dreams

The following symbols all indicate your dream is about the above for various reasons. Complete descriptions are given in the Dream Symbol Reference later.

Spiritual Healing

Alaska pipeline

Coal mine

Color gold

Electric socket

Food

Gas station

Generator

Gold

Gold coins

Goldfish

Hands

Hands-on healer

Healer as a guide

Oil tanker

Power plant

Power source

Powerful car or motorbike

Powerful horse

Solar panel

Sun

Waiter serving food or drink

Rheumatic Healer

Copper

Copper Coins

Crystal Healer

Diamonds and other crystals

Psychic Surgeon

X-Ray

Looking inside a person's body

A *jewelry shop* also indicates your spiritual side. Pay attention to what the shop keeper directs you to as this will reveal your spiritual gifts to you. If the shop keeper does not want to sell you something it means you do not have that ability and you are being politely asked not to develop it.

A *silver chain* is a very strong symbol and means that you are obliged to develop your psychic ability – you are chained to it. Most likely you are to use this to help yourself and to repay your karmic debts to others.

To dream of *gold* or anything that is gold in color indicates that you are a hands-on healer. This is the same ability Jesus uses in the bible to heal others. Hands-on healing involves channeling energy through your body and projecting that life energy into your client.

Dream: The Silver Chain

I enter a jewelry shop to buy a gold chain. The jeweler offered me a silver chain. I refused it as I only wanted a gold one. The shopkeeper would not give me the gold one and kept saying the silver one was already mine!

The Silver Chain – The Analysis

In this dream the shopkeeper is a guide because he has a title and as in any dream whatever a guide says is infallible. He is telling the dreamer that she does not have a healing ability (the gold chain is not hers) but she does have a psychic ability (indicated by silver). What's more, it is her karma to develop her psychic ability. It is shown as a chain because she agreed to develop this ability before she was born and to use it to help others. This is how she planned to repay her karmic debts in this lifetime. The dream shows that she no longer wants to do this and instead wants to change her method of paying her karma to healing others. Her guides, through the guise of the shop keeper, are telling her she cannot switch.

In reality this woman had trained in BioEnergy healing. The BioEnergy healing she learned is done through reestablishing the flow of energy from the crown chakra through to the base chakra and clearing out any blockages found. All manipulation is done through manipulating energy around the person and there is rarely any physical touch between the healer and the client. After working at this for a while she had to keep taking breaks from a few days to a few weeks as she kept getting ill herself. This in itself is a sign that she was on the wrong track and is a karmic way of being pushed away from something that is not on her spiritual path.

I have seen situations like this a number of times with people who already work in the spiritual field. They have invested time and money into their training and are understandably reluctant to drop their source of income. In all cases they are already aware that they have a different gift but they do not put the appropriate value on it. In this case the woman knew she was psychic but could not see how she could make a living from it. It is ironic, I know people who have the healing gift and they do not see how they can make a living from it. The grass is always greener on the other side!

The **ocean** symbolizes spirituality and life. Life is a spiritual journey so expect to see other symbols in the dream indicating your spiritual gifts or giving advice on your life journey.

To dream of a **teacher** means that you are a leader / spiritual teacher. Spirituality is expression of the soul so you will teach others to express what is in their core either by example or through instruction. If the teacher in the dream is working with groups it means you are to use your gift with groups. A spiritual teacher empowers others to deal with their problems.

School, being a place of learning, symbolizes learning about yourself with a view to improving yourself.

Dream: The Fake Ocean

I was back in the science room at the middle school in my home town. My teacher, a woman, was there saying something. Then I looked at the back half of the science room and it was just a huge opening to the ocean. The waves were very dark blue and white on top, but in a strange way they looked two dimensional, like the waves used in sets for plays. The sun was burning behind the water but it looked fake too. I went out into the sand. There was a huge sandcastle taller than me. Someone pushed me and I fell into it.

An **opening** is exactly what it sounds like – you are being asked to create an opening in your life for the subject matter of the dream.

The **sun** is the life giver for planet earth. Without it life on earth would not exist and if it were to stop shining tomorrow life on this planet would disappear almost instantly. In dreams the sun represents healing energy and it means you have a hands-on healing ability just like Jesus uses in the bible. Hands-on healing involves channeling energy through your body and projecting that life energy into your client.

A **sandcastle** asks you to be creative with your spiritual approach. It means this because a beach is the approach to the sea (spirituality) so indicates spiritual approach.

Dark blue or **navy,** a mix of blue (philosophy) and black (negativity), indicates a negative philosophy of life or attitude towards the subject matter of the dream while **blue and white** asks you to lighten your attitude or philosophy with regard to the subject matter of the dream.

The Fake Ocean– The Analysis

The dreamer holds a scientific viewpoint on the world (in science class) and sees activity in the spiritual field as fake (ocean is fake). The dreamer is a spiritual teacher (teacher in dream) and also has a hands-on healing ability (sun burning) but, as expected, she sees healing as fake too (sun looked fake in dream). Her negative philosophy with regard to spirituality is pointed out (dark blue waves) and the dream is asking her to lighten up on that (white on top of waves).

Beaches, being the approach to the sea, represent the dreamer's spiritual approach. The dream asks her to be more creative in her approach (sandcastle) and to include healing and spirituality as part of her reality. Do not see it as a fake with no depth (two dimensional). The irony is that the dream ends by predicting that someone will push the dreamer into the spiritual field and when this happens she will let go of her conditioning and just fall into it.

The dream shows that the dreamer's conditioning comes from her upbringing as it places her back in her hometown. The teacher being female emphasizes that spiritual teaching works through female energy but it is also a clue that the conditioned viewpoint comes from the dreamer's mother.

Passing is sometimes a pun on death, as in my mother passed away.

A *spirit* in a dream is exactly that – a spirit. If you can see them in your dream you have the ability to see spirits while awake. While this may sound scary, with a little education, it becomes a blessing.

Sitting on a floor in a dream brings you back to your childhood as this is when you used to sit on the floor.

Dream: Passing Spirits

I was sitting on the floor in an empty train carriage with no windows. The train was moving at speed. There were double doors that did not open but twice from nowhere a spirit passed close by and went through the doors. As the spirit got to the doors they swung open and in a flash he was gone into darkness. As the door swung shut a detailed x-ray of a skeleton momentarily appeared across both doors.

A *train carriage* is a common symbol for the womb and is bringing you right back to before your birth and early childhood. The train is still about your life journey but the very start is being emphasized as being important. Carriage is a common term referring to babies - for example, miscarriage and baby carriage. It is common in these dreams to show the conditions of the womb by their being no windows in the carriage. While it may seem ridiculous that you cold have any memory or lasting effect from that time in your life, look at the message in the dream to see why it is important enough for you to be getting a message about it now.

An *X-Ray* indicates that you have the gift of psychic surgery. This is an unusual gift so look for it in more than one dream to be sure. Psychic surgery has two forms. One is where you place your hands physically inside a client you are working on and remove cancers, growths and blockages. In the second form you place your hands on the client just as you would for hands-on healing. In this form in addition to healing energy flowing into the client it will also feel like spirit hands are working inside the client's body directly under your hands. It literally feels like the clients skin under your hands is being massaged from underneath.

Darkness: The dream is about your feeling of not knowing where you are going or how to get to where you want to go with regard to the subject matter of the dream. Other symbols in the dream will tell you what you need to move out of the dark.

Passing Spirits – The Analysis

The train journey tells us that the dream is about the dreamer's journey in life. However, the dream's entry point into his life is back in the womb (train carriage with no windows). If this symbol was missed we still know it brings the dreamer back to very early childhood because he is sitting on the floor. The floor, including sitting on it, is a huge part of a baby's world. So the time period the dream is focusing on is from before birth to very early childhood.

While it may seem strange that a dream could be pointing out something as far back as then looking at the other symbols we quickly see why. Twice while in the womb a spirit passes close by the dreamer and enters the spirit world through doors which cannot be opened physically. This means that while in the womb the dreamer had a close brush with death on more than one occasion.

We can see that this is by design because of the symbol that appears across the doors immediately when it happens – the x-ray. A child is a spirit just beginning their journey of life (train journey). When that journey gets off to a very rocky start like this, the spirit can pull back from the physical plane. They do not pull completely back out of the body and end up keeping one foot in the spirit world and the other on the earth plane. As a result they do not bond well with the earth plane but the bridge they built during the brush with death allows this dreamer to retain two spiritual abilities while incarnated. The first is the ability to channel (double doors to the spirit world in the dream). The second, which is rare, is the ability to perform psychic surgery (the x-ray image). This allows the dreamer to see beyond the physical. He can literally look inside a person's body and scan for problems that may be manifesting there.

In reality this dreamer's mother discovered she was pregnant again at age 44. She did not want another pregnancy or child and tried to induce a miscarriage by digging a vegetable patch in her garden! She did not induce a miscarriage but almost ended her own life as well as the baby's. She was rushed to hospital where she had to remain for nearly five months before the baby was born at seven months – two months premature. Both survived. Shortly after this dream he cut-the-ties with his mother. Until then he was angry at her and the world but never understood why!

His is aware of his ability to see physical problems within the body but has not used it for a long time. Mostly this would happen spontaneously rather than under his control. However, he uses his channeling ability on a regular basis.

To dream of a *trick* indicates a level of mistrust or lack of belief in the subject matter of the dream.

The symbol *treat* most likely means you have a hands-on healing ability which you can use to treat others.

To dream of a *doctor* means you have a healing ability. However, in dreams this means you have a hands-on healing ability like Jesus practices in the bible

To dream of someone *snooping* shows a level of mistrust with regard to that person or to the subject matter of the dream

Dream: Trick or Treat Doctor

I dreamt that my doctor came to our house to Trick or Treat on Halloween night with a little girl. I felt that he came (since he lives an hour away) only so he could snoop. I remember handing him a brown and gold candle that was mine.

To dream of *hands* indicates you have a hands-on healing ability. With this healing you channel energy through your hands into your client.

Candles indicate you have an intuitive / psychic ability. With your light you can see where others can not.

Gold and brown as a combination requests you to view hands-on healing as practical.

Trick or Treat Doctor – The Analysis

You have a spiritual healing ability in your hands. This is given by no less than four symbols; the doctor, the color gold, the mention of hands/handing and the word *treat*. The candle says that when using this ability you will get flashes of insight for the person you are working on. Brown asks you not to deny your spiritual healing ability.

I really love this dream. I particularly like the pun on treat alongside doctor, the color gold and the mention of hands. It is hard to argue against the meaning of it. Straight away we know the dreamer is a healer. However, the trick part is that she's not convinced that there is such an ability. Is it really a trick? This philosophy shows up again with the color brown being mixed with gold. The brown here asks her not to deny her gift. Her next step is to overcome her materialistic view that was picked up from her dad at the age of the little girl in the dream.

15. Absent Healing, Hypnosis & Projection

So many of our dreams at first seem impossible, then they seem improbable, and then, when we summon the will, they soon become inevitable.

— **Christopher Reeve**

Having the ability to levitate or fly like a bird is by far one of the most common themes in dreams. Here the dreamer remembers they have the ability to fly and they either do it effortlessly or spend the rest of the dream trying to get properly off the ground. When the flying is successful the dreamer always awakes feeling refreshed and indeed that is one of the functions of this type of dream. The flying symbolizes that the dreamer has a strong mind which gives them unique abilities. They obviously cannot fly but the flying indicates they can project their mind anywhere or onto anything he or she wants.

If you have this ability the most practical aspect of it is that it can be used to view a problem in an enlightened way and thereby mentally rise above it – which is what the levitation symbolizes in the dream. You can literally focus on something that has been bothering you, regardless of how long it has been, and mentally leap beyond it by capturing a higher perspective on it. It is easy to engage this ability but you have to consciously do it and tendencies are to unconsciously hang on to problems and stay bogged down by them. Once you get an enlightened perspective on your problems, their significance melts away. From your high vantage point you can see that instead of facing the problem head on, there are many avenues around it, or indeed you may see that it is not really a problem deserving of the attention you were giving it.

Astral traveling in dreams symbolizes the same thing. Astral traveling is where

Summary

► Astral projection is indicated by flying in dreams and is one of the most common dream themes.

► Absent healing is the ability to send healing energy to someone remote.

► Hypnosis, astral projection and absent healing come as a set. If you can do one you can do all three.

► When you have this ability, persistently thinking ill of others can incur karma as it affects their health. Your dreams will warn you when this is the case.

you know in the dream that you are a spirit and you have temporarily left your physical body for this experience. In fact even if you are unaware of your spirit body, it is your astral body in the dream that is flying because only it can. Your astral body is the spirit body that resembles your physical being. This is the spirit body that leaves your physical body when you die.

In astral traveling you project your consciousness into the astral body and detach it from your physical body. It is never fully detached except at death and remains connected to the physical body even when astral traveling. Even if you are not consciously aware of it, you astral travel every single night while asleep. It is during these escapades you converse with your guides and other friends who are also astral traveling. This is why you can dream of a friend you have not seen in a long time and they contact you out of the blue the next day. It is not out of the blue. You both organized it during your astral travels and you partially recall it in a dream. Advice received from your guides while astral traveling also shows up in your dreams. Memories of events you witnessed can also show up and give you a spooky deja vu feeling when you hear about the event on waking the following morning.

It is possible with practice to astral travel while awake. Both the USA and USSR acknowledge they had teams of spies engaged in this during the cold war. The first step is to move your consciousness from your physical body and into your astral body. At this point all sensations and emotions are now felt through the ast ral body and nothing is felt through the physical body. This is the state drug induced anesthetic achieves, allowing the body to be operated on without pain. There have been many reports of people witnessing their body being operated on from above the operating table. In these cases the person has also taken the step of detaching their astral body to float above the physical. They witness the operation without any pain. It is only when consciousness returns from the astral body that physical sensations and the accompanying pain can be felt again. Some hospitals have ongoing studies on these reports and to discern fact from hallucination, have a number written above the lights of the operating table that can only be seen when looking down. If the patient mentions the number in their report of events, their experience is taken more seriously.

Whether you can astral travel or fly in your dreams, it means you have all four abilities associated with it. The first which I have already covered, is the ability to get an enlightened perspective on things by mentally rising above a situation. The remaining abilities of hypnosis, projection and absent healing are covered in turn now.

Astral Traveling

For an exemplary book on astral traveling read *Journeys out of the Body* by Robert A. Monroe. The book also gives techniques for how to achieve it.

Hypnosis

Most people are only familiar with the stage hypnotist but this gift is useful for a wide range of things. It is often used to help eliminate phobias and is even used in place of anesthetic during operations! Hypnotists sometimes claim differing reasons for why their target enters a trance. In reality the hypnotist is projecting their mind onto their client. It is their strong mind that works the magic to put the client into the trance state and change their thinking. Their mind is projected over the mind of the client and while engaged the client is literally thinking what the hypnotist wants them to think. When they are brought out of the trance they have new thought patterns laid down that will hopefully allow them to overcome their fear of flying or whatever it is that caused them to seek help. Regardless of tools such as a swinging watch or rotating disk that a hypnotist may also use to help trigger the trance state, it is their ability to project their mind that is the essential ingredient.

Projection

An elderly Native American Indian was being interviewed on a popular national radio show in Ireland and he was asked about smoke signals and how to interpret them. He explained that a tribe could be fairly scattered and if a message was to be sent out a person with the ability to project their mind would go to a high point and send up smoke signals. The smoke signals were not the message. The smoke simply let every-one know that there was someone projecting a message from that point and they tuned into him or her to get it. Non-Indians could never decipher the system of communication as they always focused on the physical smoke.

While hypnosis works on an individual, projection can target any number of people or animals. The person transmitting pictures the message in their mind briefly and does this repeatedly over a period of time. The message is only focused on for a few seconds and then a break of 15 seconds or more is given. Then the message is focused on and beamed out again. Try this on your dog if you have one. When you want to call your dog in, imagine a big juicy steak in their dog dish. Do it briefly twice in a row with a break of 15 seconds. You have to be in a meditative state for this to work but if you practice meditation you can switch into this state on demand.

Projection commonly compliments a teaching ability. If you could see it clairvoyantly, sparks are flying from the lecturer and popping over the heads of the attendees. While in the presence of the teacher they fully understand what he is explaining. However, when they leave and try to explain their understanding to someone else they find their level of understanding is diminished. The projection still benefits them because they know they have the capacity to understand what was being explained and only have to close the gap between what they recall and their understanding at the time.

Absent Healing

In the bible Jesus uses this ability to heal the centurion's servant. If you fly in your dreams you have this ability too. If you are Christian, remember that in your bible Jesus says anyone who believes is capable of performing the miracles he performed and can even do greater ones than he did (John 14:12). Despite this endorsement, the idea that somebody can heal you without touching you or even being near you just does not sit well with many and they choose to see it as a scam. That is understandable from their point of view but if you have this ability you've a lot to gain by opening your mind to it. Do not let others decide your mind and put you off developing this gift or any other gift your dreams inform you of in your dreams.. When your friends and family realize you can do this, they will reach out for your help when they need it.

With absent healing you tune into the person to be healed. You remotely diagnose their condition and then focus on the areas of ill health and correct those one by one by simply picturing that part of the body restored to perfect health. There is a very good course available throughout many countries called 'The Silva Mind Control Method'. This course teaches you how to focus your mind to achieve many different objectives. As part of the course they also show you how to develop absent healing.

A word of warning is needed here. If you have this ability and you think ill of someone else you can incur karma as your thoughts could negatively affect the other person's mental and physical health. Odd annoyance does no harm but if you repeatedly think ill of someone you are unconsciously using your ability to harm them.

Dream Symbols for Absent Healing, Hypnosis & Projection

The most common symbols for this ability are flying and astral traveling in a dream. The flying symbolizes projecting your mind with ease. A vampire also symbolizes it as they can fly but the additional warning here is that you are causing harm to others through using this ability. This could be inadvertent if you were unaware until now that you have it but nonetheless you are incurring karma from how you think of others.

A billboard or poster that beams out into the public indicates projection. Indeed a projector in your dreams would indicate this. Look for puns in the name like an overhead projector which emphasizes head and above (spiritual dimension). A blackboard also indicates you have this ability and emphasizes you are to use it to teach others. TV stations and radio stations are powerful symbols for these abilities as this is where the signals are broadcast or projected from.

A hypnotist in your dreams indicates you too are a hypnotist. If the hypnotist is a TV personality it is even stronger as TV personalities also indicate these three abilities in dreams as they are projected into your home from a distance. Dreaming of Dr. Phil from the American TV show also indicates it but would have an emphasis on using your mind projection to help break negative thought patterns and encourage positive thinking in others you work with. This ability compliments counseling work very nicely.

Remember that once you have one of these abilities you have all of them. They come as a set.

Quick Symbol Reference for
Absent Healing, Hypnosis & Projection Dreams

The following symbols all indicate the above for various reasons. Complete descriptions are given in the Dream Symbol Reference later.

Billboard

Hypnotist

Looking inside a persons body

Puns on the word poster

Radio station

Television station

TV personality

Since you cannot physically fly, to dream of *flying* symbolizes that you have a strong intellect which you can use to mentally rise above a problem. In the dream, when flying you are looking at things from a higher perspective. This is a very practical ability and you are most likely aware you have it. When you've had enough of a particular problem you can step back and consciously decide to see the bigger picture. You will almost always feel exhilarated upon waking from a flying dream. This is because all your problems have become smaller through your dream.

If someone is *behind you chasing you* it means something from the past still has a power over you today. While you may feel you are past it the dreams shows that you are still expending energy trying to get distance between you and it. The feeling that comes up in dreams like this is they key. The dream is attempting to show you that there is a link between the past trauma and that feeling today. If it is a parent it means that you still have issues with that parent today.

Dream: Fear leads to Flying

I experience a recurring dream with my parents in it. They are behind me, trying to get to me and I am overwhelmed with fear. I run so quickly to get away, but cannot run fast enough. Just before my mother (usually), gets to me, I flap my arms and fly away. But the race is usually still close; my mom is hot on my trail. There are typically many obstacles in my way. Sometimes the ceiling is so angled or bumpy I can't find my way outside to get free. I recently developed the ability to carry someone with me in the dream, this is my sister. I picked her up with my legs like a bird and took off flying away from our mother.

Ceilings can symbolize a limitation as in; I reached the ceiling of my ability. As they are always above your head ceilings can symbolize the mind and / or spiritual aspects of yourself. A high ceiling asks you to create a greater space in your mind for the subject matter of the dream. A low ceiling lets you know that your thinking on that subject matter is restricted.

Heat can be about negative emotions from others. To feel heat from someone would indicate they are angry at you. To direct heat at yourself, e.g. sun melting your car, would indicate you are frustrated over something.

Fear leads to Flying – The Analysis

These dreams are about the dreamer's relationship with her parents. Something involving them in the past (they are behind her in the dream) is still getting to her today. The dream puts most focus on her mother with the dreamer only barely keeping ahead of the problem. In some of her dreams she does not manage to get free. This means the trauma is still affecting her life today. The method of escape is flying. In dreams this symbolizes mentally rising above a problem. The many obstacles are symbolic of the depth of the problem she is trying to rise above. The ceiling also has to do with the mind and free thinking so here when it is bumpy or angled it means that her free thinking is still sometimes obscured by the events from the past. It is also symbolic of conditioning picked up from her mother. Picking her sister up is positive and is symbolically healing her (picking her spirits up) at the age of her sister in the dream. It can also indicate helping her work through a common ordeal.

A spiritual ability that comes with a strong mind like hers is an enlightened intellect. She is the way she is today for a reason. How she got that way seems and is horrific from a human perspective. Spiritually, however, it is not and allows her to retain specific spiritual abilities. She can use her mind to get the bigger picture on challenges in her life. It is like she gets to a point where she has just had enough and decides, "I'm not having this problem anymore." She can then sit and think and see her path away from the problem. Along with that ability comes the ability to project her mind onto others. For example, she would be good in sales or marketing! This is how hypnosis works and is also how absent healing works. She can, with her eyes closed, imagine someone's health problem and then imagine herself mentally restoring them to health. The effect is immediate. The person she does this for will report instant improvement.

In reality the dreamer grew up in a dysfunctional, abusive household. She felt she had made great strides in dealing with her past and is confused as to why she has these dreams. Essentially this happens because the trauma is still subconsciously affecting her decisions in life today. Most likely affecting how close she lets others get to her. This is a defense mechanism employed to good effect as a child. Later in life, however, any therapy that deals with the issues must also include restoring the connection to herself. This connection is restored when she is comfortable being herself and honest with herself about her feelings in any situation. She does not necessarily need to share her feelings with others, although that is great if she can. Acknowledging them is the first step away from rationalizing her way through life - always in the head and using logic to make choices.

Happiness is a feeling and no amount of logic brings it into your life. To get into that space you must listening to your open heart and following its advice. As this dream shows, closing your heart to suppress trauma only works for a time. It must be dealt with in therapy. When you can look to the future with a sense of optimism because you feel good today - you have made it.

16. Spiritual Teaching and Leading

Selfishness is not living as one wishes to live; it is asking others to live as one wishes to live.

— Oscar Wilde

Teaching and leading are the same in spiritual terms. To make reading simpler I only use the term teaching but realize the word leading can be substituted. Spiritual teaching can be done in any field. It does not refer to a person in authority. If you have this gift you probably already work at teaching but you can be unemployed or at the bottom level of the hierarchical structure in your organization and still be a teacher. Spiritual teaching is about how you help others and is natural for those with the gift. A spiritual teacher empowers others to deal with their problems themselves rather than dealing with the problems on their behalf. Through being empowered, people are freed from their current problems and can deal with similar problems in the future should they arise again. Empowerment helps them grow through them and gain experience in the process. They can see what held them back and have learned about themselves either directly or indirectly through dealing with them.

Spiritual teaching works through our female energy and much like counseling is done with compassion, requiring an open and non judgmental heart. Female energy allows a teacher to listen, forgive and lead with their heart. Unresolved issues with your mother can inhibit the flow of female energy within you and stifle your full potential with this gift. This would likely show as being selective about who you help or an unwillingness to listen to someone looking for help or judging that they are incapable of being helped.

It is always appropriate to help someone change their behavior by helping them to see why they have it in the first place. What is inappropriate is to change someone's behavior through methods that mask the underlying cause. That

Summary

► Spiritual teaching is about empowering others to deal with their own challenges. It does not refer to being in a position of authority nor does it refer to religion.

► If you have this ability it shows up in your dreams. Your dreams will also show you how to use it.

► Teaching and leading use female energy. They require compassion and listening.

140

may seem to help the individual but it wrecks the karmic relationships they have with those close to them and can even block them from achieving their life purpose. It is like they are living a lie like a wolf wearing sheep's clothing.

At one point this was true of me. I had been meditating twice a day to keep myself calm and stress free among other things. After nearly two years of doing this I went for my first ever psychic reading. I was completely skeptical but the reader proved his ability instantly by accurately describing my character. He said I was a very angry and vindictive person but was suppressing that part of my nature through meditation. He went on to explain that the resultant effect was that my children were missing out on conditioning they specifically chose to pick up before being born. He said I would block much of their life purpose and mine unless I stopped meditating. I was dumbfounded because he was correct about my underlying nature and the meditation. I thought the meditation was making me a better person but he accurately pointed out it was me living a lie. I subsequently stopped meditating and my angry nature returned. I later cut the ties with the help of therapy and found that I was calm and stress free without the need to meditate. The difference was that cutting the ties dealt with the source by removing the underlying conditioning that caused me to be that way. Dealing with anger and vindictiveness was part of my life purpose. I had to pick it up as a child and then when I was able to acknowledge it as part of my nature, I had to do something to eliminate it. That is spiritual growth in operation.

When I first started learning about the topics in this book, I kept it hidden from everyone around me. I never spoke up even if somebody asked me about something directly. Only those very close to me knew I was into dream analysis. I naively thought that I could incur karma by changing a person's perspective on life. If they were meant to live their life a certain way and they changed because of something I said I thought that would be bad, even if they changed for the better. Later when I discovered through my own dreams that I had the teaching gift I realized I was incurring karma for not divulging what I knew and helping others when asked!

Dream Symbols for Teaching / Leading

Dreaming of the president or leader of a country indicates you have this gift. If the leader is male it is common for the dream to introduce you to the leader's wife thus emphasizing that leading works through your female energy. The same emphasis can be shown by the leader turning their left ear to listen to you as the left side of the body can also represent your female side in dreams.

Dreams of spiritual leaders particularly those higher up the chain of the relevant denomination also indicate this gift. Dreaming of Mary, the mother of Jesus, is a very common symbol for this. Dreaming of Jesus, any of the apostles, prophets, the pope, a bishop, canon, priest or rabbi, etc. all indicate this ability regardless of whether they match with your chosen faith. Dreams of saints and angels indicate the ability. National patron saints such as St. Patrick indicate it too but also highlights that leadership is part of your identity – it is your calling. Constantly dreaming of friends who share the names of the apostles like John, Peter and Simon can also be enough to indicate this.

Spiritual teaching is associated with the seventh chakra – the crown chakra. This chakra is located at the very top of the head and is partially outside of the physical body. It points upwards to the heavens connecting you to the higher spiritual energies and is often depicted as being purple (violet) or white. Dreaming of the color purple is sufficient to say you are a spiritual teacher. In addition to its association with the crown chakra it has a strong association with leadership, royalty and religious dress. In Roman times only leaders and boys under 17 (potential future leaders) were allowed wear the color purple.

Quick Symbol Reference for
Spiritual Teaching and Leading Dreams

The following symbols all indicate the above for various reasons. Complete descriptions are given in the Dream Symbol Reference later.

Bishop	Puns on the word mass (influencing the masses)
Color purple	
Groups	Queen
Leader of a country	Spiritual leader as a guide
President	The pope

To dream of the *queen* means you have a teaching / spiritual leadership ability. Each of us has both male and female aspects. Leadership uses the female aspect. This is why the Queen is commonly used to indicate this gift.

Dream: Royal

The Queen and Prince William were watching a presentation I was doing.

To dream of a *royal prince* means you are a spiritual leader and teacher. This works through empowering others to deal with their own challenges and is a female energy gift. Since a prince is male it means you lack confidence at this time with regard to being a leader.

Royal – The Analysis

This dream is elegant in its simplicity. The Queen is a very common symbol to indicate that you have a spiritual teaching and leadership ability. This is because spiritual teaching works through your female energy and requires a compassionate heart.

So why have you got Prince William on the scene? He is male but will become leader one day. So he represents your current position. It is inevitable that you will use your spiritual teaching and leading skills. This does not mean you need to be in a position of authority. It can fit in with any line of work you do. Prince William is on the scene for another reason. We get confidence and belief in ourselves from our male side. His presence in your dream when the queen alone would suffice means that you currently lack confidence with regard to this role. You don't need to worry about that. Just like Prince William you will find your place.

Of huge significance is the fact that you are giving a presentation. This in itself indicates teaching but consider who is in your audience. The fact that they are there to learn from you rather than the other way around highlights how important your gift is to your audience.

To dream of the *president* or leader of a country means you are a spiritual leader. Spiritual leaders lead through empowering others to tackle their own challenges. This gift works through our female side so quite often either the leader is a woman or the leader's wife is introduced in the dream.

A *split level* floor in a dream is often used to indicate what you should step up to. You are being asked to aspire to what is symbolically represented on the raised part of the floor. For example, if a movie star is on the raised part of the floor, you are being asked to develop your channeling ability.

A *raised bed* is more likely to be about meditation or spiritual matters. When this is the subject matter the bed is often not in a bedroom.

Dream: Mary Robinson

I was in a room with Mary Robinson (the president of Ireland), her husband, and others. There was a split level floor. In front of me on the higher floor level was a bed. Mary Robinson was casually lying on her side on the bed, raised up on her right elbow with her head lying in her open palm.

Mary Robinson – The Analysis

This dreamer has a spiritual leadership ability which is symbolized by the president in the dream. We all have male and female energy within us and spiritual leadership works through the female side. This requires listening to people. Two things emphasize the female side. Firstly the president is a woman. Notably this particular president advanced gender equality in Ireland, including encouraging women to take political leadership roles. As such she is a very powerful guide in the dream. Her presence is asking the dreamer to be like her and use her female leadership ability. Indeed with the split level floor and the leader being on the raised portion the dream is asking her to step up to her ability.

The bed in this dream symbolizes the spiritual nature of the dreamer. We are most in tune with our spiritual nature when our bodies are asleep. That's when we dream and when we leave our bodies to astral travel and communicate with other spirits. It is also a symbol of relaxation so the dreamer is being asked to relax into this role. It is not stressful leadership like leading a country. Spiritual leaders empower others to be able to deal with their own challenges in life. You can not preplan spiritual leadership rules to give to people. This method requires female energy listening skills. This is emphasized in the dream by the posture the president has adopted. In this position her right hand is covering her right ear. The message is to listen to her female side as only her left ear (female side) is uncovered.

In reality this woman is at a senior management level in the state's public transport system. Her empathic nature causes her to be deeply moved by people's problems and she gets great satisfaction from helping others. In return she asks the people she has helped to repay her by helping someone else should they ever get the opportunity to do so.

17. Writing

Morality, like art, means drawing a line someplace.

— **Oscar Wilde**

When you first start to write, it may take you some time to find your own style. Do not be disheartened. I started by writing a weekly column about dreams. It took me several attempts to find the style that worked for me. The feature articles wrote themselves but columns that included dream interpretations were terrible. I sent my first draft to my editor and she was kind enough to tell me it didn't work. I rewrote it and sent that off. She still didn't like it. On my third attempt, and this had taken weeks to rewrite over again, I decided it probably wasn't going to work and while the columns were a good idea I hadn't the skill to pull it off. Then I came up with the formula for putting the dream, my interpretation and my comment separately. It became a winning formula for me because I finally hit my style. I could interpret the dream as needed and then separately comment on any issue I wanted that I felt was warranted. I knew it worked and when I sent it to my editor I already knew it was fine. She loved it. The funny thing is that there was no difference in what I was saying in the three styles but only the third style allowed me to put myself in the writing.

If spirituality is expression of the soul you can see then how writing allows for and indeed demands that expression. I know a number of people who have written books but none of them have made money out of it! They did it because it called to them. For me, I have wanted to write this book for years but never made the time for it. I wrote plenty but not a book. Fortunate coincidence got me started on this book. For me it is consolidation of my experience. I started out thinking it would be a brain dump or partial history of my experience but it is neither. It is a present day experience in tapping into what it is I think I know. It sparked off such a flurry of thought and inspiration that I now carry around a notebook to jot down things that spring into my head. It might be an idea on how to approach a

Summary

▶ Writing is a spiritual gift and is as unique to an individual as their fingerprint.

▶ If writing is one of your gifts your dreams can even tell your target audience.

▶ Writing is quite often combined with an intuitive or channeling ability.

145

topic I'm stuck on, or it might be a memory of a dream I once did that either suits a chapter perfectly or makes me think of a new chapter. The inspiration may be turned on, but even with concrete ideas I still find times when I sit in front of my screen for four days in a row, and have only written a single paragraph. Other times I sit down and the writing just flows onto the page. I get volumes written in a single day. On those days I usually end up deleting the paragraph that took four days!

How you write depends on what you are writing about and why you are writing it. Some topics require a measure of sensitivity while others lend themselves to humor and satire. While it is great to have complete editorial control over the content and style of what you write, it is rarely the case. Unless you are self publishing, several constraints will be placed on you, including but not limited to the length of the piece, whether you can write in the first person, the target audience, the style of your writing and the perspective from which you are writing. Indeed whole sections of what you want to include can be scrapped by the editor. Don't view such situations as a problem. It may very well be that what appears to be an imposed constraint is an enlightened soul opening the door on the very avenue you need to explore, or to put it more bluntly closing the door on the avenues that would lead you astray. Consider that wisely before dropping a project. The book you are going to write may be further down the road and right now you are getting paid opportunities to learn different styles.

Your style will be a combination of many things including sense of humor, prose, poetry, simplicity of language, ability to explain difficult topics, or many other things. It is best not to compare yourself too closely to other writers that you like. They may have a style that does not work for you and as long as you try to write like them your writing will not flow. Forget how everyone else writes and find your unique style. It is this unique style that makes writing a spiritual thing. Expression of the soul is what life is about and when you tap into your style you are allowing your soul expression. The connection made will come across to your readers as a connection with them.

Automatic Writing

Another form of writing is automatic writing. This is where you distract yourself from the awareness of what you are writing and just let your hand write away. For example, read a newspaper or book while at the same time have a pen in your hand, deliberately have the notepad out of your field of vision and write automatically.

Dream Symbols for Writing

Writing is easy to spot in dreams. If you dream of a writer or poet whether it is a modern day writer or Shakespeare you have the gift. Following the rule that anyone with a title is a guide and you have whatever ability a guide displays in a dream it clearly means you have a writing ability. If you are lucky they may even tell you what to write about by focusing on a topic themselves.

A common symbol is a writing implement that is special in some way. The fact that it is special emphasizes the special nature of the gift. You may dream of entering a shop that specializes in pens to find the pen that is perfect for you. This dream is encouraging you to find your unique way of writing. The shop keeper may even offer you a particular pen. Whatever is unique about the pen offered is a clue to tapping your ability. A pen with a light built-in tells you that your intuition (the light) will engage when you are writing. A silver pen would indicate the same thing. A gold pen tells you that writing will be healing (gold color) for you in some way. The price of the pen can also be significant. If you are told the pen costs $3 you are being asked to commit (number 3) to writing – to put your mind body and soul into your writing. Your reluctance to pay the amount asked is an indicator of how likely you are to agree that writing is your gift.

A less obvious symbol is to dream of a desk lamp attached in place of your arm or somebody else's arm. The attachment shows that writing is part of your makeup. You can't remove it from your being – if you did you wouldn't be complete. It would also mean that your writing works through your intuition. You will get a feeling or an impulse about what it is you are to write or how to write it. When you see gifts combined like this the spiritual journey is learning how to integrate both abilities. Don't expect them to immediately blend together. Take time to work them together.

There are many creative writing courses out there and invariably they are run by writers who have made it themselves. You'll hear many words of wisdom on these courses as very few people start out knowing exactly how to make it work. You can either empathize with or be saved from the same frustration the facilitator went through in the beginning. You'll also hear about how to write and what to write about. It rarely works the way you intend. Many of the articles I have written started out as something completely different when I sat down at my computer. In many cases I had to change the title completely! Some years on I now find that I do write about what I sit down to write about. But I think that now I am more tuned in to what wants to be written and I now know it in advance. I never succeeded when struggling to go against what was coming.

Quick Symbol Reference for Writing in Dreams

The following symbols all indicate the above for various reasons. Complete descriptions are given in the Dream Symbol Reference later.

Author as guide   Poet or writer as a guide

Fountain pen   Special pen

Magic pen

To dream of a *writer* or *poet* means you have a creative writing ability and you are being asked to use this in your life as a means of connecting with your inner core. Through writing you will find your distinctive style of expression and expand your understanding of yourself. For example, to dream of writing mathematical equations would mean that through the deduction process engaged in while you write you will expand your awareness of yourself.

Gifts in dreams are normally given by guides. Being given a gift symbolizes you were bestowed with a special gift at birth. The specific ability may or may not be indicated by the gift itself but it will be shown by other symbols in the same dream.

Dream: Talking with Robert Bly

I was sitting, talking with author and poet Robert Bly. Then a woman called my attention to two guests (a man and a woman) who had brought me a gift and she was angry I was ignoring them. I was also flustered as I was enjoying my talk with Bly. The gift was a pair of earrings which were huge and looked like mini crystal chandeliers. I thought to myself, "I can't wear these things. I wouldn't be able to hold my head up with all that weight."

Earrings indicate you have a channeling ability where you can communicate with spirits. This is not as frightening as it sounds. There are many TV shows now where the host does this and from these you can see how natural the ability is.

Chandeliers are a source of light and also contain crystals. Light sources indicate you have a psychic / intuitive ability. This comes as a feeling where you just know something without any logical reason for knowing it. The crystal component of the symbol emphasizes the preciseness of your ability. It is or has the potential to be crystal clear. The word chandelier can also be used in dreams as a bad pun on channel(er) so indicates you are a channel.

148

Talking with Robert Bly – The Analysis

Robert Bly in the dream indicates that the dreamer has a creative writing ability. He is a guide in the dream (has a title), and as with any guide the dreamer has the same ability he does. The rest of the dream will then be a comment on how best the dreamer can tap into his potential as a writer.

The woman represents his mother and she is shown to be an angry person (exactly as the woman in the dream was). She is pointing out a man and woman who are together. This is a request for the dreamer to balance the male and female sides of himself. To help him in this regard he needs to look at how his relationship with his mother causes him to ignore the female side of himself now. The female side is to do with emotion, the heart, intuition and philosophy of life. Essentially the best formula is for his heart and head to work together.

The gift of a pair of earrings is specifically pointing out a spiritual gift he has – the gift of channeling. This works for him through hearing guidance from the spirit realm and through inspired writing. The size of the earrings is asking the dreamer to pay heed to this ability. In the dream they can not be ignored so do not ignore it in reality.

It is interesting that at the start of the dream the dreamer is dialoging with his guide. This is exactly what channeling is. The reference to not being able to hold his head up is likely to mean that in his writing he will record this type of dialogue and it is perhaps this that makes him feel he can not hold his head up.

In reality the dreamer is trying to become a writer so this dream is very poignant. The dream is accurate about his mother too as in his words, "my mother is an angry woman and this has caused me problems." The dream tells him to achieve balance within and to write from the heart. The anger in that relationship inhibits the flow of his gift now so doing a therapy like cutting-the-ties would be very useful at clearing these problems. This is would stop him feeling like there is a weight dragging him down and allow him to hold his head up high.

A *shop window* is often used in dreams to encourage you to adopt a better outlook towards the subject matter of the dream. Shop windows usually have bright and inviting displays that make everything look attractive.

A *fountain pen* indicates that you have a gift for writing. A fountain is a source so a fountain pen implies that you have a creative writing source that you can tap into. This dream is asking you to create space for it in your life.

A *shop owner* is a guide in a dream. Listen at what he is saying or what he is encouraging you to do. In reality this is what your guides are saying you have a responsibility to do.

Dream: The Fountain Pen

I was looking at fountain pens in a shop window. One could do all types of writing including wide filling and fine writing. The shop owner told me it cost $3. I did not buy it.

You have a creative *writing* ability.

Three is a symbol for meditation and commitment – putting your mind, body and soul into the subject matter of the dream.

The Fountain Pen – The Analysis

This dreamer has a strong creative writing ability (fountain pen). Prices on symbols in dreams often indicate the effort required to develop what it symbolizes. Here the price is £3 so the price being asked to develop her ability is commitment. The dreamer shows her reluctance to develop her ability by refusing to buy the pen. In fact her reluctance is explained by her expression – I did not buy it - an expression commonly used when you do not believe what you are being told. The dreamer clearly does not buy into the message of the dream that she has this ability. However, it is her guide (shop owner) that tells her she has the ability so there is no question about it. The fact that it is a shop also means that she is responsible for developing her writing ability. The pens laid out in the shop window are enticing her to view it as something nice to have and to commit to developing.

18. Prophecy / Fortune telling

Always forgive your enemies; nothing annoys them so much.

— **Oscar Wilde**

Prophecy is where a person has the ability to predict the future. This is the gift that most people think of when anyone mentions communication with spirit or any type of divining such as tarot cards. However, this is not as common a gift as you would expect, when for example, compared to channeling. A little more than one in twenty of us have it. The reason for the low percentage is that you do not need to be prophetic if you have certain other gifts. If you can communicate with your guides then only they need a handle on predicting the future and you get the benefit.

You are prophetic if you have prophetic dreams. However, not all dreams that appear to predict the future are actually doing that. When we sleep we travel to the astral plane and meet with other souls, both living and in spirit. On this plane we may agree with them to do certain things or to meet them on the physical plane. The next day the old school friend we dreamed about calls us out of the blue and we are amazed because we dreamed they would call! Our dream clearly did not predict the future, but from our normal limited perspective on things we think it did. Dreaming of an event that is happening while we are asleep is also not predicting the future. There are several ways we can get informed about such events while we are asleep. Astral traveling as just described is one. A common one for many people is to know who is calling when the phone rings. Again that is not prophecy because the person that pops into your head is already tuned in to you. This is more likely to indicate that they have the gift of projection than anything else. Projection is described in a separate

Summary

▶ The gift of prophecy is one of the most practical gifts there is when you use it for yourself.

▶ You do not need to be prophetic if you can talk to your guides. They already are.

▶ Prophecy is not about foretelling disasters.

▶ Envisioned outcomes are not set in stone. The outcome can be altered.

▶ Your dreams predict the future in symbolic form even if you are not prophetic.

chapter.

The easiest way to tell if your dream is prophetic is by how it feels. Prophetic dreams feel different from a symbolic dream. If you are prophetic you are most likely already aware of this feeling. If not, and you already know you are prophetic, look out for it the next time you think you had a prophetic dream. It is unmistakable to the point that I have never had to describe it to anyone. You just know it was 'one of those dreams'. Knowing the difference in feeling between symbolic and prophetic dreams will put your mind at rest if you chance to dream about your child having an accident. You will be able to tell it was not a prophetic dream!

Dream Symbols for Prophecy

This gift is very easy to recognize in dreams. The most obvious symbol for it is a crystal ball, as it is clearly associated with telling the future. Dreaming about going to a fortune teller is another, as the fortune teller is a guide and you always have the same abilities that guides display in your dream. Having dreams where you just know what is going to happen next in the dream, demonstrates the gift in operation. This might be dreaming about driving somewhere and just knowing what will be around the corner before you get there. Dreams give expression to the aspects we are ignoring in waking life, so in this case the dream allows the dreamer to exercise their prophetic ability that they are not tapping into in reality. Dreams of high flying birds can also indicate this gift, with eagles being the most common. The concept here is that the eagle flies at such a great height in the sky it can see the past, present and future from its vantage point.

Nostradamus is probably the most famous person with this gift, having predicted the exact manner of the death of the king of France. There are many who will argue whether he was prophetic or whether he was just trying to write a best selling book. Regardless of that, if you dream of him you are prophetic. But don't look at this gift as the ability to predict disaster. It has a very practical application in everyday life. If, for example, you are considering making a significant move, such as a house move or career change, your prophetic ability will kick in automatically and tell you exactly why not to do a particular thing. It is probably unique in that way, as most methods of getting information do not reveal the precise details of why not to do something. It comes as a complete knowing and requires no analysis. To you it is an immediate and certain fact, and while you can try to explain it to others you have no reason for knowing it, and therefore no reason can be given. Prophecy does also tell you which avenue is positive to choose, but in these cases it comes more as a feeling of knowing that avenue has life attached to it. It does not give the same precision as when you are told why not to take a particular route, although it may give some important details.

Dreams predict the future

Your dreams predict the future in symbolic form regardless of whether you have the gift of prophecy. They predict the future based on conditions prevailing today and the events which led up to them. This is not remarkable in itself when you consider that dreams take everything about you into account! It is similar to your doctor looking at your past history of illness and asking you specific questions before coming to a considered opinion of your current problem. Past, present and future are intermixed in dreams, so the future is typically indicated by showing something happening further along the road, with the road indicating the passage of time.

All events in your past, even while in the womb, go to make you the person you are today. So if, for example, your diet is unhealthy and you do not exercise, your dreams can predict future heart difficulty unless something is done to improve your situation. You may get the same prediction even if your diet and exercise program are good, because of non-physical problems. Alternatively if you are eating food which your body is allergic to, the dream can predict problems in the colon.

In all cases dreams show the prediction, the cause and what needs to be done to prevent it. It is important to realize two things. Dreams can predict illnesses even twenty years ahead of their onset. Also, these are only predictions. The predicted outcome can be avoided or brought about based on how you react to the information provided to you by the dream.

Quick Symbol Reference for Prophecy in Dreams

The following symbols all indicate the above for various reasons. Complete descriptions are given in the Dream Symbol Reference later.

Color soft or pearl white	Fortune teller as guide
Crystal ball	High flying birds
Dreams where you just knew what would happen next	Prophetic dreams
	Nostradamus as a guide
Eagle	

Flying symbolizes that you have a strong intellect which you can use to mentally rise above a problem. When flying, you are looking at things from a higher perspective. This is a very practical ability and you are most likely aware you have it. When you've had enough of a particular problem you can step back and consciously decide to see the bigger picture. You will almost always feel exhilarated upon waking from a flying dream. This is because all your problems have become smaller through your dream.

In mythology an *eagle* is said to fly so high that it can see the past present and future from its high vantage point. Due to this an eagle in a dream indicates that you have the gift of prophecy. However, it is unlikely that this is the only symbol indicating prophecy in the same dream.

Being *at the top of a very high mountain* can indicate that you have reached or will reach a point in your life where you can see where you are going. This type of dream can also indicate you have the gift of prophecy as you have such a clear view of everything around you from your high vantage point.

Dream: Flying with an Eagle

I was on top of a mountain on a sunny day and I jumped off of it. I was flying, very, very high over lots of mountains that were brown and green. I felt very light and free when I was flying. After sometime, this big eagle joins me for the ride and we fly together. He leads me to a point where there is a valley and I land in front of a fortune teller's table. She has a sort of a stand that she sells jewelry. She says to me: "Take these earrings and put them on you." They are beautiful earrings and they have opals and rubies on them. I put them on and she says that I will look and hear much better with them. In my dream, I actually felt very beautiful after putting them on.

To dream of a *fortune teller* means that you have the gift of prophecy. This is not a very common gift even though public perception is that everyone who is psychic in any way can tell the future. The fortune teller may offer you a gift in the dream to highlight that this is indeed your gift.

Jewelry is often used in dreams to highlight your spiritual gifts and that they are the most precious part of your nature. You use them to repay your karmic debts and achieve your life purpose.

Earrings indicate you have a channeling ability where you can communicate with spirits. This is not as frightening as it sounds. There are many TV shows now where the host does this and from these you can see how natural the ability is.

Flying with an Eagle – The Analysis

This dreamer has a number of abilities. The most prominent in the dream is the gift of prophecy which is indicated by the eagle and again by the presence of the fortune teller later in the dream. Flying in a dream allows the dreamer to mentally rise above her problems to get a higher perspective on life. This means she has an enlightened intellect which she can use to rise above her problems in daily life. Indeed being at the top of the mountain at the start of the dream backs this up.

Dreams often indicate the future by introducing something into the same scene later in the dream. In this dream the eagle is introduced *after some time*. This means that the dreamer's prophetic ability is coming but not quite here yet. She may already be using it now but it will become more prominent later.

The fortune teller is a guide in the dream and is showing her the precious nature and value of her gifts by having precious jewelry laid out on a table. As is typical with guides she gives her a gift of earrings. Earrings are symbolic of channeling so the dreamer also has a channeling ability which is connected with her prophetic ability. The beauty of the earrings asks the dreamer to see the beauty in her abilities. In the dream she accepts this and symbolically realizes her self worth and the value of her gifts after putting them on.

The fact that the guide is selling jewelry shows the dreamer, by example, that she is to use her abilities in public (sell her gifts to others).

In reality the dreamer had recently changed her diet to cleanse her body by eating only healthy foods and excluding meat. This is working for her as the dream starts out with the healing symbol of the sun. Also when looking down while flying she sees brown and green mountains which symbolizes that her colon and blood stream are being cleansed.

19. Relationships

When a woman marries again, it is because she detested her first husband. When a man marries again, it is because he adored his first wife. Women try their luck; men risk theirs.

— Oscar Wilde

Your life purpose is unique. Your intention in being here is to discover and eliminate the limiting conditioning that obscures your awareness. Dreams keep you true to this purpose, commenting on all aspects of your life, including relationships. To understand a dream's perspective I first want to describe how relationships help you on your quest towards awareness.

Your relationship with your partner

Relationships are a shining star when it comes to discovering limitations. If you are like most people, the biggest problem is that you tend to spot only your partner's limitations while glossing over your own, and your partner does the same. In relationship counseling the therapist is greatly aided when you list the problems you are having with your partner. When you see the counselor taking notes, they are not writing them in the column as issues for your partner. They are writing them in your column as issues you need to deal with. While this may seem unfair, your list is pointing out to the therapist exactly what pushes your buttons. Each button reveals limiting conditioning in your nature to be examined. This is regardless of what you have on your list. Let's take a strong example. Suppose you have on your list that your partner has cheated on you. You cannot see how that points to a limitation on your part. However, your limitation could be showing loyalty where it is not warranted. That limitation makes you stay in a dysfunctional relationship

Summary

▶ Your parents and your partner are instrumental in helping you achieve your life purpose.

▶ We often learn most about ourselves from the most difficult relationship.

▶ We subconsciously choose a partner with the same traits as the parent we have most issues with.

▶ Negative conditioning from parents can be cleared.

and find fault with your partner each time they cheat, rather than addressing the issue of misguided loyalty. Everyone is different and a skilled therapist will unearth what is needed for you to be free from conditioning that limits you.

Of course relationships are not always on the rocks. With all the baggage cleared, relationships provide the best space in which to grow. Feelings are shared openly and unconditional love creates a space in which to expand your knowledge of yourself. You feel free to open up and share things that you have never shared with anyone else. Sharing is therapeutic in itself as you have to identify and focus on the issues you are sharing in order to express them. You may never have done that before in your life and with the right person it feels like a burden lifted. Someone who loves you is now helping you to carry the weight. You treat your partner with the same respect they give you. Allowing them to be who they are teaches you their strengths and weaknesses. The freedom to be who you are teaches you your strengths and weaknesses and has far reaching spiritual value. You become strong within, knowing and respecting your boundaries and theirs. At the start of each relationship you expect nothing less and so does your partner. Yet this type of relationship is rare because you choose your partner's traits years before you meet them!

In the counseling field it is observed that we choose as a partner, a person with the same traits as the parent we have most issues with. If you have issues with your mother you will select someone just like her. If you have issues with your father you will select someone just like him. This is regardless of whether your partner is a man or woman. You and your partner are drawn together by your energy fields and your energy field was shaped by your childhood. So too was your partner's. The shapes fit together like two pieces of a jigsaw puzzle. However, the two shapes were created by children and when the honeymoon period has passed childhood conflict awakens. Your friends may have seen it all the time but for you the immature nature you perceive from your partner comes like a bolt of lightening. Maturity is what is called for. It is time to grow through the difficulties in the relationship. If you fail to do this your next partner will be similar to your last because you still look for a fit to the jigsaw puzzle you hold onto. To make spiritual progress you must be around someone who can push the buttons your parent installed! The intention is that you grow tired of having your buttons pushed and deal with the underlying issues. This invariably involves looking at life shaping events in your childhood and clearing their negative effects one by one.

Your parents and your partner are instrumental in helping you achieve your life purpose. Your parents give you the conditioning, including positive traits, and your partner is a peer with whom you can face the resulting issues. Life is a spiritual journey towards awareness and most people are unlikely to stop and question life when everything is going well. Without questioning, you learn nothing about yourself. The karmic path ensures that conditioning gives you the opportunity to ask the right questions for your growth.

Your relationship with your parents

From the human perspective we see conditioning coming mostly from childhood. We look at ourselves and say, "I am this way because of what happened to me when I was thirteen. Nobody knows what it is like to be me or what I went through. The system and society failed me. That is why I am the way I am." However, that only appears correct from the human perspective. From the spiritual perspective there is more to the picture. You choose your parents! To understand why, you need to look at the rest of the picture.

You are a spirit and will always be. Through actions on your part you have lost awareness of who you are. The same is true for everyone on the planet, many of whom have regained their former awareness to differing levels. As a spirit you need to question and eliminate the limiting beliefs that obscure your awareness. In some cases a physical life helps in this process. You may have had several before this one. In each physical life you focus on one or more limiting traits that form part of your nature that blocks your awareness. By necessity, the incarnation process allows you to start each physical life with a clean slate. However, you want to mark this slate with specific negative traits that form part of your nature in the spirit world. One way of doing this is to pick parents whose behavior will condition you the way you need to be. If being judgmental is one of your negative traits you may pick a parent with that trait. Given that this is your natural inclination you will easily copy it from your parent. Once copied, your physical existence is deliberately tainted by this limitation. However, the usual intention is that something will cause you to acknowledge the limitation during your physical lifetime, take appropriate steps to eliminate it, and thus free your spirit from its grasp.

The design of your life before being born is so comprehensive it allows you to pick up any conditioning you need to deal with. Sometimes the purpose of conditioning is to push you in the direction you need to take in life, rather than to allow you transfer an existing negative trait from the spirit world to the physical. In both cases there usually comes a time when it is appropriate to free yourself from the conditioning. In some ways this is much easier to do on the earth plane than in spirit. The density of the physical world allows spirits who are at different levels of awareness to sit beside each other. Each physical life invariably includes planned encounters with souls at a higher level of awareness with intended beneficial effect. In the spirit world you may be completely unaware of spirits at higher levels of awareness. Your viewpoint forms your reality and need not be argued with anyone. Another benefit of the physical plane is the ability to focus on only one specific trait or just a few. The physical density and design of the human body allows for blocking memories from past lives and leaving behind some of your negativity. Thus being lightened from some of your burden, leaves you free to work on the task at hand.

Another useful feature of the earth plane is the illusion of time passing. You live only in the present moment. If I ask you to change something you can only change it in the present as you only exist now. You do not exist in the past. If I ask you to change a behavior in the past you cannot do it. Similarly you do not exist in the future. If I ask you to change something in the future you also cannot do that. You must wait for that future point to become 'now' and then do it because you only exist and have control in the present. You can never exist in any other time. You can reflect on the past and future but cannot live in it. True you did experience the past but it was the present when you were experiencing it. Life in spirit is an ever continuing experience in the present moment. For this reason it is possible to remain stagnant for eons in terms of progress towards awareness. On the earth plane, this is unlikely as change is constant. The feeling of time running out spurs many people into facing and dealing with issues they know they must.

From a spiritual perspective you must copy into the physical plane, the negative traits that must form part of your conditioning in this physical lifetime. Parents are used as the easiest method for doing this. Indeed this is part of their life purpose too. Later, in adult life, you get opportunities to acknowledge this conditioning. You may not take them. You may not see that you are vindictive. The nature of conditioning is that you are blind to it until something opens your eyes. Free will allows you to close your eyes again in denial. Hopefully that is not your case and you embrace the opportunities granted you. Depending on your circumstance all this may seem crazy. However, the traumatic events in each lifetime are ultimately healed, either here or on the spirit plane, as you progress towards awareness.

Your relationship with your children

When you ignore opportunities to acknowledge and eliminate the effects of negative conditioning, you are destined to pass it on to your children. While most individuals feel affected by issues with their parents, they argue that they do not pass on what they suffered to their children. For the most part that is true. We tend to protect our children from the issues which most affected us. If your parents were overly strict with discipline and never allowed you go to the late night dance you may compensate by allowing your children that freedom and only occasionally discipline them. When they do incur a restriction, the memory of your childhood may cause you to let them off half way through it. However, your children may perceive their freedom as a lack of loving concern on your part for what they do and where they are. The hazy discipline can teach a lack of respect for your boundaries and lead to enormous problems in later teenage years. You have conditioned your children as a direct consequence of the conditioning you received. Indeed you have completed a cycle. Your children may in turn condition their children exactly as your parents conditioned you, when in later life they realize the hardships they put you through as a result of the freedom you gave them.

The cycle of traits being passed on from generation to generation is called family karma. As part of their life purpose, your parents have a spiritual contract to condition you a certain way so that you have the potential to achieve your life purpose. The contract with you was made before they were born. In turn the contract you have with your children was made before you were born. Family karma is an obligation you have to your children. The obligation is simple. You are to be the person you are because their life purpose is counting on it. If you are an angry and bitter person then be an angry and bitter person. To be anything else would not be true to your nature and denies them theirs.

When your eyes are opened to your negative traits the situation remains the same. You must still remain true to your nature. Never suppress it. For example, I unwittingly discovered that meditation suppressed my angry nature and so meditated for years. At the time I believed the meditation made me a better person as it allowed me to be more tolerant of others. However, meditation for that reason meant I was living a lie. Like taking drugs, my behavior was altered but my nature was not. Just like awareness it was merely obscured temporarily. When I stopped meditating my angry nature returned to the surface and I had learned nothing about myself during the intervening period. Then I discovered the therapy Cutting-the-ties. Within eight weeks my nature was fundamentally changed. The anger was gone. What's more, I did not have to perform any daily ritual to remain changed.

Instead of finding something that suppresses your negative traits, select a therapy to help you eliminate the negative effects of the conditioning that produced the traits. Once freed, your nature changes just like mine. Instead of being angry you may become a loving, supportive person. Then you can be loving and supportive with your children and remain in keeping with your contract of being true to your nature.

I want to return to an earlier point about how being yourself in a relationship can have far reaching spiritual value. On the earth plane we can mask our thoughts and feelings and present an illusion to others of who we want them to believe we are. That is possible only because of the density of this plane and is not possible on the spirit plane. If you can be truly open with even just one person on the earth plane it prepares you greatly for life in spirit where all your thoughts and feelings are open.

Relationships in dreams

Once a dream features your partner, it is about the nature of your relationship. For that reason this subject matter is by far the easiest to spot. From that point on, however, the dream is symbolic like every other dream. For example, to dream of your partner dying in a car crash does not predict the death of your partner. Rather it symbolizes apprehension about losing your partner. The loss can be through any means, such as a break up. This is a common dream if you have previously gone through a difficult relationship and now feel you are finally with a decent person. This dream is only triggered after you decide you will do what it takes to keep the relationship going. Rather than being a bad omen, the dream indirectly shows your commitment to your partner. However, the dream is asking you to enjoy the relationship in the present moment and not spoil a good thing with constant concern over losing this one.

In some cases your partner may not behave as themselves in your dream. They might leave you stranded while on holiday, for example. Again the dream is not predicting this behavior, rather the dream uses your partner to raise issues that need healing with another important person of the same gender. For example, one woman had recurring dreams of her husband leaving her stranded in a difficult situation. In one dream he left her stranded at a music festival. Being happily married the dreams puzzled her. In

160

reality her father died four years before she wrote to me. She was very close to him and moved home when he was diagnosed with cancer. The dreams started four months later when he died and symbolized her distress at being left on her own. The dreams show she needs to heal the ongoing effect of her father's passing as this is subconsciously affecting her relationship. One man she deeply loved left her – the fear is that it could happen again.

When searching for solutions to save a failing relationship, your dreams need not include your partner. One couple in just such a predicament discussed having another child to help save their marriage. However, after a dream where the woman found herself in a hospital delivery room with a doctor who was ready to shave her genitals using a saw, hammer and other builders' equipment, she changed her mind. The dream showed that in her case, having a baby to build up the relationship was a dramatic step.

Dreams frequently set out to heal you of past relationships that were traumatic. When trauma is not healed, all future relationships are affected by it. A woman whose relationship with her fiancé finished badly could not understand why she kept dreaming of being with him, being extremely happy and them laughing together. This is a classic healing dream. It is not so much the events in life that shape you, rather it is your reaction to the events and what you hold onto from them. Therapy brings us to a point where we can see that we are indeed holding onto something that affects us negatively and we can then hopefully let it go. Dreams do the same and sometimes short cut the process by replacing negative memories with positive ones. The positive events in dreams are taken from reality but are sometimes exaggerated to amplify the healing effect. Here the dream asks her to remember the good times when they were happy together rather than the end of the relationship. It is better to hold onto that and let that influence current relationships.

Another woman was severely traumatized by her boyfriend's death as she was standing next to him when he pulled the trigger and killed himself. In her words;

I dream I am taking care of a deceased boyfriend who has come back to life but carries the wounds from his self inflicted gun shot wound to the head. I can see the wounds, stitched, and I clean them. I carefully reposition him so he is comfortable. We talk at length, and I caress his face. I ask him why he did this terrible thing to me. Why he felt he needed to leave me. I fix him lunch and feed him. I bathe him and change his sheets. I see his mother scolding me and telling me to be careful with him! I can smell him. He wears the glasses that he used to wear. I

Men in dreams

Male characters may indicate your reaction to

► men in general

► that particular man

► the male aspect of yourself

► your father

► intellect, idea or mode of thought

► healing agent, guide or entity

► a former life

161

brushed his hair. It is way too real. The strangest part is that my current hus-
band is in bed in the next room in my dream. I find myself going back and forth
from room to room in my dream. I feel the love in my dream that I had for him
all over again and wake up grieving for him all over again after 28 years.

This dream was twenty eight years after the event. Obviously having the dream means she is still affected. You are everything in your dream so reading it from that perspective we can see what the dream is doing. In bringing her deceased boyfriend back to life the dream symbolically restores life to the part of her that died as a consequence of the trauma. In tending his wounds she is symbolically healing the wounds and scars left on her. Since his death she became a nurse and symbolically uses her healing ability in the dream when she feeds him. Again the healing is for her benefit. Bathing him also cleans her wounds and scars and brushing his hair symbolically reorganizes her tangled thoughts around the event. Moving back and forth between her deceased boyfriend and her husband shows her current relationship is impacted by past events. Indeed linking everything else in the dream to this last part shows the whole purpose of the dream is to heal the trauma from her past relationship so that she is freed to be herself in this one.

The birth imprint and parental relationships in dreams

The birth imprint has such an impact on shaping your personality, philosophy of life and self esteem that it shows up repeatedly in your dreams and in many guises. Buildings in dreams symbolize the body and moving into a building and exiting again (often by a different means) symbolizes entering into your mother's body and being born. Movement downwards also symbolizes your move onto the planet. The downwards motion symbolizes moving from a higher vibration to a much denser / lower vibration. A common symbol for this is an airplane landing and indeed your arrival as the theme of the dream is further emphasized by airport arrivals being where you meet up when your plane lands. The plane does not have to land at an airport to still have this meaning. A crash landing, for instance, indicates your arrival was difficult and you may even have had a brush with death.

Arriving at a station by train also indicates the start of your physical life. So too does a ship berthing in a harbor with berth also being a pun on birth. Claustrophobic spaces, often with no windows, are indicative of the womb and signify being in your mother's womb. Symbols are often combined in dreams. For example, a descending elevator is moving down and also claustrophobic. Another example is journeying on a train carriage with no windows. The train, the claustrophobic room and indeed the pun on carriage all point to carriage of a baby.

You are everything in your dream so any party celebrations indicate your birth. A common birth symbol is Christmas – the birth of Christ. Dreams that feature the birth imprint often reflect the reaction of your parents to your arrival. A woman sitting at a cash register means you mother put a price on her love – she did not love you unconditionally. A man dressed in dark brown indicates dad had a materialistic view of the world which you either copied or were negatively affected by. Exiting an elevator and being ignored by everyone shows you did not get the attention you needed as a child. A man saying you are in his way indicates dad did not want a baby.

Healing agents

Supportive helpful characters frequently feature in your dreams to heal the negative effects of the parent with the same gender. Healing agents always go the opposite way to that parent. For instance, a woman wearing pink or offering flowers, symbolically brings the love mother was unable to provide, while a man cleaning windows heals a negative outlook picked up from dad.

Issues can be picked up at any age. Since dreams mix the past, present and future they show the approximate age through various methods. Anything behind you indicates the past so if the man cleaning windows splashes your back with soapy water he is a healing agent attempting to cleanse issues connected with dad from your past. If your seven year old daughter falls down it symbolizes mother failing in her parental role (falling down on the job) when you were seven. A man chasing you with a knife indicates you are still affected today by anger (knife) displayed by your father in the past (behind you in the dream). Watching stars collide indicates a clash of ideals with a parent. The exact issue is not always shown in dreams. This is particularly true when you have a conscious memory of the events.

Clearing conditioning

Dreams point out issues with the express purpose of showing that they still affect you today. Their ongoing impact can, for example, make you feel unworthy of love, feel lacking in self esteem, angry, feel unimportant or a feel like a doormat. Dreams set out to heal past relationships so you are freed from their negative influence. Realizing that dealing with issues picked up from parents is part of your life purpose is important to give you the freedom to look at them openly. Many adults avoid healing these issues. They try to suppress the memories, telling themselves their parents did their best, the pain involved is too much or they are nothing like their parents. Others feel that never talking to the parent involved is dealing with the issue. Unfortunately it is not. The pain that brings a person to making these decisions is real and the reaction is understandable. Dealing with issues, however, does not mean discussing them with your parent or even having to face your parent. Successful therapies involve looking at yourself and discovering how you are still carrying the negative influence. Once acknowledged, the therapy helps you overcome the negative impact. Counseling with a competent therapist and cutting the ties that bind are both effective at stripping

> ## Women in dreams
> Female characters may indicate your reaction to
> ► women in general
> ► that particular woman
> ► the female aspect of yourself
> ► your mother
> ► emotions
> ► healing agent, guide or entity
> ► a former life

away the negative effects of traumatic relationships. Cutting the ties can be done alone and is described on my website.

It is always appropriate to cut the ties with your parents. However, it is not always appropriate to cut the ties with your current partner. Due to the way life is planned in spirit, many relationships are karmic. This means you could have an obligation to your partner. Cutting the ties clears the conditioning affecting the relationship but does not free you from the obligation. Being asked to sign anything in a dream with your partner reminds you of your spiritual contract to them. At some point in life your karmic debt may be paid and you are free at that point to cut the ties with them. Counseling works in a different way and is unlikely to break a karmic bond as your guides can greatly influence what you get from it.

The karmic link may be to a previous life where your partner failed you or you failed them in some way. For example, if your partner killed you in a former life, part of your purpose in this life may be to clear your sense of betrayal. To achieve that you planned to get into a relationship where that feelings is pervasive. From your limited perspective you cannot see that you must get to that point in order to free yourself from the chains of the former life. Your partner's part in the contract is to evoke those feelings. If they fail to do so they are failing in their spiritual obligation to you and you may fail to achieve part of your life purpose.

There are many effective therapies that help clear negative conditioning. In choosing something, try to find a therapist recommended by a friend. If you saw your friend change for the better that's a good sign.

To dream of your *partner* means the dream is primarily about the nature of your relationship. The rest of the symbols in the dream will expand on the theme.

Wandering in a dream signifies you currently have not focus in life with regard to the subject matter of the dream. Set a goal to work through the issues that are holding you in this space.

Dream: Ex Partner

I was in the garden of an ex partner of sometime ago. I was wandering up a curving path when I saw in amongst some bushes the face of my ex partner. I could not seem to reach where the face was appearing and it was very dark all around the head.

When *dark* refers to night time, *darkness* or being *in the dark*, the dream is about your feeling of not knowing where you are going, or how to get to where you want to go with regard to the subject matter of the dream. Other symbols in the dream tell you what you need to do to move out of the dark. For the same reasons dark can also symbolize depression; for example, this would be indicated by dreaming of the upstairs of a house being in darkness.

Ex Partner – The Analysis

Your dream is saying that you have not gotten over this **partner**. While the dream shows darkness around his head it means there is still a dark cloud around you with regard to the relationship. This often indicates you are being dogged by depression or dark moods. Not being able to **reach the face** is symbolically saying that "you need to face up to the break up of this relationship". Since the break up you have not refocused your life but are **wandering** along a path.

It would help you cut the ties with your ex boyfriend. When you are completely over him, you will likely dream of the positive aspects of this relationship as pleasant memories are healing and effective at bringing passion into future relationships.

In reality the dreamer hit a deep depression when her relationship ended two years ago and it lasted a considerable time. She has pulled through that and is now getting her life back on track. The dream shows there is still some work to do in order to move on.

Dream: Alone

I was at a party with my boyfriend, at an old house my grandparents lived in until I was 5. I came into the room and saw a blonde girl sitting on his lap and holding his hand. They both just glared at me. I glared back at my boyfriend.

The scene changes to my other grandmother's apartment in the same town and I am there alone. Then my boyfriend and this very blonde girl and her friend are climbing over the balcony to get into the apt. I let them in. And he is talking about how he doesn't love me and never has been happy and she makes him happy.

This whole time, this very blonde girl with a pink ski hat on is clinging to him very sexually and......my teeth start to fall out. Literally fall out of my head into my hand. I can't catch them fast enough. They are overflowing into my hand. Very clean teeth, no blood not really any pain - just teeth falling and falling. I'm holding out my hand to show my boyfriend but he doesn't care. He just goes on and on and I can't really understand his words but it is all about how he's leaving me.

The scene changes and I am talking to his mother on the phone. She is defending him saying it is his nature. The scene changes again to riding on a train or subway but I am in a compartment alone.

Alone – The Analysis

I received the dream nearly ten years ago and to this day it evokes great sadness when I read it. I simply want to dive into the analysis and show how dreams link many layers of our lives together so I leave looking up the symbol reference as an exercise.

Starting off the dream is about the dreamer's relationship as her partner is there. Immediately the dream links issues in her relationship with issues in the past; specifically age 5 because of the location. Also the party symbolizes her own birth, so while it may not be conscious in her mind, the issues go back further than age 5. Her boyfriend and the blonde girl also symbolize her parents. Of significance is that they glare at her and are obviously inconsiderate of her feelings. This paints a very bad picture of childhood and shows the foundation of her problems. The dreamer glaring back shows that she has copied these traits to some degree. At this stage of the book it must be realized that was meant to happen.

The location changes to an apartment. This highlights that the result of her early childhood years was that she suppresses her feelings / has locked away her heart. While the apartment is sufficient to indicate this, the balcony reinforces that she lives life rationally – devoid of emotion. Two women appear with her boyfriend in this setting. This is to give expression to her emotions as she does not do it enough in reality. The pink ski hat shows that she did not bond with her mother. Pink alone indicates this but the reference to ski or snow shows that her mother was emotionally cold towards her. This could already be deduced from earlier.

Now we come to the crux of the present day problem. Her teeth start falling out. This signifies she feels incapable of raising children. Animals carry their young around with their teeth so losing teeth would destroy their ability to raise young. She tries to show her boyfriend her problem with raising children (showing him the teeth that have fallen out) but he does not care. This does not mean that in reality he does not care. It simply means that she has fears with regard to raising children and wants him to understand. Since, in the dream, he next says he is leaving, we can deduce her fear of bringing children into the world is compounded by the fact that she feels she will lose her partner if she persists with not wanting any. The dream links the difficulty in communicating this with him to communication problems with her mother (talking to a mother on the phone).

The dream ends with the dreamer feeling everything is falling apart and going through life alone (a train journey on her own). That is her greatest fear.

In reality this dreamer left home when she was 16 and moved 3,000 miles to get away from her mother. She became harsh, promiscuous and bitter. Until her current relationship she did not have the slightest idea of how to love someone. At the time of this dream she was in a very close, respectful and loving relationship for two years. It is understandable then, why dreams would encourage her to use the support in this strong loving relationship to heal the past. Indeed, healing the past would improve her relationship as it would eliminate her fears.

This dreamer, due to her long history of isolation, has a strong counseling ability and although it is very unusual, she is intimately aware of all her problems and where they come from. By introducing grandparents twice the dream is telling her that she will make a *grand* parent but she still does not feel that. In reality her boyfriend wants a house full of children but due to the pain of her childhood she feels she could not make a good parent until she has successfully dealt with the issues around her mother. She is afraid it will be a disaster like her family and feels desperate to not let that happen. At the same time, her greatest fear is to find herself alone again.

In her own words; "No matter how close I feel to my partner or how much better our relationship becomes each day, somewhere deep down I am afraid it will not last forever. And someday sooner or later I will be that same 16 year old girl fending for herself and shutting out the world, unable to really love anyone."

20. Psychic Development

The true mystery of the world is the visible, not the invisible.

— Oscar Wilde

Although strictly not related to dreams, I include this section for those who, having discovered from their dreams that they have specific spiritual abilities, want a taster of how to develop and use them. The exercises here are intended to be light hearted and fun to try on your own or with like minded people. I can testify that they all work as I have used them so many times over the years. The exercises are in a specific order starting with the easiest. I deliberately do not have lengthy explanations as the main goal is to try the activity. Here is a list of what you can try.

► How to feel the aura with your hands

► How to see the aura

► How to see angels

► How to feel your angel's presence

► How to protect your aura.

► Clearing your aura. This is very important if you are doing any exercises where you are trying to communicate with spirits or angels.

► Communicating with your angels using physical feelings

► Communicating with your angels using a pendulum

► Closing down

► Color breathing

► How to do hands-on / spiritual healing

The Aura and Chakras

The Aura is an electromagnetic energy field that surrounds all living things. In humans, energy is fed to the body through seven main energy centers or chakras. The energy is used within the body and unprocessed energy emanates through the skin (not the pores) to form the aura, which has five layers.

Kirlian photography, which was invented in Russia around 1939, enables pictures of the aura to be taken. More recently, Neil Gershenfeld, a physicist at MIT Media Laboratory, has developed an electromagnetic field camera to track the aura around the human hand. Connected to a computer the camera can distinguish the hand from any background and accurately determine its posture and the screen object to which it is pointing. Such a device could conceivably replace the computer mouse.

A healthy aura includes all the colors of the rainbow. When there is a physical, emotional or spiritual imbalance this can be seen in the aura as impure colors. These impurities can be seen in the aura far in advance of any physical symptoms of an illness. Unless the source of imbalance is dealt with, physical illness can manifest. Through scanning this energy field, healers detect imperfections that reflect physical or emotional problems in their client and through channeling energy into their client's body they can restore the balance so the body can heal itself.

Many clairvoyants who can see the aura clearly, claim that problems show up in the outer layers of the aura first, and work their way inwards through the other layers, eventually manifesting as a physical condition in the body. Armed with this knowledge, some therapies locate the source of a physical problem in the aura and clear that. Once cleared the physical body is capable of restoring its own health.

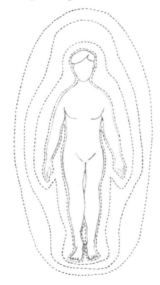

Figure 13-1 The Human Aura

The Main Chakras

The word chakra means wheel or vortex. The seven main chakras in the human body are each a centre of spinning energy. The location of the chakras is indicated on the diagram below. The first chakra is located at the base of the spine and the seventh is at the crown.

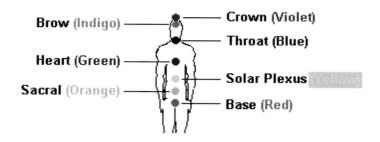

Figure 20-2 The Location & Colors associated with the Chakras

Everything in the spirit world comes down to energy. All work with the spirit world, whether it is channeling or healing, is through tuning into or manipulation of energy. This energy is all around us and we are plugged into it through our chakras. By way of analogy, a chakra can be likened to a transformer. For reasons of efficiency, electricity is delivered through the national grid at a very high voltage. However, this voltage is too high to deliver directly to a house. Apart from being dangerous to humans, it would burn out any appliance connected directly to it. To resolve this, transformers are used to step down the high voltage from the national grid to the correct voltage for the appliances in our house. In a similar way, the chakra steps down the high vibration of power around us, to a level suitable for our bodies. Each chakra steps down the power to the suitable level or vibration that is needed for the organs and glands that it feeds. The higher the chakra, the higher the energy it works with. This is mirrored by the frequency of the color associated with each chakra. For instance, the base chakra is the lowest and is in harmony with the color red. Red is the lowest frequency of light in the visible spectrum. The highest chakra is the crown chakra. This is in harmony with the color violet, which is the highest frequency of light in the color spectrum.

Clairvoyants see or feel these vibrations as different colors. The colors are those of the rainbow, or as would be seen by placing a prism in the path of a beam of white light. If you cannot see the chakras you can use a pendulum to locate them. This is more easily done with a partner. Have your partner lie down. Hold the pendulum over the centerline of their body and move it very slowly from the base of their spine to the top of their head. When the pendulum is directly over a chakra it will spiral in harmony with the energy.

Activity 1 - How to Feel the Aura

Using the correct technique the aura is easily visible. Although my courses are about Dream Interpretation I started showing people how to see and feel the aura to overcome their skepticism when discussing the spiritual dimension of dreams. This article focuses on feeling it. I always enjoy this part of the course because it is something that works for everyone. People get totally charged at the magic and simplicity of it. I urge you to try this one. It will only take five minutes but could very well change your life by opening you up to a whole new dimension.

Find a partner who wants to try this with you. Only one of you will be able to feel the aura at a time so take turns. While doing this make sure you can see a clock or watch with a second hand. Assuming you are the one going to try it first, here is what to do. The pictures correspond to the steps.

1. Join your hands together at chest height as below.

Figure 20-3 How to feel the aura – Join hands together

2. As in figure below, have your partner place their hands over yours so as to keep your hands together. For a period of at least one minute but not more than 90 seconds, try to pull your hands apart while your partner applies pressure to stop you. Make sure to put effort into pulling your hands apart. This will hurt your arms but is immediately worth it.

Figure 20-4 How to feel the aura – Pull hands apart

3. When the time is up, have your partner completely remove their hands and step back several feet from you. Move your hands to just above waist height and hold them parallel six to nine inches apart. Hold this position. See figure below.

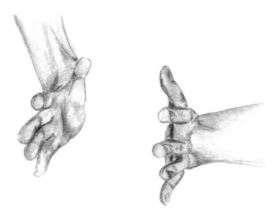

Figure 20-5 How to feel the aura – Hold your hands 6 to 9 inches apart

What you will feel

You will feel like you are holding magnets in the palms of your hands and that they are repelling each other. Ever so gently, moving just a fraction of an inch at a time, move your hands closer together and then further apart. Don't let them get any closer than two inches. While moving them together try to detect the point of strongest pressure where your hands are repelling each other. Stop the movement at this point and then gently move your hands further apart and then back to this point. The pressure will increase as you 'collect' the energy with your hands. This point of maximum pressure marks one layer of the aura.

Now move your hands to just over hip distance apart. Let the energy build up between your hands so you can feel it again. Now gently bring your hands closer again remembering to keep them parallel. You will feel another layer of the aura at a distance from between 24 inches to 14 inches. The distance varies from person to person. Once you detect this point collect the energy again by gently moving your hands further apart and then back to that point.

If you have difficulty

The most important step is where you try to pull your hands apart while your partner stops you. This gets the blood and energy flowing down your arms. To increase the flow push apart with your fingers as well as your hands. If it does not hurt you are not doing it hard enough. If you cannot feel it let your partner take a turn. When they feel it they can help describe to you how to feel it more easily.

How to improve your new ability

After resting for a while stand up and hold your hands as in Figure 5 above. Just allow the energy to build up and you will begin to feel it within one minute. You do not need to do the previous steps again. Repeat this the following day. From then on you will always be able to feel the aura by just holding your hands parallel and letting the energy build up.

Activity 2 - How to See the Aura

It is best to do this with a group of six or more people but techniques for seeing the aura alone are described later. Choose a room that has a plain white or pastel colored wall. Dim the lights to where the room is darkened but you can still walk around comfortably. Wait until your eyes have adjusted. Have one person, the subject, stand still against the wall. Have the subject keep their eyes closed so as not to distract the focus of the viewers. See figure below. The viewers should stand or sit in front of the subject at a distance of about 6 to 10 feet. Glasses do not need to be removed by anyone.

Figure 20-6 How to see the aura – Have subject stand against a wall

What you will see

You will see a bright haze around the subject's body (see Figures 7 and 8). This is particularly easy to see around the head and shoulders. Some in the group may see colors but do not worry if you cannot. Help others by describing what you see. Take turns as the subject and notice the differences between the auras. You will notice that some people's auras are easier to see than others.

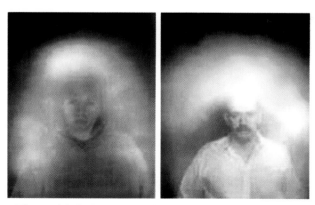

Figure 20-7 How to see the aura – What you will see

173

How to see it

Look slightly above and between the subject's eyebrows. Let your eyes relax and do not try to see the aura. When practicing, it is initially harder to see it if you look directly where it is. The aura will just seem to appear around the subject. This can take from 10 seconds to 2 minutes depending on the viewer. When this happens do not look directly at it or it will 'disappear'. Instead, train your eyes to see it by keeping your focus on the subject as described. After you have trained your eyes to keep the focus you can look directly at the aura without losing it.

If you have difficulty

While looking at the subject, think of something or someone that makes you feel good (your small child, for example). The aura is particularly easy to see around the head, shoulders and hands.

Trying this alone

With conditions the same as described above, put a potted house plant at eye level in the subject's place. Use a fast growing plant if possible. When looking at the plant open your heart to the wonder of its creation. How simple, yet beautiful, it is. When your heart connects with this you will see the plant's aura. When you have succeeded at this step you can look at your own aura using a mirror in place of the plant. The distance in the mirror is doubled so don't sit so far away! Look at yourself just as described above for looking at the subject.

Activity 3 - How to see Angels

When you are comfortable with seeing the aura, begin to look slowly around the subject. You will see at least one but usually more outlines, just like the aura. They can be anywhere within 3 feet of the subject and may be lower than shoulder height or high above the person. You should be able to look directly at these once you keep your eyes relaxed. When you see one, point it out to others so they know where to look. Pinpointing the location is good feedback for all involved, so that you know you are actually seeing something. Angels usually move around slowly during this period and in different directions. This happens while the aura remains in a fixed position. While beginners looking at the aura can sometimes convince themselves they are seeing a contrast image or trick of the light, it is hard to say this when looking at angels.

While I can see angels, I do not see much detail. However, if there is a clairvoyant in your group, whether they are aware they are clairvoyant or not, they will see great detail. They can describe facial features, clothes and colors. This always makes it more interesting. Clairvoyants can also see features and colors in the aura itself.

Now here's something to spice it up. Have the subject ask an angel to occupy the same space as their aura. Then while everyone is looking at the aura have the subject walk away. Do not let your eyes follow them. It should be easy to see an angel that remains in the person's place.

174

Activity 4 - How to Feel the Presence of your Angels

It is very easy to feel the presence of angels and it only takes ten minutes for the exercise. As with many of these exercises this one is much easier to do in a group but will work on your own. The advantage of a group is that you can compare what you are feeling. Once one person makes the connection they can describe it to others in the group. Here is what to do.

- ▶ Arrange your seats in a circle in a quiet room, preferably with wooden floors. Close any windows and doors so there are no draughts.

- ▶ Sit in a comfortable upright position and close your eyes.

- ▶ Very quickly take note of how your body feels. Pay particular attention to how your skin feels – are you warm or cold, etc?

- ▶ Relax and mentally ask your guides to enter your aura.

- ▶ Now you will notice a coolness starting at the level of your feet and moving slowly upwards. You will feel this with the same strength; regardless of the type of clothes you are wearing (jeans, skirt, etc.). Everyone in a group situation will feel the coolness at the same level in their body at the same time. It feels like you have your legs dangling in a pool and that you can sense the currents in the water.

- ▶ Allow the feeling to rise up your body and see how far you can bring it. Around waist level or stomach level is good for most groups.

What you are feeling is the energy of your angels. It is very calming and very obvious. You may get a shiver down your spine or some other feeling in your body immediately prior to feeling the coolness. These are the trademarks of your guides. If you are getting a one to one reading you should feel this energy much more strongly than when trying it alone or in a group. The Psychic will bring the energy level up to at least the brow chakra and you can feel this yourself as a buzzing sensation in your brow chakra while you are connected for the reading. If you are trying to feel this and you do not, there are two main reasons. The first is that you are too concerned about the questions you are asking and the second is that the Psychic is not connected with the Spirit world herself. Once you get this feeling at any point in the reading you can relax with the quiet knowledge that the information you are receiving is being channeled. You do not need to feel it all the way through the reading.

When I am doing radio shows where people phone in with their dreams, I wear a jacket in the studio because of how cold I get! I would literally be shivering without it. The feeling relaxes me though, because I know my invisible helpers are working with me to interpret the dreams.

Activity 5 – Clearing your Aura

This is necessary before any communication with your angels; otherwise you cannot be certain who is answering your questions. It could be your own bias or it could be another spirit having fun influencing you when they have no idea of the correct answer. Over time you can become very proficient at clearing your aura and do it with just a thought.

I describe a number of ways to do this. They all work just as effectively as each other but you may have a preference for a particular method.

Clearing your Aura by feeling the presence of your angels

You may already have tried this method. *Activity 4 - How to Feel the Presence of your Angels* clears your aura. It is the slowest way to do it but does have the advantage of relaxing you while you do it and that helps with the subsequent communication.

When clearing your aura with this method, notice that at some point in the exercise you feel a shiver down your spine. That is the point at which your aura is cleared. If you do not feel it, your aura is not clear so persist with it. It does not matter at what point you feel that shiver. You may feel it before you begin the exercise. Once you do, you can skip the exercise as your aura is clear and you will not feel the shiver again. Try to notice what causes you to feel the shiver and see if you can trigger it another way. Once you can trigger it, you have found your method for clearing your aura.

Clearing your Aura by stimulating your spiritual chakras

This method always works, even for the beginner. It works by focusing on your spiritual chakras, which are the throat, brow and crown chakras. Follow the instructions and illustrations until you feel a shiver down your spine. You will feel the shiver typically within ninety seconds. For clarity front and side view are shown. Your feet never move during this exercise.

► **Step 1**. Referring to the figure below, raise your hands to your brow chakra. Move your hands in small clockwise circles for a few seconds. This opens the brow chakra.

Figure 20-8 Clearing your aura – Move hands to brow chakra

► **Step 2**. With one hand over the other slide your hands in a slow steady motion from your brow chakra, over the top of your head, down the back of your head to the back of your neck. While doing this repeat mentally, "I cleanse my aura

176

in the name of love".

Figure 20-9 Clearing your aura – Slide hands to crown chakra

Figure 20-10 Clearing your aura – Slide hands down to back of throat chakra

▶ **Step 3**. Slide your hands from the back of your neck to your throat. Keep repeating the mental phrase.

Figure 20-11 Clearing your aura – Slide hands to front of throat chakra

177

► **Step 4**. Sweep your hands from your throat downwards by your side as if shaking water from your hands and fingertips. If you have not felt a shiver down your spine move your hands back to your brow chakra and continue from step 2 above. Note you do not need to rotate your hands over your brow chakra again.

Figure 20-12 Clearing your aura – Sweep hands down by your side

From anywhere after 30 seconds you will feel a shiver down your spine. This shiver is what you are waiting for. It does not matter how long it takes; keep up the exercise for five or ten minutes if it takes that long. Once you feel the shiver your aura is cleared and you can stop. This exercise works by stimulating your three spiritual chakras as your hand movements repeatedly cover your brow, crown and throat chakras in turn.

Clearing your Aura by grounding yourself

I discovered this method of clearing my aura accidentally and this is how I always do it now. It may only work when you have cleared your aura many times by other methods, so do not be disheartened if it does not work first time for you.

With your eyes open or closed, simply imagine that you are standing on two light pads that are strapped to each foot. Now imagine a shaft of white light emanating from the sole of each foot and moving downwards at incredible speed towards the center of the earth. As it nears the center imagine the center of the earth as a ball of blue neon light and see the two shafts racing towards it. They pierce the center to form solid shafts of white light from your feet to the center of the earth. Right at this point you should feel the shiver down your spine.

Given time this method works instantaneously, reliably and repeatedly. If you ground yourself you feel a shiver. If you do it again you feel another shiver. When I am being interviewed or working in person with someone, this is the method I use. Nobody knows you are doing it.

Activity 6 - Closing Down

Activities such as meditation or channeling also open the aura. We are all aware of the need to take care of our physical body but many people engage in activities which exercise the spirit body without properly caring for it. In a meditative state we assume a posture that encourages energy to flow through us more freely. We also use our mind to raise our vibration to connect with a higher plane. Whether we realize it or not, this opens our aura and chakras more than any other exercise. When finished the exercise, it is necessary to close ourselves down but most practices omit this step. Closing down is described next. It is NEVER a good idea to remain open like this.

How to close down

Stand up straight. With your eyes closed, imagine a golden light coming from the sky right above you and shining straight through the centre of your body and into the ground. Now, starting at the top of your head, imagine that a strand of this light is moving in a clockwise direction around you. Imagine the light is gently moving downwards as it swirls around you. As it passes each chakra, it closes it to the level required to operate on the physical plane. You do not need to worry about what that level is. Trust that the light knows what it is doing. The light then moves into the ground.

That's the whole exercise. It takes less than two minutes to do. Do it immediately after your development exercise or following all discussions your group may have after the exercise. Try to not talk about any of your spiritual experiences after you have closed down as this will open you up again. If you do, simply close down again when you are done.

Activity 7 - Communication with Angels using Physical Feeling

Full dialogue with my guides was always the ultimate goal for me. I wanted clear, concise communication that left no room for mistakes. Many of the development exercises I have covered are precursors to this goal. I describe two methods of communication, which while not full dialogue are another step on that path. They let you receive simple yes and no answers from your guides to precisely phrased questions. It will work well in advance of full dialogue and teaches you to focus properly on the questions you ask. For the purpose of this exercises it is best, but not necessary, to be alone as this will remove any time pressure you may feel when others are present.

There are three parts to communication and none can be skipped. They are

1. Clear your aura.

2. Communicate using any method that works for you.

3. Close down.

Clearing your aura and closing down are described earlier. Allow that you are only learning this process and go easy on yourself. When communicating in the beginning, you may only get a few answers (typically less than 7) before you notice the answers have become blurred. This is normal and is due to issues with keeping your aura clear. Over time this problem diminishes.

How to do it

This exercise works well either sitting down or standing up. With your questions prepared, wait until you feel the presence of your angels as described above. When you are comfortable that they are present, ask your angels to give you an obvious feeling that indicates a positive response from them. Take time to notice a change of feeling in your body. It can be different for everybody but is always distinctive enough for you to spot. For example, I feel a positive response as a coolness that sweeps down my spine. Over time this has become more noticeable for me.

▶ Clear your aura using any of the techniques. Regardless of the technique, you must get a shiver down your spine which indicates you are grounded.

▶ Ask your angels to give you an obvious feeling that indicates a positive response from them. Take time to notice a change of feeling in your body. It can be different for everybody but is always distinctive enough for you to spot. For example, I feel a positive response as a coolness that sweeps down my spine. Over time this has become more noticeable for me.

You are trying to spot something that is subtle and can be tricky until you know what you are looking for. To help you spot it, ask your angels to remove the feeling, then wait twenty seconds and ask them to give it to you again. Keep doing this until you spot the signal and are comfortable with detecting it.

▶ Ask your question and wait. If you get a positive response, the answer is *Yes*, if you do not, the answer is *No*. It is up to you to phrase the question so it can be answered with a simple yes and no. If the question is ambiguous the response will not come. With practice it will be so obvious you can ask a silent question in a crowded room and be sure of their response. The method used to indicate a positive response will never change for you but still ask for the feeling each time you begin asking questions so that you know your connection is clear.

If you find yourself getting nowhere, take a break and come back to it. Always make sure your aura is clear as this is the only time the signal will be clear. If it is not clear your own bias and other spirits can affect the answer!

Activity 8 – Communication with Angels using a Pendulum

A pendulum is a balanced weight on the end of a thread or flexible fine chain. It does not have to be made of anything in particular, although crystal pendulums, such as quartz, are the most popular. Their weight is also not important but they must be able to swing easily and freely. Once you try the exercise you will discover what weight works best for you.

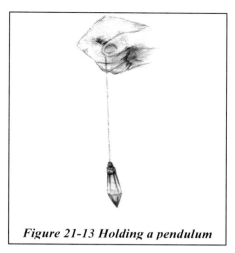

Figure 21-13 Holding a pendulum

► Clear your aura using any of the techniques.

► Hold the pendulum thread comfortably in your hand. There is no set way to hold it – all hand positions work. Hold the pendulum steady, acting as if your life depends on the pendulum not moving.

► Ask your angels to show you a *Yes* answer on the pendulum. Remember to act as if your life depends on the pendulum not moving. The pendulum will slowly start to spiral in a clockwise direction. See the figure below. Do not be fooled. You are moving the pendulum but you are not doing it consciously. By attempting to hold the pendulum steady you are removing your conscious mind from the answer. Your angels are then free to gently influence the movement of the pendulum in the appropriate direction. Clockwise is the typical direction for the answer *Yes*. Although it is possible for it to be different for you, it is most common for a clockwise spiral to indicate yes. It could also be indicated by a back and forth movement or left and right sideways movement. Whatever it is for you it is likely to remain that way every time you use a pendulum.

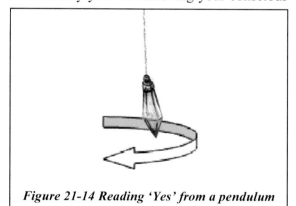

Figure 21-14 Reading 'Yes' from a pendulum

► Now stop the pendulum from moving and ask for a *No* answer. Holding your hand steady you will see that the pendulum begins to move in an anti-clockwise spiral. See the picture below. This is the movement you get when the answer is *No*.

Figure 20-15 Reading 'No' from a pendulum

▶ Formulate a question clearly so that a simple yes or no is the only appropriate answer. Keep this and only this question in your mind and hold the pendulum steady. Again it helps to pretend that your life depends on holding it steady.

The pendulum will move to indicate a clear answer. If the pendulum does not move or does not indicate a clear yes or no, then change how you phrase the question. When I first did this I was surprised at how often I thought I had reduced the question to a simply yes or no answer, when in fact the question was ambiguous. This is an exercise in teaching you how to formulate your questions and your angels will be unswerving in it. When the question is ambiguous it means you have not fully focused on the issue. Once you have been doing this for some months, your angels will be more forgiving and answer the question as you intend it. However in the beginning they use the opportunity afforded them to help you train your mind.

Once you have your answer, formulate another question and wait for that answer.

In the beginning you may only get a few answers (typically less than 7) before you notice the yes and no have become blurred. This is normal and is due to issues with keeping your aura clear. Over time this problem diminishes but even a seasoned dowser always starts their set of questions by clearing their aura and asking for a yes, reading the pendulum, asking for a no and reading the pendulum. If yes and no do not come out properly on the pendulum, they clear their aura again or wait for another time. The last thing wanted is to get a lot of answers that mean nothing because your connection is not clear. When I know my connection is clear my first question is always, "Is it appropriate to ask questions with regard to this subject matter at this time?" It is possible to have a clear connection but your angels or the angels of the person with you may feel it unwise to divulge the answers being sought.

Activity 9 - Protecting your Aura

There are a few techniques here, all with the purpose of protecting your aura. This by necessity is personal, so you would only do these on your own.

Your aura is controlled by how you feel. If you are fearful or feeling depressed, your aura becomes quite small and can be hard to see. If you are feeling very positive your aura expands to a great size, becomes full of light and is very easy to see.

Protecting your aura in a relationship

Normally your aura is sealed, but feeling affection towards another person causes your aura to open up to theirs. Most of us are familiar with the effects of this. When you are connected you feel happy when they are happy. Conversely you feel sad when they are sad. You are literally feeling the emotions in their aura. This is welcome when a relationship is going well but adds to the pain when it is not. In the latter case, in order to reconnect with your feelings, it is often necessary to take a break of a few days away from your partner, and from anyone who would try to influence you in any way about your relationship. This will allow your aura to become clear of their influence. In this isolated space you can reconnect with your feelings and this will strengthen your aura. You can then re-enter the same space your partner occupies, with a renewed ability to distinguish your feelings from theirs.

Protecting your aura from the influence of others

This exercise works well for partners, your boss or anyone who rubs you the wrong way. It must be done before you meet the person, so I suggest you do it first thing in the morning before you get dressed. Close your eyes and imagine your aura around you. Notice its oval shape and imagine this shape filling with very beautiful and warm light. Fill it outwards from your body in all directions rather than from the bottom up - as if your body is the element of a light bulb. Now imagine a golden seal forming just on the inside edge of your aura. Imagine the seal hardening so that nothing can get into your aura. The seal acts like a mirror reflecting away anything that comes near you. You feel totally protected inside a cocoon. Now imagine the seal becoming soft and bright but it still works with the same effectiveness. You now control what can get into your aura and unless you allow it, all negative feelings projected at you simply bounce off your aura.

Activity 10 – Color Breathing

This is a beautiful and simple exercise which takes only a few minutes, has immediate effect, and has many practical applications. Refer to the Color Healing Chart below to see the effect each color has. If, for example, you are feeling run down and want to pick yourself up, you could breathe red to energize you. You can do this with your eyes open but preferably sitting down with your eyes closed.

Imagine a beautiful cloud of red floating in front of you. Look at the pure color, vibrant and rich. Now breathe in slowly inhaling the beautiful red cloud into your lungs. Hold the breath for a few seconds and breathe out slowly. As you breathe out imagine

183

all negativity, such as things that have upset you, depression, etc. leaving you. You may see this as an impure color or grey breath as you exhale. Now breathe in more of the beautiful red cloud. Feel your lungs absorb this red color. Now as you exhale your breath is clearer. Keep breathing in and out, drawing in more of the red cloud each time. Feel the red move all around your body as your blood carries it from your lungs. Feel your body wakening and energizing. The red is spreading through your whole body and is now passing through your skin and into your aura. Soon your aura is filled with this beautiful red color. You now feel full of energy. Before finishing, seal the color into your aura by imagining a silver lining around your aura. This holds the red in for a lasting effect.

This technique works equally well for calming (use blue instead of red); before interviews when you want to be open to new ideas (use orange), etc. Feel free to mix colors. For example, blue and yellow relax your body and stimulate your intellect during exams.

Try it now to show yourself the power of color. You may only need to take 12 breaths for a lasting effect.

Color	Healing Effect
Violet	Brings spiritual peace. Heals insomnia, tumors of the brain. Calms highly-strung, excitable people.
Indigo	Develops psychic perception, intuition, Heals eyes, ears, nose and mental problems.
Blue	Fights infections. Heals throat, fevers, etc.. Gives peace of mind.
Green	Creates balance of energy. Heals the heart, circulatory system. Helps you overcome fear of giving, sharing, adaptability.
Yellow	Heals nervous system, elimination, liver, intestines, pancreas. Balances adrenal glands, heals skin troubles, diabetes. Stimulates intellect.
Orange	Help digestion, assimilation of new ideas, removes repression and inhibitions. Broadens the mind, helps you cope with life and career.
Red	Heals the creative, reproductive systems. Stimulates circulation of blood and flow of adrenaline. Energizes, gives confidence and courage.

Activity 11 – Channeling Healing Energy

There are many types of hands-on healing. Popular forms include Reiki and Bio-energy. The healing I describe here, however, is completely controlled by spirit. The therapist channels healing energy into their client but does not focus the energy with any intention. Their focus is simply on being an open channel for the healing energy. Spirit uses the energy channeled to heal the client in an appropriate way.

If you have already discovered from your dreams that you are a hands-on healer you will find that this technique works instantly for you. Find somebody to practice with. They don't need to be ill for it to work and it does not affect anyone negatively. Here is how to do it. Referring to the diagram follow these steps.

► Have your client sit in a comfortable position with their back straight. Refer-ring to the figure below, stand behind them and place your hands on their shoulders. Now imagine a beautiful light coming from the soles of your feet and moving directly downwards to the centre of the earth. Imagine the light reaches the centre of the earth and joins with a beautiful neon blue glowing light there. You may not feel anything the first time you try this but with prac-tice you will feel this connection being made.

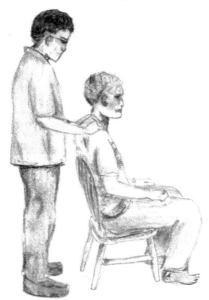

Figure 20-16 Spiritual healing

► Now imagine neon blue earth energy moving upwards within these rays of light and flowing through your body to your crown chakra.

► Imagine now that your body has become like a magnet and feel it attracting a ray of golden light from the very centre of the universe. This light travels to you and connects with your crown chakra. Imagine this golden light moving down the back of your head, across your shoulders and down to the level of

185

your heart but still covering the whole width of your back, where it meets with the blue earth energy coming up.

▶ Now imagine the golden energy flowing from there down the outside and top of your arms and spreading into your hands covering them entirely. At the same time imagine the blue earth energy flowing under your arms to your wrists.

▶ Finally imagine only the golden energy flowing from the centre of your palms into your client. While you may not feel this at first you should feel it before the end of this exercise.

You have now started channeling healing energy into your client. It can actually take the energy a couple of minutes to begin to flow so relax and just let it happen. As the flow increases you will feel as if your hands are in a pair of very large gloves that give you a strange pins and needles sensation.

When I started doing this type of work I did not feel much beyond the sensation in my hands. Now I can feel spirit hands working underneath my client's skin pushing and pulling. This is a very physical feeling and many clients will comment on it if they feel it happening to them. Whether your client feels anything or not does not affect the healing they receive so do not worry. Once you can feel it, trust that everything is working as it should.

If you get a sense that you need to move your hands to another location on your client's body ask their permission, lift your hands and move them gently to that location. Let the connection adjust for the new position and the energy will begin to flow again.

Typically healing will require you to channel energy for about 20 minutes. At no point do you try to imagine your client being healed as this inhibits the flow of the energy. Trust that spirit will guide the energy to where it is needed, and work the healing for your client. Your purpose in the equation is to channel the energy for spirit. If it is not in the life purpose of the client to be physically healed then that particular healing will not happen, but spirit will use the energy to help them in some other way. A healing always takes place.

As you become more in touch with the healing energy, you will begin to notice that spirit guides the energy around your body in different paths depending on your client's ailment. Sometimes you will feel energy moving down both arms, other times you will only feel it in one arm. When a blockage is being cleared in your client, you will feel it as energy moving from your client to under your arms and down the front and sometimes the back of your legs into the ground. This is an extremely important connection and is opened when you imagine the light coming from the soles of your feet at the start of the session. It prevents you from picking up the blockages you are clearing from your client. In time you will feel this connection even when it is not being used to ground negative energy. It can feel a little different for different people but it always feels like something is grounding you. When you are used to feeling it and find it missing during a session stop working. This means you have a block within yourself

186

that you need to clear. To continue to work while you have this block can cause you to become ill. Do some gardening or go for a walk in the park to restore your ground connection again.

Once you can feel the flow of both energies, experiment and develop your own style with this. Also, depending on your client you may find it better to have them lying down rather than sitting. In all cases it is best for your feet to be firmly on the ground to maintain your ground connection. One healing that requires a significant change in your posture is when working on a fever. When doing this type of healing, only place your right hand on your client and point your left palm towards the earth, (i.e. your left palm is parallel with the floor. During the session imagine energy flowing from your left palm into the earth.

When practicing, pick a friend who is healthy and practice just feeling the energy flowing. When you can feel the flow, you can begin working on people with ailments. Ailments do not need to be physical. For example, this type of healing is very effective at lifting depression.

Dream Symbol Reference

0

Zero is the perfect symbol with no beginning or end and as such in dreams it indicates God, ideals and goals. For example, 70 would indicate Spiritual ideals and 30 would indicate commitment to your goals.

1

One is a male number and indicates individuality and creativity. These are two sides of the same coin. The more individual you remain the more creative you are as you do your own thing rather than follow the crowd. This number can also indicate that you are being selfish with regard to the subject matter of the dream. This number will almost always be shown with other numbers and is usually first. For example, catching the 17 bus tells you that your spiritual journey (7) is unique (1). One can also indicate commitment – being at one with yourself.

10

Ten which indicates completion as it is at the end of the set of individual numbers.

12

Twelve indicates being judgmental as there are twelve people on a jury.

2

Two is a female number and indicates balance, sharing, give and take and two way communication. Two way communication is important for channels (mediums) and as such they will often have dreams littered with the number two, such as, the number 2 itself, weddings, twins or two of anything. Dreaming of the number 2 is not enough in itself to indicate that the dreamer is a channel but it is a very good indicator. The balance indicated by this number can be about communication in your relationship or anything else that is unbalanced in your life. Highways are often used to indicate balance in dreams with emphasis being given to the two way flow on the road. This refers to balance in your heart. Do you share your feelings honestly? Do you always take or do you give too much of yourself?

3

Three has to do with commitment to the subject matter of the dream. It stands for mind, body and soul and is a request to commit mind body and soul to improving yourself in the direction indicated in the dream. Three will often appear in dreams about the heart as people who have suppressed their feelings often lack passion and commitment for new things in life. It is also similar to a broken 8 in appearance and 8 always symbolizes the heart. A triangle or pyramid also indicate commitment and request the dreamer to meditate on the subject matter of the dream.

4

Four indicates limitation. For example, catching the number 4 bus would indicate the dreamer is limiting their life journey through their actions or thoughts. A box or square also indicate limitation. This number is very common in dreams and is usually linked with other numbers. A choice between the 23 and 24 buses to Parnell Square reminds you that you have a choice between committing (3) to keeping balance (2) in your life or limiting (4) that balance (2). The rest of the dream indicates where the balance is required. In the previous example it is between work and the dreamer's relationship (as symbolized by the Irish patriot Parnell).

5

The number *five* indicates the karma path in dreams. Literally you are experiencing your world through the five physical senses alone. Dreams with the number five quite often show what you are obliged to develop on this path so look for other symbols to indicate this in the dream.

6

The number *six* indicates the dharmic path in dreams. Six symbolizes going beyond the five senses and karma and experiencing life as a spiritual journey in a state of Grace. Choices are made through the heart and the path in life you follow is the path you know is of most benefit to you spiritually. This way of living has a strong connection to life, the spirit world and a great sense of purpose. To others it can appear irrational and crazy at times but

that is because they are still experiencing life through karma.

7

Seven always indicates spiritual enlightenment. Your spiritual center is your seventh chakra which is located at the very top of your head.. A dream where you catch the number 37 bus to church is a request to commit (3) to developing your spiritual side (7 and church). Paying $47 for something indicates that the dreamer is limiting (4) their spiritual nature (7) by not putting enough energy (paying for something) into developing it.

8

Eight, is the only balanced number and indicates expansion through balance of the heart. If you turn 8 on its side you get ∞. You can easily imagine balancing that shape on the end of your finger. It is also the symbol for infinity which indicates limitless expansion. Eight features in dreams about the heart and circulatory system. The symbol itself is made of two circles and anything circular in a dream symbolizes your circulatory system.

9

Nine is not very common in dreams and indicates that you are spiritually advanced. It is a reminder to follow your life purpose because within this lifetime you have the potential to repay all your karma and make this your last necessary earth life. It does not mean you cannot come back for another earth experience – rather that you do not have to. If you dream of 9 you would find yourself naturally drawn to learning about spiritual matters.

ACTOR / ACTRESS

A *movie actor* or *actress* indicates that you are a channel / medium The words a movie star says in a movie are given to them. In a similar way the words a channel passes on are also given to them.

A *TV actor* or *actress* indicates that you are clairvoyant. You have clear vision as symbolized by the television which is used to view them.

AFFAIR

If you are *having an affair* in a dream, you are being asked to get intimately in touch with your male side if you are having an affair with a man, or your female side if the affair is with a woman. Having an affair with a person of the same gender means the same thing. We all have male and female aspects to ourselves which have their own unique traits. For example, compassion, listening, leadership and your philosophy of life work through your female energy. Confidence, belief in yourself, feeling worthy of the space you occupy, career, ambition, sex drive and spiritual healing work through your male energy. The dream may be triggered due to an imbalance which is affecting your ability to develop or move forward in an aspect of your life.

To dream of *your partner having an affair* is not a prediction or confirmation. It merely means that your dream is trying to get you to work through your feelings for your partner. It can be triggered if you had or considered an affair in this or a previous relationship?

AFRICA

Africa, being the origin of the human species, is about getting to the root of an issue. This meaning does not hold if you are from Africa.

AGGRESSION

See *Anger*.

AIR BAG

Air bags symbolize your lungs.

AIR BLOWER

An *air blower* symbolizes your lungs.

AIR PUMP

Heart, circulatory system, emotions. See *Pumps*.

AIR VENT

An *air vent* symbolizes your respiratory system and is common in dreams of asthmatics.

If smoke is getting into the air vent the dream is asking you to cut out smoking or remove yourself from smoking environments.

AIRPLANE

Airplanes being lofty, can indicate being up in your head or too logical with regard to how you go through life or with regard to the subject matter of the dream. Come down out of your head and let your heart have a say in decisions too.

An *airplane arrival* or *landing* signifies your birth - your arrival onto the planet.

An *airplane crash* signifies a difficult birth - one that was either emotionally traumatic or life threatening.

An *airplane departure* signifies the beginning of a new project or phase of your life. Often these dreams show what is holding you back from the new project. For example, to dream of your partner forgetting your passports for the flight signifies there are problems in your relationship and you are blaming these for not taking the jump.

A *fighter plane* indicates you are an angry person – ready with a verbal arsenal to win arguments and defend your space. The dream will likely say how this came about and will be encouraging you to soften up.

AIRPORT

An *airport* signifies the start or end of a phase of your life journey. Arrivals commonly signify your birth and departures signify a new project. See *Airplane*.

AISLE

Dreams that draw attention to an *aisle*, particularly, but not confined to, a church, indicate you are a channel. You can communicate with spirits. Puns on the word aisle also indicate this.

ALARM

An *alarm system* is a symbol for the immune system. The immune system is constantly on alert looking for intruders (germs).

Trying to *reset an alarm* can indicate MS (Multiple Sclerosis) or other autoimmune disease. It is thought that MS results from attacks by an individual's immune system on the nervous system. Resetting the alarm is a symbolic attempt to restore the immune system to its proper function.

ALASKA

If you have never lived in *Alaska* to dream of it means that you are emotionally cold towards yourself and others. You need to be warmer.

ALASKAN PIPELINE

An *oil pipeline* symbolizes that you are a hands-on healer. The huge quantity of oil flowing through the pipeline is a great source of power. Like the pipeline you have a source of power within you. This power can be channeled into others by placing your hands on them and letting the energy flow.

ALCOHOL

Alcohol is commonly referred to as spirits and can indicate your spirits or your spirituality. For example, a dream with a nail where the nail is on a bar stool is a pun on denial (the nail) of spirituality (bar).

Drinking alcohol in a dream is about repression of feelings as drinking suppresses your sensitivity.

ALIEN

Aliens, the extra terrestrial kind, when helpful, remote, friendly or in authority signify your guides or guardian angles. They show up as aliens in your dream because you are not quite sure that you are the same as them. When you become more comfortable with the fact that you are, dreams of them as aliens will diminish. The only difference between you and them is their state of awareness and the fact that you currently inhabit a body.

Aliens, when threatening, signify entities such as malicious spirits or illness. Going to bed in an angry mood can trigger dreams where you are fighting off aliens when you end up on a low level of the astral plane.

ALLIGATOR

To dream of an *alligator* indicates that you are either too assertive (your bite is too large) or the opposite; you need to drop your timid nature and stand up for yourself. You will know which applies to you. This dream is healing and intends for you to get renewed strength to get a grip on things. Sharpen your teeth and like the alligator do not let go once you have sunk your teeth in. You should only bite off in life what you can chew but the first part is also to be able to take the bite at life. See *teeth* for more.

An *alligator in a swamp* represents your colon. Here the alligator symbolizes a health warning so look to the other symbols in the dream to indicate what you need to do to prevent it.

AMUSEMENT PARK

An *amusement park* is healing for depression or a request to enjoy yourself. Parks symbolize your heart so an amusement park is trying to put a sense of fun and amusement back into your heart.

ANGEL

Angels in dreams represent your guardian angels (guides) in reality or a positive guiding force in your life. They are the only infallible character in dreams so always follow their advice. Quite often they remain silent preferring you to figure out what they deem is important. This can be indicated by what they are doing, what they are wearing, what they are carrying or by who is with them in the dream.

ANGER

Anger commonly shows up in dreams to do with patience and the digestive system. Eating while angry is very bad for your digestive system. Emotion charges the food you are eating like a homeopathic remedy. Eating in a posi-

tive frame of mind programs the food to heal your body. Eating while angry or depressed programs the food to cause problems.

An *angry* man in your dream can indicate your dad was an angry person. Similarly an angry woman indicates your mother was angry.

ANIMAL

One interpretation for *Animals* is that they represent your human nature (animal nature). We are animals and part of the animal kingdom. As such we have animal instincts that are part of our nature. Do you suppress part of your animal nature? To dream of an *elephant*, for instance, means that you hide your sensitivity by displaying a thick skin (see *elephant*). You are a sensitive animal and there is no point denying it – it is part of your nature so accept it. To dream of a *sheep* indicates you are timid or don't do enough for yourself (see *sheep*). If you dream of an *alligator* or *crocodile* means that you are either too aggressive and need to stop snapping at others or that you are losing a grip on things (once a crocodile has a grip on you they will not let go) and need to sharpen your teeth so you can take a good bite at life or be assertive when you need to be.

The significant thing is that as an animal your instincts can guide you through a given situation and quite often this is the right thing to do. Our animal side is also instrumental when it comes to having fun. Fun is a spontaneous thing and that's how instincts work. To dream of a *lost dog* returning asks you to let your mental guard down and trust your instincts.

To dream of an *animal dying* can be about letting your animal nature die. It can also be about your body's immune system fighting off disease. To dream of dead **mutated animals**, **crows**, **badgers**, **snakes**, **worms**, or other animals that are **carrion** is good. Here the animals represent a serious health threat such as cancer and them dying or you killing them in a dream shows your immune system is up to the task of fighting off the threat. To dream of these animals laying eggs, warns of a disease spreading within your body. The rest of the dream will say what it is that is allowing the spread. The good news is that dreams warn of disease before it manifests so there is plenty of time to take remedial action. It also needs to be pointed out that to occasionally dream of health threats is fine. It becomes serious when you consistently dream these symbols.

Rabbits and *animals with young* symbolize your reproductive system.

Slow moving animals indicate that you have a slow moving colon and need to do something to speed it up.

Talking animals indicate that you need to express yourself.

Look up other animals by name to discover their meaning.

ANTIQUE FURNITURE

Antique furniture indicates ideals. It is always good to have ideals and goals, however, if the ideals are not part of your life purpose and are hindering you in any way, your dreams will show this. Moving your parents' furniture or furniture that looks like theirs into your house is a common theme here. A clash of ideals is indicated in this case, if you find yourself having to be careful not to hit against the furniture, or find yourself moving it around looking for space for it..

APARTMENT

Apartments symbolize your heart, circulatory system and emotions. Typically it means that you separate yourself from your feelings. Literally you and your emotions are apart – you are not conscious of them. At least with regard to the subject matter of the dream, you are being too logical and need to involve your heart more in the decision making process.

APOSTLE

To dream of an *apostle* means you are a spiritual teacher / leader. This does not mean in a religious way. Spirituality is expression of the soul so you will teach others to express what is in their core.

APPROACH

Approach in dreams is a request for you to get closer to whatever is the subject matter of the dream. For example, if you dream of approaching a person in body armor, the subject matter of the dream is *not allowing others to get close to you*. In this context the approach asks you to allow others approach you – allow others to get close to you.

ARCHWAY

An *archway*, particularly when cut through a green hedge, is a pun on artery and therefore implies your circulation system.

ARENA

An *arena* symbolizes conflict either within yourself or with others.

ARMOR

Protective *armor* indicates that you do not allow others to get close to you.

This is always about your heart and emotions. The idea is that by keeping people at a distance you cannot get hurt. The dream shows you this, to ask you to open up and allow others to get close. It is not healthy for your heart to suppress your feelings over a long period of time. Ideally you are open and honest about your feelings both to yourself and to others.

ARMY
Armies can indicate the bodies defenses in action against an invading bacteria or virus. They can also indicate conflict either within or with others.

A subversive or ***underground army*** can indicate a serious threat to the body such as cancer.

Army uniforms indicate you have a regimented way of thinking that needs to change. In the army troops are trained through boot camp to not question the orders of their superior regardless of the threat to their own life. Green army uniforms ask you to listen to your heart rather than your head.

ARROW
An ***arrow*** indicates you are a counselor as it symbolizes helping someone find the direction they need to take.

ART GALLERY
An ***art gallery*** symbolizes ideals or goals. For example, to dream of arguing with the male owner over a painting indicates a clash of ideals with your father.

ARTIFICIAL LIMB
An ***artificial limb***, such as an artificial right leg, means you are following convention rather than letting your

natural abilities support you.

ASTRAL TRAVELING
Astral traveling symbolizes that you have a strong intellect which brings with it the gifts of absent healing, projection and hypnosis. Quite often it is a request to rise mentally above a problem. See *Flying*.

ATTIC
An ***attic*** symbolizes your mind or brain in dreams.

AUBURN
Auburn, being a dark red, indicates frigidity. Red is the color of the base chakra and indicates sexuality in dream. Dark shades indicate fear so the combination shows fear linked to sexuality.

AUNT
Your ***aunt***, as your mother's peer, symbolizes your mother and female side in a dream. For example, her dying in a dream asks you to let the negative influence of your mother die.

To dream of your sick or ***deceased aunt*** receiving a transfusion and coming back to life, asks you to rediscover and nurture your female side.

AUTHOR
An ***author*** symbolizes you have a creative writing ability and you are being asked to use this in your life as a means of connecting with your inner core. As an author, you will find your distinctive style of expression and expand your understanding of yourself.

AWAKEN
To ***awaken*** in a dream is very positive and symbolizes having your eyes

195

opened to the reality of your life. This is invariably associated with reaching a level of spiritual awareness that puts you on track for achieving your life purpose.

BABY

Dreams of a *baby* or babies can be triggered when you are trying to have one. The dream can also be about influences you picked up as a baby.

To dream of a *baby* or babies, particularly when given one or asked to mind one, means there is something in your life for which you have responsibility. Just as a baby needs nurturing and care, you are obliged to do what it takes to look after or develop whatever it is. Once the attention is given the outcome is always positive.

To dream of you or someone else *giving birth* means a new aspect of yourself is about to be born. As above, it is your responsibility to develop this side of yourself. This is always a positive dream, as to allow a new aspect of yourself to flourish you must let go of whatever kept it suppressed. This dream usually comes after doing some developmental work on yourself.

To dream of someone *nursing a baby* or doing so yourself, asks you to provide the correct nurturing environment to develop a new aspect of yourself.

A *baby with a special ability* means that you have a sixth sense in line with what the baby is portraying in the dream. For example, if a newborn baby can talk it means you have a special communication ability – you are intuitive / psychic and you are being encouraged to do something to develop and use it.

A *stillborn baby* means that you are

not doing what is needed to nurture a new and positive aspect of yourself. Don't be disheartened by this dream but take it as a strong message that you need to make more of an effort.

BACK

Your **back** is most commonly about your past as like your past it is always behind you.

Washing your back whether deliberately or inadvertently is about the need to cleanse some baggage you are carrying from the past. For example, a window cleaner spilling soapy water on your back is a request to cleanse issues from the past.

Looking over your back or *looking out a back window* means that you are focused on the past. Something in your past has you looking back at it all the time. You may not be consciously aware of it but whatever you are doing today is controlled by something from the past.

If *someone has their back to you* it means the person they symbolize in the dream turned their back on you. At least that's your view of it, but when it comes to your life you can only see it from your point of view. If the person in the dream is a woman, this is most likely going to be your mother. If the person in the dream is a man this is most likely going to be your father.

BACK DOOR

A *back door* indicates your rectum - the back door to your body. Houses, buildings and cars represent your body in dreams and various parts of the house represent various other parts of your body.

196

BACK GARDEN

The *back garden* whether it is your childhood house or not is often about the past. However, in dreams about your health the back garden is also about your colon or elimination system. For example, to dream of soggy newspapers in the back garden indicates mold is growing in your colon – often indicative of candida albicans.

A *back garden path* is always about your colon or elimination system. If it is a cement path the dream is saying that food is caked onto the walls of your colon and you need to do something to eliminate it.

BACK HOE

A back hoe symbolizes your digestive system. This is because these vehicles are associated with working with dirt or dirt tracks.

BACK PASSAGE

A *back passage* is about your colon or elimination system.

BADGER

A *badger* represents the elimination system for two reasons. The first is the black and white color combination which indicates the colon. The second is that the badger is a carnivore that digs into earth to find prey. As a result a badger can indicate a health warning with the colon. Try to eliminate or cut down on food items referenced in the same dream.

BALCONY

Due to its height, dreaming of being on a *balcony* means that you operate from your head. Logic and analysis are your methods for determining your actions. The dream points out your position to ask you to come down from your head and include your heart in the decision making process.

An *important figure above you on a balcony*, particularly someone with a title or who speaks with authority, is in the dream to guide you. Their advice is infallible. Sometimes they take on a negative position to show you how you are acting with regard to the subject matter of the dream.

BALD

To dream of being *bald* indicates you are refusing to think about the subject matter of the dream. If someone else in the dream is bald it can mean the same thing. However, it could also be about how someone else is affecting your thinking.

BALL

A *ball* represents an ideal or a goal. Anything circular in a dream can symbolize this. A soccer game, for example, represents your pursuit of goals.

BALLOON

A *balloon* represents an ideal or a goal. Anything circular in a dream can symbolize this (see numbers) but a balloon is also something you look up to - symbolizing a request for you to aspire to achieving your goal.

BAMBOO

Bamboo, being wooden and a long tube, indicates your colon. It can also indicate you are a channel as it is a tube that is open at both ends.

BANK

Banks control the flow of money in circulation and as such they symbolize your heart, circulatory system and emotions. A bank can also symbolize your emotions and in this case is most likely about suppressing your feelings.

A *bank account* also indicates your feelings but in this case the attention is being drawn to how balanced your heart is. Do you share your feelings or do you hide them from others? Constant suppression of emotions can lead to physical problems with your heart and circulatory system.

An *overdrawn bank account* means you are being asked to address the imbalance as a matter of importance.

A *bank robbery* is not what it appears. With the bank symbolizing your heart the 'robbers' are forcing you to give from your heart. However, in your case the feeling in waking life is that when you give you get nothing in return – this indicates an inability to share.

A *river bank, earthy and muddy* indicates your colon. Quite often these dreams link the state of your bloodstream with the state of your colon reminding you that what you eat ends up in your bloodstream. In particular, foods that your system cannot digest or eliminate properly build up toxins in your colon which then seep into your bloodstream.

A *river bank, green with clear water* indicates your heart, emotions and bloodstream.

BANNER

A *banner* is symbolic of a title or qualification. Usually in dreams it is indicative of a perceived need for a qualification to feel entitled to do what you are already capable of.

BANQUET

To dream of a *banquet* is a request to

be selective about the food you eat, and to eat what is required to keep your body healthy. Do not starve yourself. This is a common symbol for people who are damaging their body through excessive dieting.

BAR

Bars symbolize socializing.

Getting drunk in a bar symbolizes repression of feelings as alcohol desensitizes you.

BAREFOOT

Being *barefoot* in a dream indicates having cold feet with regard to the subject matter of the dream. The subject is given by other symbols in the dream. For example, finding yourself barefoot in the lobby of a hotel with your partner, is about how your reception at birth (hotel) is holding you back from moving forward (barefoot) in your relationship today (with your partner in dream).

BARN

A *barn* symbolizes your digestive system or colon. For example, steaming hay in a barn or a moldy barn indicates you have the condition candida albicans.

BARRIER

A *barrier* that acts like a fence means you suppress your feelings. This is used to mark your personal space. In dreams this is a symbol of sharing and indicates suppression of feelings. You do not share your feelings with others and more importantly you do not acknowledge your feelings yourself. Feelings come from your heart and persistent suppression can lead to health problems in this area. Also look for symbols to do with your head such as roofs or being up a height as these dreams are often asking you to move your centre of consciousness down from your head and into your heart.

A **barrier** at a check point such as a customs post is about expanding your consciousness. See *Customs Post*.

An **obstacle on your path** acting like a barrier indicates that you are blocking your progress with regard to the subject matter of the dream. This is regardless of the fact that you did not put the obstacle there in the dream. If you know who put it there then you are letting the influence of that person block you from doing what you need to do. If it is non-personal, such as wet cement on the pavement, you need to improve the health of your colon in order to continue in the direction of your goal.

BARRISTER

Anyone with a title in a dream is a guide and you always have the ability they are displaying in the dream. A **barrister** is the senior counselor in a court of law. The dream is saying that you have the ability to counsel others. You are a counselor. Quite often in these dreams a woman will appear prominently.

BASEMENT

A **basement** indicates your subconscious or something that is below your conscious awareness. It is buried below a level which you can see.

BASKET

A **baby basket** indicates your reproductive system and uterus in particular.

A **flower basket** can also indicate your reproductive system.

BASKETBALL

A **basketball** signifies ideals / goals. Career is indicated by the black and orange color combination so the dream may refer to your career goals.

A **basketball game** is about how you pursue your goals in life.

BAT

A bat that flies signifies you have an angry or negative mind with regard to the subject matter of the dream. It also signifies you have special abilities – see **Flying** for more.

A **bat** or club indicates that your male side controls your attitude to life or the subject matter of the dream.

BATH

A **bath** can represent the uterus. This is because water represents life and a bath is a vessel that holds water.

For the same reason as above the **bath plug hole** can represent the cervix.

A **dark shadow** coming from the bath plug hole can indicate a condition such as endometriosis.

Being a place of cleansing a **bath** can also represent the need to eliminate some idea you are holding onto or indeed physical elimination.

BATHROOM

A **bathroom** represents purity, cleansing of ideas or attitudes and physical elimination. This is particularly true when attention is not drawn to a specific device in the bathroom.

In dreams about the physical body the **bathroom** can also symbolize the liver, kidneys or colon. Emphasis is often given to specific items in the bathroom in this case. In this case the **bathroom taps** would symbolize your kidneys. The *waste pipes* and *drains* represent your colon. The *toilet bowl* represents your bowel. Any sort of *straining device*, particularly one using organic material would indicate your liver.

Bathroom walls indicate the walls of your intestines. If the paper or plaster is falling off the walls it indicates the lining of your intestines is damaged.

BATHTUB

A *bathtub* can represent the uterus. This is because water represents life and a bath is a vessel that holds water. A dark shadow spreading from the plughole can indicate endometriosis.

Being a place of cleansing a *bathtub* can also represent the need to eliminate a negative influence in your life.

BATON

A *baton* is a male symbol and indicates that you have a male energy approach to life or the subject matter of the dream. You need to restore balance between male and female aspects of yourself. Female energy allows you to forgive, listen, have two-way communication, lead and more. All aspects worthy of developing.

BATTERY

A *battery*, being a pump, represents your heart and circulatory system since the heart is your body's pump.

A *dead battery* or *battery trouble* means you are not doing what is required to keep your heart engaged and healthy. We easily accept that our heart needs the right diet and exercise but forget that our heart also needs emotional expression for optimum health.

BAY

A *bay*, being part of the sea where life originated, represents your life. It can also be about your spiritual life since ultimately life is a spiritual journey.

BAY WINDOW

A *bay window*, particularly if it is in your mother's house, represents the womb. The dream is showing you how you are still affected today by something from way back in the past. Because these dreams are about being born, they often include symbols that indicate something precious you brought with you on this life journey. It is something that for you, gives expression of your soul and makes you feel connected to life.

BEACH

A *beach* represents your spiritual approach or your approach to life itself. The sea represents life since that is where life on earth began. The beach is the approach to the sea so symbolically represents your approach to life. Any unpolluted water in a dream can also indicate your spiritual side.

BEAR

A *bear*, due to its brown color, symbolizes your elimination system.

BED

Beds symbolize your reproductive system, sex, rest, meditation and astral activities.

A *bed* can symbolize your reproductive system since most procreation takes place in one.

Beds also symbolize your sexuality. This can occur if you repress your sexuality. This is nothing to do with sexual preference. For instance, if you view your gender in a negative way as a result of past trauma, present career or any other reason, your dreams will consistently ask you to accept your sexuality as a fundamental part of your nature. For example, *driving a bed* down the street is asking you to get in touch with your sexual energy and include it in your pursuits. Don't confuse this with sexual preference. Our creative energy is intricately linked with our sexual energy and is affected by any blocks we may have in this area.

A *raised bed* is more likely to be about meditation and spiritual matters. When this is the subject matter the bed is often not in a bedroom.

For obvious reasons *beds* can also indicate you need rest.

BEDROOM

A bedroom, like a bed, symbolizes your reproductive system, sex, rest, meditation and astral activities. See *Bed*.

A *bedroom* symbolizes your reproductive system as sexual activity takes place there.

A *communal bedroom* indicates the uterus in particular as the uterus is the only place in the body where another person can sleep.

A *dirty bedroom* indicates you see sex as dirty. This could be due to an overly strict or religious upbringing that puts a stigma on the sexual act.

A *stain on the bedroom floor* indicates you feel guilty with regard to sex. This could be due to an overly strict or religious upbringing that puts a stigma on the sexual act. It can also be triggered by strong religious beliefs where indulging in pleasures of the body is seen as evil.

Bedrooms are also a place for rest and sleep and as such can symbolize meditation and astral activities. When this is the case, other symbols in the dream will indicate which activities.

Someone breaking down your bedroom door to attack you can be indicative of sexual abuse.

BEHIND

When a dream places something *behind* you, it is symbolically putting it in the past. This is in much the same way you would encourage someone to deal with a traumatic event and ask them to put it behind them. In other words do not keep looking at it day after day.

If someone is *behind you chasing you.* it means something from the past still has a power over you today. While you may feel you are past it, the dreams shows that you are still expending energy trying to get distance between you and it. The feeling that comes up in dreams like this is the key. The dream is attempting to show you that there is a link between the past trauma and that feeling today. If it is a parent, it means that you still have issues with that parent today.

BEIGE

Beige symbolizes the need for tolerance / acceptance. Quite often beige appears in dreams as an antidote to white. It asks the dreamer to be less critical of themselves and others. A woman wearing a beige blouse in a dream asks you to accept your mother as she is. Through doing this you are developing tolerance and growing through it. Parents are always the most difficult to deal with. Life is designed to be that way. I will accept my mother / father if they will just …. fill in the blank yourself. That intolerance will cause you to dream of beige or cream. If a person tells lies about you do you set out to correct your image in their eyes of everyone they spoke to? That will cause you to dream of beige or cream. Don't focus on controlling others. Rather, focus on being the person you know you are.

BELFAST

Belfast is noted the world over for the opposing views of it inhabitants (Unionists and Republicans). As such in dreams, it symbolizes that you are at polar opposites with regard to the subject matter. For example, if you and your partner are traveling to Belfast it means you and your partner are polar opposites in the relationship – this leads to major conflict.

BELL

A *door bell* ringing is a request to open the door on an opportunity that has come your way. If the door is at the front of the house the opportunity is something new in your future. If the doorbell is at the back of the house the opportunity has to do with resolving something from the past.

A *church bell* is a reminder that life is a spiritual journey. You are being asked to favor the spiritual path at this time

BENCH

To dream of a *bench* can indicate that you are judgmental with regard to the subject matter of the dream.

BEREAVEMENT

Bereavement symbolizes your need to eliminate negative influence from the past. An aspect of you has to die be-

fore another aspect can find expression. For example, to dream of the death of your father means you need to eliminate the negative influence of your father.

BERTH

To dream of a *berth* or berthing a ship or boat is a pun on birth and is about the start of your life journey.

BIBLE

The *bible* symbolizes spirituality or religion. These are not the same thing. Spirituality is expression of your soul and includes things like writing, singing, music, teaching, leading and more.

BICYCLE

Bicycles represent your heart, circulatory system and emotions, due to the fact that balance is required to use them. Your heart requires balanced sharing of feelings.

BIG WHEEL

A *big wheel* or *Ferris Wheel* is likely to be about being caught on a karmic cycle. This is where you miss the opportunities in life to repay the karmic debts you owe. The result of which is the need to plan another life to pay the debts you had planned to pay this time around. A Big wheel journey symbolizes this perfectly as it just does a complete cycle and you end up back where you started.

BILLBOARD

A *billboard* projects a message into the minds of others and in dreams symbolizes that you have the power to project your mind. This can be used for a number of things.

The first is that you can use your

strong intellect to rise mentally above a situation. You don't always do this though!

Another thing it is useful for is hypnosis, where you project your mind onto a client to help them 'think' their way through an issue. Literally your thoughts direct the thoughts of the client.

Another use, although controversial in some circles is absent healing. Here you project your mind onto the client and use your thoughts to think them well. The connection between the brain and the immune system has been established. Absent healing projects positive healing thoughts onto the client with the intention that the healing takes root.

Lastly this strong mind can be used to project thoughts to others, including groups of others. See flying.

BINDING

Binding indicates karma you are bound to. For example, to dream of holding a book whose binding is not complete indicates you are obliged through karma to give channeled readings. Readings will complete your karma.

BIRD

Birds often symbolize goals or ideals as they are something we usually have to look up to. This is true even if the bird in the dream is on the ground or dead.

In mythology an *eagle* is said to fly so high that it can see the past present and future from its high vantage point. Due to this an eagle in a dream indicates that you have the gift of prophecy. *High flying birds* indicate the same thing.

An *ostrich* indicates there is something you are refusing to face.

A *dead bird*, other than a crow or other carrion bird is a request to put life into the pursuit of your goals. Don't just sit and wait for them to come to you. You need to get the off the ground.

A *chicken* indicates your relationship, as chicken is often used as a term of endearment.

A *frozen chicken* indicates that you are being cold in your relationship and need to be warmer towards your partner.

A *crow* or other *carrion bird*, because they eat dead and rotting flesh, can represent cancer. Bear in mind that dreams warn of cancer in plenty of time to do what it takes to prevent it from developing. A crow burrowing into a part of your body indicates where the cancer is likely to present itself. If left untreated it will continue to cause more and more harm to the body.

A *dead crow* is a good symbol and indicates that your immune system is successfully fighting off the cancer cells.

A *crow* can also represent depression. In these dreams the crow is more likely to be on its own and circling overhead, perhaps over the rooftop of a building. In this case you often feel fear when facing the crow. The crow often appears alone as that reflects how you are at present.

A *bird flying on one wing* is a symbol for alcoholism due to the phrase, "A bird never flew on one wing." This is a common response when asked if you need another drink. This dream shows you a bird flying on one wing to encourage you to say no to the next drink.

BIRTH

To dream of you or someone else *giving birth* means a new aspect of yourself is about to be born. As above, it is your responsibility to develop this side of yourself. This is always a positive dream, as to allow a new aspect of yourself to flourish you must let go of whatever kept it suppressed. This dream usually comes after doing some developmental work on yourself.

BIRTHDAY

To dream of a *birthday* or *birthday present* is a dream's way of bringing you back to your own birth. This is regardless of whose birthday is being celebrated in the dream. The rest of the dream will be about how the circumstances of your birth affect you today. This can be positive or negative.

BLACK

Black on its own indicates negativity along the lines of fear, anxiety, resentment, hatred or guilt. A *black stain*, for example, would indicate guilt. When mixed with other colors, black adds a negative aspect to their meaning.

Black and white together indicates you have a tendency to see life or the subject matter of the dream in black and white terms. This comes across as being intolerant or extremist. You see others are either with you or against you. There is no neutral position allowed. You need to be more tolerant. Another difficulty with being black and white about things is that you judge things as being either in the *right* or *wrong* camp. If presented with a third option it must also fit into the right or wrong camp but only one idea can fit into the *right* one. In order to open your mind to something new, you have to first manage to move the current *right* idea into the *wrong* camp and that's a big task to ask. If you allow for more than just right and wrong you can have many shades in-between. Then you can have something that is *almost right*. Not being able to eliminate concepts that are holding you back, eventually leads the body into not being able to eliminate waste matter efficiently and manifests as a slow moving colon along with the issues that can go along with that.

Black and red together indicate anger – negative passion.

Black and orange as a color combination in dreams indicates ambition driven out of fear and always indicates career. Tigers have this color combination so often symbolize career in dreams.

BLACKBOARD

A *blackboard* in a classroom indicates you have a spiritual leadership ability to work with groups and help them to expand their consciousness to take them out of the dark. Spiritual leadership works through empowering others to achieve for themselves, rather than doing something for them. It also indicates another ability which works in combination with your leadership. You also have the ability to project your mind so that when you are engaged with others, they connect completely with what you are saying. It is like you are putting your hands inside their heads and rearranging their thought process.

BLIND

To dream of being *blind* can be indicative of you being blind in a past life. If you or someone else is blind in the dream it can also indicate you are unwilling to see or look for the solution to a current problem.

BLONDE

Blonde as a color indicates tolerance and acceptance.

If it is *blonde hair* in the dream, it signifies the character is a guide. Hair represents thoughts so the blonde hair represents purity of thought.

BLUE

Blue symbolizes expression and includes spirituality, religion, art, culture, philosophy and attitude to life itself. It is one of the most common colors in dreams and is used to show your attitude to the subject matter. If other colors are mixed with it, you are asked to do what it takes to remove them from your philosophy if they are negative (dark or polluted colors), and to add them if they are positive colors. For example, *dark blue* or *navy,* a mix of blue (philosophy) and black (negativity), indicates a negative philosophy of life or attitude towards the subject matter of the dream, while *blue and white* asks you to lighten your attitude or philosophy with regard to the subject matter of the dream.

Blue and gold asks you to regard your spiritual healing ability as positive in your life.

Blue and silver asks you to regard your psychic / intuitive ability as positive in your life.

BOAT

A *boat* can represent your physical body. Is the boat in good shape? What is the dream emphasizing about the boat?

A *boat journey* represents your life journey. Check out to see what else is significant in the dream as this is how the dream comments on where you are on your journey.

If your *partner is with you on a boat,* the dream is about your relationship.

A *small boat* can indicate you as a child but it can also indicate that you feel on your own when navigating through life.

A *speed boat*, being a source of great power, indicates you have the gift of hands on healing. Literally you have a source of great power at your disposal.

A *lifeboat* indicates you have the ability to rescue lost souls. This is an unusual gift and is used while your body sleeps. In actuality you can traverse the astral plane with ease. We all go there when asleep and souls who are crossing over after death can find themselves lost and confused. You and others like you specialize in finding them and helping them make their journey. You particularly use this when someone close to you dies. Apart from dreams of rescuing someone at sea, most people with this ability are blissfully unaware of it.

BODY ARMOR

Body armor indicates that you do not allow others to get close to you. This is always about your heart and emotions. The idea is that by keeping people at a distance you cannot get hurt. The dream shows you this to ask you to open up and allow others to get close. It is not healthy for your heart to suppress your feelings over a long period of time. Ideally you are open and honest about your feelings both to yourself and to others.

BOG
Bogs symbolize that your blood is not being cleansed properly by your lymph system.

BOILER
A *boiler* indicates your heart and circulatory system. Symbols of fire are always linked with the heart. A boiler uses fire and also pumps water out to the extremities of a building and back. The pump and circulation are symbolic of your heart and circulation system.

BOILING
Boiling indicates anger. For example, a dream of milk boiling over indicates issues with mother (milk) need to be dealt with.

BONNET
A *bonnet* or *hood* being the access to a car engine is about your heart. An *open bonnet* is a request to open up to your feelings or open your heart. Having the *bonnet* open in the rain is a healing symbol as this indicates letting life into your heart. The dream is asking you to do this in waking life.

BOOK
To dream of a *book on a specific subject* means you have knowledge of that subject area. This is particularly the case when you have the book in your hands in the dream, and even more so when it is not a book that you are familiar with, or is not available in reality.

To dream of *many books* or a *library* means you have a counseling ability.

In this case the books represent a depth of knowledge or wisdom that you have. This depth of knowledge can be used to help others deepen their knowledge of themselves. You have this counseling ability regardless of whether you have had formal training. Note that many countries require you to have a formal qualification before practicing counseling officially under the counselor banner.

Books on a table again mean you have a counseling ability (see many books above). However, in this case you are being told that you are responsible for developing this ability to a level where you can formally practice it.

A *book's binding* is about karma you are bound to.

A *book's spine* is about your spine. Threads in the spine would indicate nerves in your spine.

BORDER POST
A *border post* is where an official determines whether you have everything required in order to pass from one state or country to another. This symbolizes the transition from one state of consciousness to another. This is especially true if you are asked questions by an official at the border post. If the country or state you are moving into is bigger than the one you are leaving, your new state of consciousness is expanded. If it is smaller you are doing something that is limiting you.

It is common for the official to ask you what you will work at in the new location. They may even suggest a career and a salary. If they do, look up the career and salary in this book as they are symbolic of what you are being asked to do in order to develop your new state of consciousness.

BOTTLE

A *bottle* is a common symbol for the kidneys.

A *broken bottle* indicates damage to the kidneys. The damage is likely to be indicated by the location where the dream takes place or by food types or drinks being shown specifically in the dream.

BOUTIQUE

A *boutique* reminds you that you chose your role or attitude towards something current in your life. It is not preordained that you must only look at it from one perspective. Are you playing the role you think is expected of you? Why do you think you are entitled to the attitude you have adopted?

BOWL

A *bowl* or any vessel that carries water can represent the uterus.

A *mixing bowl* represents the bowel because it is a pun on bowel and also because food stuffs are mixed in it. The foods being mixed in the bowl are indicative of foods you are being asked to eliminate from your diet.

A *toilet bowl* can indicate elimination. If, however, there are food items blocking the toilet bowl or visible in it, you are being asked to eliminate these food items from your diet. For example, a milk carton blocking the toilet would indicate the need to eliminate dairy products from your diet.

A *cracked toilet bowl* warns of potential damage to your bowel. Again look for food items being specifically referenced or symbolized using color and eliminate them from your diet.

BOX

A **box,** being a container, symbolizes containment or limitation. It is a specifically strong symbol of limitation as it also has *four* sides and a *lid* both of which also indicate limitation. The rest of the dream will indicate what has you boxed in.

A *box*, through English slang usage, can also indicate the womb. An *egg box* in this context would indicate the ovaries or reproductive cycle. Running out of eggs in an egg box indicates the end of your fertile period for having children.

A *boxed gift* indicates it is time for you to explore a new and positive aspect of yourself. Open the box (remove limitation) to discover the gift.

A person *giving a boxed gift* is a guide. Always heed the advice they give you in the dream.

BOX ROOM

A small *box room* at the end of a hallway can represent the uterus. Indeed any claustrophobic location can but this symbol is particularly strong because the hallway also symbolizes the womb.

BOXING MATCH

This indicates you are going through a period of conflict.

When a *blow to the head* is emphasized you are being warned of potential stroke. Look for other symbols to indicate the circulatory system.

BOY

A *boy* can indicate your male side or that you had issues with your father when you were the age of the boy in the dream. We each have both male and female aspects to ourselves.

Dreams always encourage you to restore balance to this energy mix. In fact that is one of the main purposes of your life.

BRAKE

Dreams with *car brakes* normally have to do with the brake not working efficiently. This usually means that you are doing something that is blocking the achievement of your goals. You are either doing something counter productive or your fears are slowing you down from getting to where you need to be.

BREAD

To dream of *bread* can indicate a number of things. *Taking home the bread* would symbolize your income. The rest of the dream is likely to be about how your career or a financial burden is affecting something else in your life.

Soggy bread or *large amounts of bread* indicate that bread is clogging up your digestive system. If you find you have an intolerance to particular foods it can often be due to eating something, such as bread, that slows down your digestive system. Once slowed down, other foods have time to literally rot and produce toxins in your gut.

Brown bread is the Cockney rhyming slang for dead and indicates this in a dream. Something else in the dream will alert you to what you need to change in your life today.

Toast bread also is a pun on death. In this case, however, the connection with the heart is established as fire is required to make toast. Look for other symbols to indicate changes you need to make.

BREAK

To dream of being on a *holiday break* is a request to take it easy and allow some healing for your body and mind.

BREAKFAST

Breakfast is a meal time so the dream is about your eating habit or your digestive system. The word itself comes from the two words break and fast so this dream could be a request for you to eat well and avoid dieting or skipping meals. Look for someone underweight or skinny in the same dream.

BREAST

Breasts symbolize nurturing in dreams. For example, if a friend has exposed breasts in a dream it is a request for you to use your nurturing / leadership abilities in social settings.

BREASTPLATE

A *breastplate* indicates that you do not allow others to get close to you. This is always about your heart and emotions. The idea is that by keeping people at a distance you cannot get hurt. The dream shows you this to ask you to open up and allow others to get close. It is not healthy for your heart to suppress your feelings over a long period of time. Ideally you are open and honest about your feelings both to yourself and to others.

BRIDGE

A *bridge* is for spanning a divide and as such in dreams it suggests you need a reconciliation of different aspects of yourself. For example, dreams of bridges can be triggered if you are thinking of leaving work to start out on your own but are troubled by issues of confidence.

Bridges can also indicate reconciliation with others. In this case you are likely to know of the waking life issue and the person or persons involved. However, it is common to dream of the people with whom reconciliation is required. Sometimes the relevant person is shown in symbolic form. John dreamt he was trying to hurry across a rope bridge while meteorites were falling. His path was blocked by a man coming in the opposite direction. In this dream the man represents John's father, a man whom John feels has obstructed his path in life. The dream is telling John that in order to move forward he must reconcile a clash of ideals (indicated by meteorites falling) with his father.

Bridges can also indicate a transition. While on a bridge you are neither where the bridge starts nor where it leads to. It is common for these dreams to occur when going through a transition between stages of your life or doing some therapeutic work on yourself that will lead to a positive outcome.

Lastly a *bridge* can indicate that you have a counseling ability. The first rule of interpretation is that you are everything in the dream. If you are a bridge your special ability is to help people span a divide which symbolically indicates reconciliation issues whether with themselves or with others.

BROWN

Brown being the color of earth indicates you need to see the subject matter of the dream as practical. It is common to see brown alongside spiritual gifts in dreams. Here the brown is asking you not to deny your spiritual ability. The gift is practical and you need to bring it down to earth. For example a brown church door asks you not to create practical opportunities to include your spiritual aspects in your life on the planet.

Dull brown indicates negative materiality where you are too focused on earthly things. This unenlightened philosophy leads to a denial of spirit and ultimately depression. If a dull brown coat is worn by your father in your dream it means that you picked up your materialistic philosophy of life from him.

Brown can also indicate issues with your colon.

BRUISE

To be *bruised* in a dream indicates emotional trauma. While the trauma is likely to be in the past you are dreaming about it because it is still affecting your actions today.

BUDDHA

Buddha symbolizes your spiritual level in a dream. You are either at an enlightened level of awareness or have the potential to reach that stage in this life time. Buddha is also particularly known for his spiritual leadership so it also means that you have that ability.

BUFFET

To dream of a *buffet* is a request to be selective of the food you eat, and to eat what is required to keep your body healthy. Don't starve yourself. This is a common symbol for people who are damaging their body through excessive dieting.

BUG

Bugs represent things that are bugging you in reality.

BULDOZER

A *bulldozer*, like any other earth moving machine, is about your colon and elimination system. This is due to the colon being the dirt track of your body.

BUNSEN BURNER

A *Bunsen burner*, being a flame source, is about your heart and emotions. If the dream is highlighting a physical problem with the burner, it is about your physical heart otherwise the dream is focusing on your emotions and is most likely asking you to be more openly expressive.

BURGER KING

To dream of *Burger King* or any fast food restaurant is about the need to speed up your digestive system. It is a symbolic antidote to a sluggish digestive system with *fast food*. To emphasize the healing the dream will often place you in the drive through which provides *faster* fast food and is usually very brightly lit in the dream.

BURGLAR ALARM

A *burglar alarm* symbolizes your immune system. For example, repeatedly *trying to reset a burglar alarm* in your dream can indicate an auto immune disorder such as multiple sclerosis (MS).

BURIAL PLACE

A *burial place* indicates the digestive and elimination system. This is regardless of whether the burial place is for an animal, pet or human. The color brown (see colors) and the earthiness of the burial place are sufficient to indicate the digestive system. Any dream where digging into the earth / dirt is involved implies the dirt track of your body, which is your colon. However, a morbid symbolic link exists because both the digestive system and a burial place are used to receive dead meat.

BUS

Dreams including a *bus* are often about your life journey especially if it is a *school bus*.

The *bus number* is significant in commenting on how you are currently doing on your journey. For example, a number 17 is about your individual spiritual path, whereas a 47 indicates that you are limiting your spiritual journey.

Getting the *wrong bus* means you are being asked to change your direction in life. Again the bus number or the bus's destination will indicate the specific change to be made.

If the bus does not go where it should or takes an *unexpected route* you are again being asked to take stock of where you are going in life. Is where you are going in line with what your dreams are asking you to do?

Getting off a bus can indicate birth through symbolically showing you enter into the world. The rest of the dream will comment on the circumstances of your birth and how it affects you today.

A *bus stop* is where a journey starts and ends and as such can indicate the beginning or end of your life journey or a phase of your life journey. This is not usually a health warning.

Being upstairs on a *double decker bus* indicates that you tend to rationalize decisions rather than follow your heart. Literally you live in your head, upstairs in your body. The dream is encouraging you to listen to your feelings.

Waves washing over the top of a bus indicate you rationalize, due to some previous emotional turmoil, the idea being that closing your heart and retreating into your head will protect you from similar pain in the future.

An *open top bus* is asking you to open your mind to new things.

To dream of a *bus driver*, whether you are the driver or not, means you have an ability to work with groups of people in a counseling or coaching fashion. Like the bus driver you can bring the group from where they are to where they need to be.

Waiting in line for a bus means you have a sluggish digestive system. Literally food is waiting in line in your colon instead of traveling at normal speed through it. The dream is asking you to do something to speed it up. For example, remove the foods from your diet that slow it down. The foods in question are often indicated in the same dream. See the chapter on *Digest This* for a complete description.

A *bus* can sometimes be used as a pun for bust and therefore be about how loved and nurtured you felt from your mother. For example, a dream where a Fiat Bambino car had crashed across the front of a bus told the dreamer that she wasn't planned. From her mother's perspective she was an accident that she was forced to take responsibility for. The dreamer, at age 45, was still affected by this reception at birth.

BUS DRIVER

A *bus driver* indicates you have a leadership / teaching ability that works well with groups. It means this because a bus driver takes many people from where they are to where they need to

be at the same time.

CAGE

A *cage* symbolizes your heart and emotions. Specifically it means that you suppress your feelings. You keep your heart in a cage so that others cannot get close to you. The logic behind the action is that if people cannot get close they cannot hurt your feelings. Over time you can become so good at suppressing your feelings that you do not even acknowledge them to yourself. For example, a dream where a woman reluctantly releases you from a cage means that you are reluctant to open up or share your feelings with others.

CAMERA

Being a device for reproducing images a *camera* indicates your reproductive system.

CANADA

Canada indicates expansion of consciousness through dharma or compassion. This is often referred to as living in a state of grace and is the way Jesus proposed we live. On this path you choose what you know will be spiritually beneficial to you and not necessarily what is logical. This meaning does not hold if you are from Canada.

CANDLE

Candles indicate you have an intuitive / psychic ability. With your inner light (candle) you can see where others can not.

CAR

A *car*, being a physical structure, often represents your body. In dreams where it does represent the body there is often emphasis on a particular part of the car or type of car.

Car can be a pun on Karma and indicate that you are on a karmic path. The dream will show you what is holding you on this path and what you need to do to move past it.

A *car battery* represents your heart or circulatory system since a battery is an electron pump, the heart is your body's pump.

A *dead battery* or *battery trouble* means you are not doing what is required to keep your heart engaged and healthy. We easily accept that our heart needs the right diet and exercise, but forget that our heart also needs emotional expression for optimum health.

A *car choke* is a pun on choking or suppressing the expression of feelings from your heart. You need to be more honest with your feelings.

The car *engine* represents your heart as the engine is the heart of the car. Trouble with the engine is a health warning to do with the heart and circulatory system.

A *bonnet* or *hood* being the access to the engine is also about your heart. An *open bonnet* is a request to open up to your feelings or open your heart. Having the *bonnet* open in the rain is a healing symbol as this indicates letting life into your heart. The dream is asking you to do this in waking life.

Oil is to the engine as blood is to the heart and so indicates blood in a dream. The most common symbol with oil in dreams is the *engine leaking oil*. This represents anemia as anemia is a loss of red blood cells.

The *car roof* is about the brain or mind. An *open top car* is asking you to open your mind to something new in

your life. If you have recently 'made up your mind' about something you are being asked to think again. If something has come your way and you are dismissing it, you are being asked to think again. The rain coming into an open top car is asking you to open your mind to letting life in. This is true even if in the dream the rain gets in because the roof won't close. This is saying, "Don't close your mind."

The *wing mirror* represents your reproductive system as a mirror reproduces images. It is unlikely to only have one symbol indicating the reproductive system so you may find the car is *Morris Minor* or other car that is no longer in production. The symbolism in that is that such cars are no longer being reproduced which is again pointing to a reproduction system – yours. Another pun in the Morris Minor name is the word minor which means child which yet again points to your reproduction system. A mirror on a *Fiat Bambino* would also be the same as Bambino means child in Italian. Lastly a *rear view mirror* also means your reproductive system because of the mirror and the pun on rear or rearing. You are being asked to look at (view) something in the past that is causing you to have issues with having or raising children. The issue itself can be any number of things and is likely to be given by other symbols in the same dream.

Headlights would indicate the eyes as they allow you to see. However, they also indicate an intuitive ability as they allow you to see in the dark. So while others can't really figure out what is going on, your intuition kicks in and you appear to get direction out of nowhere.

The *trunk* represents two things. Firstly it can indicate your stomach / digestive system as the trunk is so commonly used to hold grocery items. Your stomach is the first place your body holds food when you put it into your body.

The *trunk* can also indicate the womb for this reason. Viewing the car as symbolizing the body, the trunk is a small place within the car, with no windows and which is used to transport smaller items. The womb is a small place with no windows which is used to bring smaller bodies onto the planet. In these dreams it is also common to find yourself driving the car out of an underground car park into the daylight. This dream can be about your own birth.

The *windshield* protects you from the weather, in particular the rain, and so in dreams it indicates protecting yourself from life. The dream is asking you to get more into life. Don't just wait for things to come to your door. Do something to bring the fun back into your life.

Dreams with *car brakes* normally have to do with the brake not working efficiently. This usually means that you are doing something that is blocking the achievement of your goals. You are either doing something counter productive or your fears are slowing you down from getting to where you need to be.

Car *tires* represent your circulatory system as due to the tires being circular and the fact that they need to be pumped, they are analogous to the heart being a pump. The tires being flat would mean there is little emotional expression in your life. You are just plodding along with no real passion on

a daily basis.

Tire lug nuts indicate the immune system. The lug nuts keep the tires safe on the car. Since tires represent the circulatory system, the lug nuts represent what keeps the circulatory system healthy and that represents the immune system.

The *steering wheel* represents two things. Firstly the circulatory system due to the wheel's circular nature and secondly, it is a reminder that you have the ability to control the direction of your life. If you are having problems driving, when the *steering is fully locked* while driving around corners, it indicates your alcohol consumption is inhibiting the direction in which your life is going. The pun here is *locked* referring to being drunk.

Driving a car is about striving towards your goals as we use cars to take us from where we are to where we need to be. Symbolically this indicates moving towards our goals. A goal can be an obvious target like getting a qualification or a specific job. It can also be something less tangible like wanting to be a more attentive parent. See *Driving* for more.

A *powerful car* indicates you are a spiritual healer. You have great power running through your body (car).

CAR PARK

A *car park* symbolizes you have a choice of roles or attitudes with regard to the subject matter of the dream. For example, to dream of parking your white car and choosing a cream one asks you to drop your controlling nature (white) and adopt a more tolerant one (cream).

CAR UNLOCKED

To dream of your *car unlocked* is a request for you to go ahead and let your guard down. If things are stolen from the car, it shows that you expect to lose out if you are open. If the dream shows nothing was stolen it is much the same and shows you that you will not lose out if you open up.

CARRIAGE

A *carriage* such as a train carriage is usually a pun on being in the womb. As adults not involved with psychology or therapy, we can find it difficult to believe that we have any memory from that far back in our life, but we do. We perceive with more than our brains, particularly when under 2 years old, and can carry emotional scars from the womb if we nearly lost our life through a mis*carriage* or felt threatened with abortion.

CASH

Cash can be indicative of the amount of energy you are willing to commit to the subject matter of the dream or it can be a request to commit energy to it.

Petty cash often indicates that you do not value the subject matter of the dream. For example, to dream of a silver box with petty cash inside, says that you view intuition (silver) as petty or that the information you get that way is petty. Hardly worth sharing because it is of no real value. You need to place a far higher value on your ability.

A *woman at a cash register* indicates your mother placed a price on her love.

CASTLE

A *castle* symbolizes past life influences, given that it is unlikely you live in one now! It can often mean that your attitude towards the subject matter of the dream is out of date.

CAT

Cats often indicate your gut or stomach. Cat gut is used for many things and we also have the expression *my stomach is cat*. In these dreams, other symbols for the digestive system will often occur such as dreaming of *a cat in the kitchen*, references to biting or the mouth or references to particular foods. As with most animals the location of the cat is most significant. Kitchens always indicate the digestive system as a kitchen is linked with eating and food preparation. A *cat being eaten by a snake* or being chased by one is a warning of stomach cancer. A *cat climbing the wallpaper* or scratching you is indicative of acid reflux.

Cats, especially if black, can also indicate guilt due to the fact that the cat-o-nine-tails was used on ships to purge sailors of their sins.

A *cat in the bedroom* or scratching a bed post would indicate guilt with regard to sexual activity.

A *cat in the bedroom wardrobe* indicates that guilt (the cat) is affecting your attitude (clothes in wardrobe) towards sex (the bedroom). This can even be the other way around where your attitude towards the sexual act is causing guilt. For instance, if you were sexually abused in your childhood this could cause you to adopt a distasteful attitude towards sex which causes you to feel guilt because you don't want to have sex with your partner.

CAVE

A *cave* is a good symbol for the womb and brings you back to when you were in your mother's body.

A *cave* can also indicate a feeling of isolation or an introverted nature.

CAVITY

A *tooth cavity* is about problems with your reproductive system. If you do not currently have a problem the dream is a warning of a problem manifesting.

Large cavities in dreams symbolize your lungs and respiratory system. Your lungs are a large cavity in your body.

CEILING

Ceilings can symbolize a limitation as in *I reached the ceiling of my ability*. As they are always above your head ceilings can symbolize the mind and / or spiritual aspects of yourself. A high ceiling asks you to create a greater space in your mind for the subject matter of the dream. A low ceiling lets you know that your thinking on that subject matter is restricted.

CELL PHONE

A *cell phone* indicates you are clairaudient. Clairaudience is a gift where you literally hear messages from the spirit world. Mostly the messages are heard as lines from songs popping into your head. The segment of the song will repeat over and over making you wonder why you can't get it out of your head. Once you accept it is a message it immediately changes to a line from another song or stops if it is the end of the message. It can also work through hearing lines from movies.

CEMENT

Cement or a *cement path* is typically about your colon or elimination system. The dream is saying that food has hardened in your colon and is caked onto the walls. You need to do something to eliminate it. This inhibits the flow of waste matter and the absorption of nutrients through the walls of the colon.

CENTRAL HEATING

Central heating is an excellent symbol for your heart and circulatory system. Buildings represent your body and the central heating system circulates throughout the building from a central location (your heart).

CHAIN

A *chain* represents a karmic obligation. For example a silver chain indicates you are obliged to develop and use your psychic ability to help others.

CHAIR

A *wooden chair* symbolizes your colon and elimination system as it is where you park your bottom!

CHANDELIER

Chandeliers are a source of light and also contain crystals. Light sources indicate you have a psychic / intuitive ability. This comes as a feeling where you just know something without any logical reason for knowing it. The crystal component of the symbol emphasizes the preciseness of your ability. It is or has the potential to be crystal clear.

The word *chandelier* can also be used in dreams as a pun on *channeler* so indicates you are a channel.

CHANNEL

To dream of a *channel* means that you too are a channel – you can communicate with spirits. Puns on the word also mean this. For example, the English Channel or Channel Islands.

CHASING

If someone behind you is *chasing* you, it means something from the past still has a power over you today. While you may feel you are past it, the dreams shows that you are still expending energy trying to get distance between you and it. The feeling that comes up in dreams like this is the key. The dream is attempting to show you that there is a link between the past trauma and that feeling today. If it is a parent it means that you still have issues with that parent today.

CHEST

A *chest* that is essentially a large spatial cavity, such as a wooden chest or chest of drawers, symbolizes your lungs as they are the spatial cavity within your body. This is especially true if the chest is described as being at chest level.

A *human chest* can symbolize your chest. For example, if a crow is burying itself into your chest in a dream it is a warning of breast cancer.

A *treasure chest* symbolizes your spiritual nature and spiritual gifts.

CHILDREN

A *child* in a dream can indicate you at that age. Commonly it will be one of your own children in the dream. A *boy* can indicate your male side or that you had issues with your father when you were the age of the boy in the dream. Likewise to dream of a *girl* can indi-cate your female side or that you had issues with your mother in childhood. We each have both male and female aspects to ourselves. Dreams always encourage you to restore balance to this energy mix. In fact that is one of the main purposes of your life.

If you dream of a *number of children* your age can be indicated by how many children there are. For example, seven children in the dream is about you at the age of 7.

CHIMNEY

A *chimney* is connected to the fireplace so in dreams, like any symbol connected with fire, it is about your heart, circulatory system and emotions. There can be a double connection to smoking being bad for your heart.

CHOPPING

Chopping symbolizes that you are angry / cut-up over the subject matter of the dream.

CHRISTMAS

Christmas is the celebration of the birth of Jesus and in dreams symbolizes your birth – the most important birth when considered from your perspective.

CHURCH

To dream of a *church*, *synagogue, mosque* or other *place of worship* means that the dream is about your spiritual side / idealism. Look for other symbols in the dream to indicate what you are being specifically asked to develop.

CINEMA

A *cinema* represents expansion of life and is present in dreams where you are being shown how to make your life into the bigger picture that is meant for you. Long before television, cinema was the means for news dispersal and letting the people know what existed in the world.

To *exit* the cinema asks you share what you know about life to others – bring it out onto the street.

CIRCLE

A *circle* symbolizes your heart and circulatory system.

CITY

Cities symbolize your mind. This is especially true for capital cities as the word capital comes from the Latin for head.

CLARINET

A *clarinet*, like any musical instrument, symbolizes that you are a channel / medium. You can communicate with spirits. A clarinet is a particularly strong symbol for channeling because it has an opening at both ends. This too is symbolic of a channel. A channel is open to the spirit world and the physical world.

CLASSROOM

A *classroom*, being a place of learning, symbolizes learning about yourself with a view to improving yourself.

CLIFF

A *cliff* indicates that you rationalize with regard to the subject matter of the dream. This may be life in general, if a boat journey or water is the main subject of the dream. Cliffs are up a height from sea level and this symbolizes your consciousness being up in your head and away from your heart. The

purpose of the dream is to point out your rationalizing nature and ask you to move your center of consciousness downwards towards your heart - listen to your heart more.

On a cliff and looking out to sea can also be about your spiritual nature and what you must overcome to achieve your life purpose.

CLOCK

In English slang the heart is referred to as the ticker. Due to this and the fact that *clocks* are circular with hands moving in circular paths they represent the heart, circulation system an emotions in dreams. This still holds if the clock is digital in the dream.

To move in a *clockwise* direction also symbolizes the heart and in this case indicates it would be wise for you to following the advise of the dream.

To move in an *anti-clockwise* direction is telling you that what you are doing is not wise for your heart.

CLOTHES

Clothes represent your attitude towards the subject matter of the dream as we dress to suit our mood or to suit the role we feel obliged to play (e.g. career). In the dream context, we are free to wear anything we want or to even wear nothing. How we dress, particularly the colors worn, can be very revealing. *Old fashioned clothing* would indicate that you have adopted an old fashioned attitude towards the subject matter. This is most likely handed down to you by one or both parents. Being given *hand me downs* belonging to your father would be clearly showing you have adopted your fathers attitude.

Being *naked* in a dream is a very

good symbol and shows that you are being asked to be yourself when it comes to the subject matter of the dream. The disturbing feeling usually associated with this type of dream, indicates the level of discomfort you would have in being yourself. If you are currently undergoing therapy in reality, this type of dream shows it is working well and restoring your sense of identity.

Washing clothes can represent anxieties with regard to the subject matter of the dream.

CLOUD

A *dark cloud* symbolizes depression. A *cloud with a silver lining* indicates you are heading out of depression.

CLOWN

A *clown* symbolizes inner sadness that is not expressed.

CLUB

A *club* is a male symbol and indicates that you have a male energy approach to life or the subject matter of the dream. You need to restore balance between male and female aspects of yourself. Female energy allows you to forgive, listen, have two-way communication, lead and more – all aspects worthy of developing.

A *dance club* symbolizes expression of your heart and indicates you need to listen to and share your feelings more.

A *club or association* can indicate your participation in the club of life. For example, wanting to cancel your membership in a club can indicate a conscious or subconscious wish to leave the planet.

COAL MINE

A *coal mine* is a source of power so can indicate you are a hands-on healer. However a *coal mine* can also be about your colon due to the fact that it is mined from the earth and the half pun coal makes with colon.

COAT

A *coat* indicates that you do not allow others to get close to you. This is always about your heart and emotions. The idea is that by keeping people at a distance you cannot get hurt. The dream shows you this to ask you to open up and allow others to get close. It is not healthy for your heart to suppress your feelings over a long period of time. Ideally you are open and honest about your feelings both to yourself and to others.

COFFEE TABLE

Due to the pun on cough a *coffee table* can symbolize the lungs. Look for other symbols in the dream to back this up. Are there vacuum cleaners, air ducts or ventilation systems in the dream?

Magazines on a coffee table indicate that you have a counseling ability. Indeed the dream is saying that it is your responsibility to develop this ability. Literally it is time for you to put this gift on the table.

COFFIN

A *coffin* symbolizes you need to eliminate negative influence from the past. A negative aspect of you has to die before a positive aspect can find expression. For example, to dream of the death of your father means you need to eliminate negative influences from your father.

COINS

Coins can represent a number of things in a dream, including energy, your heart and circulatory system, intuition and hands-on healing. The value of the coin or indeed the quantity of coins can also be the significant symbol in the dream. For example, 20 cent would be asking you to develop your channeling as a goal while 40 cent would mean you are limiting your goals.

Silver coins, being the color of the moon, indicate you have a strong intuitive ability. Like the moon you are a light in the dark. It is common to find yourself discovering silver coins in a dream or picking them up.

Gold coins, being the color of the sun, indicate that you have a hands-on healing ability. The energy from the sun breathes life into our world. Like the sun you can project energy into others.

Copper coins indicate you have a hands-on healing ability that works well for healing rheumatism.

COLOR

Colors reveal a lot about the meaning of a dream. Look up the individual color to determine its meaning.

COMMUNISM

Communism in dreams indicates sharing of feelings. This comes from the ideal of communism rather than how communism has unfolded in communist countries. The communist motto shows the ideal, *"Each one gives in accordance with his ability and each one takes according to his needs."*

COMPACT DISC

A *compact disc*, when full length, indicates you are on the karmic path. The karmic path is far longer than the dharmic path when it comes to increasing your awareness. A single release on CD indicates the shorter dharmic path.

COMPUTER

Computers symbolize logic, the brain and conditioning. This is because computers are programmed using logic to repeat the same tasks over and over. The computer itself is analogous to the brain while the software that controls it symbolizes the mind.

COMPUTER BAG

A *computer bag* represents conditioning that is holding you back. Computers indicate conditioning (they are programmed to repeat the same task over and over). Bags indicate baggage, which by themselves indicate conditioning from the past.

CONCERT

To dream of a *concert* means you are a channel. Music is inspired by the spirit world and in dreams indicates an ability to communicate with the spirit world.

CONFLICT

A *conflict* symbolizes you are at war with yourself.

COOKER

A *cooker hob*, because it is used to cook food, is about your stomach and digestive system. For example, a dream showing milk boiling over on the cooker and spilling down onto the floor indicates an allergy to milk or dairy products. It would also indicate anger (boiling) that needs to be dealt with.

An *oven* usually symbolizes the uterus.

COPIER

A *copier* reproduces copies of an original and as such symbolizes your reproductive system. Commonly to reinforce its symbolism the copier is located in the bedroom.

COPPER

Copper indicates you have a hands-on healing ability that works well for healing rheumatism.

CORRIDOR

Corridors are used to take you from one room to another. You do not remain in them for very long and as such in dreams they signify you are in a transition.

COUNCIL

Anything that includes the word *council*, including a council house, council flat, county council meeting or official all mean that you have a counseling ability.

COUNSELOR

To dream of a *counselor* means you have a natural counseling ability. Counseling works through your female energy and although it is a requirement to be trained officially in order to practice, it is not learned from books or tuition. It comes through living life on the outside always looking in at others, including your friends, and seeing their individuality and why they get on and what's going on when they don't. From a young age, friends will automatically have sought you out for advice as they are drawn by your aura.

COUNTER

A *counter* is about something you are accountable for. For example, to dream of magazines on a counter asks you to develop your counseling ability. People are counting on you to develop it. It is likely this is part of your life purpose and how you intend to repay your karmic debts.

COUNTRYSIDE

The *countryside* indicates emotions in a dream for two reasons. Firstly the countryside is a vast open space and openness in dreams is about being open with your emotions. Secondly, the countryside is mostly green and this is the color of the heart chakra.

COURT

Courts are where judgment is passed and indicates that you are judgmental with regard to the subject matter of the dream. You probably suffer most under your judgmental hammer.

COURTROOM

Courtrooms indicate you judge yourself harshly.

COURTYARD

A *courtyard* indicates you are judgmental. A *cobbled stone courtyard* indicates your judgmental nature comes from a past life influences.

CRAB

The *crab* is the astrological sign for cancer and in dreams indicates a physical health warning. It does not mean that you have cancer and it is normal for everyone to dream of cancer from time to time. Your immune system is designed to spot it and fight it off. The same dream is likely to also show what is triggering the cancer and what needs to be done to prevent it.

CRANE

To dream of a *crane* means you approach life from a logical perspective (high up in your head).

Bright yellow cranes indicate that you have an enlightened intellect and can use this to get a higher perspective on problems at hand or to improve your philosophy of life.

CRASH

A crash can symbolize stress in your life. An *airplane crash* signifies a difficult birth. Your arrival on the planet did not go as smoothly as expected. The event was traumatic due to either a brush with death or a negative emotional experience. A small / baby car crashing into a bus can indicate you were an unwanted baby. In this case the bus symbolizes feeding at your mother's bosom (bust) and picking up on her feelings about your arrival.

To dream of your *partner dying in a car crash* is indicative of a relationship which to you feels like the one you don't want to lose. It is a common dream for people who have had a previous difficult relationship. It does not foretell the death of your partner. Rather it shows your fear of losing them. The dream is showing you this fear only because it is affecting your relationship in someway. Don't put pressure on yourself or your partner because you think something will cause them to leave. Enjoy what you have now.

CREDIT CARDS

Credit cards, because of their association with banks, are about balance of the heart and sharing of feelings. Credit cards normally operate where the credit card company gives to you first and you owe them, so in dreams they indicate that when it comes to sharing feelings with people or that special person in your life, you are behind. The dream is asking you to open up and share your true feelings. What makes you happy? What makes you sad and why? Do people know the real you or only what you choose to show on the surface?

CROCODILE

To dream of a *crocodile* indicates that you are either too assertive (your bite is too large) or that you are losing a grip on things (losing your bite) - once a crocodile has a grip on you they will not let go. You will know which applies to you. This dream is healing and intends for you to get renewed strength to regain your grip on things by healing your bite. You should be able to take a bite at life and only bite off what you can chew. See *teeth* for more.

A *crocodile in a swamp* represents your colon. Here the crocodile symbolizes a health warning so look to the other symbols in the dream to indicate what you need to do to prevent it.

CROSS COUNTRY

Cross country is about opening your heart and using it to guide you in your life. Easier said than done but well worth the effort it takes to get there.

CROUCHING

Crouching in a dream indicates you are protecting yourself in some way. This protection comes at a price and the dream is asking you to deal with whatever caused you to be this way.

For example, a dream where you are crouching down protecting your three year old son says that you are protecting your inner child from an event that happened at age 3. Now is the time to look back at this time and do whatever it takes to eliminate the negative effects that you still carry with you today.

CROW

A *crow attacking* or eating something is a warning of cancer. For example, a crow burrowing into your chest is a warning of breast cancer.

A *crow sitting on a roof* or flying to or from one indicates negative thoughts.

A *large crow flying overhead* symbolizes depression.

CROWD

An *overcrowded* room signifies your lungs as it is hard to breathe in such locations.

A *crowd* standing in line or queuing symbolizes a slow moving colon.

CRUCIFXION

To dream of a *crucifixion* means you are crucifying yourself unnecessarily. This self punishment and criticism achieves nothing regardless of what you feel you have done wrong.

CRYING

Crying in a dream is healing as it symbolically gives release to pent up emotions related to the subject matter of the dream.

CRYSTAL

Crystals in dreams can indicate that you have a special healing ability that works through channeling energy through crystals. This is not a common ability and should not be taken lightly. Crystals have a natural resonance and greatly affect the energy around us and flowing through us. Using them the wrong way will not help a client. However, if you dream of crystals you are being asked to use them for healing purposes.

Crystal is often used to mean something is crystal clear. This comes from the fact that when specific properties of quartz were discovered (applying energy to quartz causes it to vibrate regularly and compressing it causes it to release energy) they were employed in tuning circuits to lock-on to exact frequencies. The result was that receivers using crystal tuning did not drift and enjoyed clarity over other tuning circuits. In dreams this often symbolizes a clear connection with a spiritual ability.

CULL

A *cull* is usually indicative of your immune system fighting off a threat of disease. For example, to dream of killing young mutated animals in the wild indicates fighting off cancer in your body as cancer is mutated cells. The animals quite often are shown as young or not fully developed as this is the stage where you want your immune system to spot the threat and deal with it. Note, however, that the animals do not have to be young – once they are shown negatively it means the same thing. Black and white or menacingly black animals mean the same thing. Overgrown animals also represent a threat and are good to kill in a dream.

CUPBOARD

Cupboards like any large cavity in a

dream symbolize your lungs and respiratory system. This is especially true if the cupboard is described as at chest level.

CUSTOMS POST

A *customs post* signifies you are ready to make the transition from one state of consciousness to another. This is especially true if you are asked questions by an official at the customs post. If the country or state you are moving into is bigger than the one you are leaving, your new state of consciousness is expanded. If it is smaller you are doing something that is limiting you.

It is common for the official to ask you what you will work at in the new location. They may even suggest a career and a salary. If they do, look up the career and salary in this book as they are symbolic of what you are being asked to do in order to develop your new state of consciousness.

CYCLING

Cycling symbolizes your heart, circulatory system and emotions due to the fact that it requires balance. Your heart requires balanced sharing of feelings.

CYLINDER

A *cylinder* indicates you are a channel / medium – you can communicate with spirits. A cylinder is typically open at both ends but does not have to be for the meaning to hold. A channel is open for communication at both ends – the physical world and the spirit world.

DAD

A dream including your *dad* is likely a comment on your relationship with him and how it is holding you back in some area of your life now. Dreams only focus on problems in your life. Although you may have had a wonderful relationship, there are still often traits or attitudes you copied that you could do without.

To dream of your *dad dying* is not a warning about his death. Rather it asks you to let some negative aspect of yourself die so that a more positive one can find expression. The negative aspect is connected with your dad that you either copied or developed as a result of your relationship. It does not matter if your dad is already dead or you have not seen him in many years. It is the effect you are carrying today that is the target of the dream. Male energy is affected by your relationship with your dad and gives you confidence, belief in yourself, creativity, individuality, various spiritual gifts and more. The dream can be about any of these.

DANCING

Dance or Dancing represents expression of feelings from your heart and is therapeutic in dreams. The dream is symbolically giving expression because you do not do this in reality.

DARK

When *dark* refers to night time, *darkness* or being *in the dark,* the dream is about your feeling of not knowing where you are going, or how to get to where you want to go with regard to the subject matter of the dream. Other symbols in the dream tell you what you need to do to move out of the dark. For the same reasons dark can also symbolize depression; for example, this would be indicated by dreaming of the *upstairs of a house in darkness*.

DARK PASSAGE

A *dark passage*, especially with dirt or dust on the floor, indicates your colon in dreams.

DAUGHTER

Your *daughter* can indicate your female side or that you had issues with your mother in at the age of your daughter in the dream. You have both male and female aspects to yourself and dreams encourage you to restore balance to this energy mix. In fact that is one of the main purposes of your life.

To dream of your *daughter dying* asks you to eliminate the negative conditioning you picked up around the age of your daughter in the dream.

DEAD

See *Death*.

DEATH

Death symbolizes you need to eliminate negative influence from past. An aspect of you has to die before another aspect can find expression. For example, to dream of the death of your father means you need to eliminate negative influence of father.

To dream of your *partner dying* is indicative of being in a relationship you do not want to lose. While it seems dramatic the dream is trying to get you to face your fear of losing your partner in order to get over it. This is a common dream when you find yourself in a relationship that feels like true love particularly when it follows a bad relationship. The most common theme is your partner dying in a car crash.

DECEASED

See *Death*.

DEFECATE

Defecating eliminates waste that would become toxic in the body if kept any longer. In dreams it symbolizes the need to eliminate an issue from the past or a negative influence in the present that is the equivalent of toxic.

DELTA

Delta is formed by sediment dropped by a slowing river and as such can symbolize the need to cleanse your colon as toxins are getting into your blood stream.

Delta can also be a pun on feeling stuck with the hand your were dealt.

DENTIST

To dream of a *dentist* means you need healing for your bite. Do you feel you are losing a grip on things? This dream can be triggered by a feeling that you have bitten off more than you can deal with at this moment in time? It is a healing dream, with the intention of giving you the assertiveness you need to deal with the situation.

If the *dentist is filing your teeth* it means that you are too aggressive or assertive when it comes to the subject matter of the dream. There is no need for you to sink your teeth into whatever it is that's going on right now.

DEPRESSION

To dream of someone with *depression* is about your existing depression or a warning that you are heading towards depression. The same dream is likely to link the depression to a particular parent by featuring them, or to a past event through symbolically representing that.

DESK LAMP
A *desk lamp* indicates an intuitive / psychic ability. However, desks are also used for writing, so look for other symbols that indicate a writing ability, such as a fountain pen.

A beautiful combination of symbols is where a dreamer discovers that a *desk lamp is part of the arm* from the elbow down. The most common desk lamps are very like an arm, with a joint in the middle where your elbow would be and a joint to control the direction of the lamp where your wrist would be. This means that you have a creative writing ability that works in combination with your psychic ability. Use both together to compliment each other.

DIAMONDS
Diamonds symbolize that you are a crystal healer. Crystal healers channel energy through crystals to areas of their client's body. Energy can be channeled into and away from the body.

DIAPER
Diapers indicate your elimination system

DIGGING
Digging to prepare a garden or grounds asks you to do the groundwork on yourself to move forward with regard to the subject matter of the dream. If the work is nearly complete in your dream it means that you have already done the groundwork and are now ready to proceed. That is a very positive indication.

Digging for buried treasure indicates you need to discover your spiritual abilities.

Digging your heels in shows that you are stubborn with regard to the subject matter of the dream.

DINING ROOM
Dining rooms signify communication and interaction in dreams. In general we share our intentions for the day and how our day went, when eating meals there. As a place for eating, a dining room can also indicate your digestive system in health related dreams.

DIRT
Dirt indicates your colon needs cleansing. Your colon is symbolically the dirt track of your body.

DIRT ROAD
A *dirt road* or *dirt track* indicates your colon. Your colon is the dirt track for waste matter in your body.

DIRTY
See *Dirt*.

DISEMBODIED VOICE
A *disembodied voice* in a dream is always a guide / guardian angel. If you can remember what they said follow their advice. They are infallible.

DOCTOR
To dream of a *doctor* means you have a healing ability. However, in dreams, this means you have a hands-on healing ability like Jesus practices in the bible.

If a *doctor is reluctant to do healing* it means your immune system is repressed or slow to act in the way it should.

DOCTOR'S SURGERY
Dreams of *a doctor's surgery* are

about your state of mind and how it influences your health or healing.

DOG

A *dog* is mans best friend and in dreams signifies your human nature (animal nature). If you disconnect from life you can find yourself dreaming of *losing your dog*. To dream of a *lost dog* returning asks you to let your mental guard down and trust your instincts.

DOLPHIN

A *dolphin* symbolizes channeling in a dream. A channel is someone who can communicate directly with spirits and Angels. Dolphins are mammals like us but live in the ocean. In dreams the ocean represents spirituality so here is an air breathing mammal that has adapted enough to travel into the spirit world.

DOOM

Dreams evoke a feeling of *doom* when this is how you normally feel with regard to the subject matter of the dream. Other symbols in the dream will tell you how to heal this in reality.

DOOR

Doors represent opportunities due to the fact that we use them to create openings in what would otherwise be an obstacle in our path. Where the door is located can be significant. If the door is ahead on your path it signifies an opportunity in the near future. A door to your right can signify the same thing but it could also be an opportunity that has already manifested.

To *close a door* in a dream means you are closing off an opportunity that you should be taking advantage of.

To *lock a door* signifies refusal to create or take an opportunity out of fear. Your protection mechanism is to avoid it. This is not good to do in a dream regardless of what you think you are protecting yourself from in the dream.

A *locked door* indicates you are blocking an opportunity in reality.

Double doors represent your heart and sharing as they allow a flow both inward and outward. Your heart needs this flow of feelings to stay healthy.

Revolving doors also symbolize your heart due to their circular movement and also because they allow flow in two directions. *Revolving doors* can also symbolize karma as it is possible to get caught on a karmic cycle where you keep messing up opportunities to clear your karmic debt.

Unusually large glass doors including sliding doors, indicate you have a psychic / intuitive ability. You are being asked to open up to using it. For example, encountering a sliding door on the public pavement asks you to take the opportunities (door) presented in public (public pavement) for using your psychic ability (glass).

Houses represent the body so the *back door* to a house represents your rectum (the back door to your body) while the *front door* can represent the vagina – the front door to the body by which someone can exit.

DOORBELL

A *doorbell* ringing is a request to open the door on a newly awakened aspect of your being. It is very common in these dreams for the doorbell to ring early in the morning or to wake you up in your bedroom. It's a very good symbol in dreams.

DOUGHNUT

To dream of a *doughnut* is a pun on 'Do Not' and is asking you to avoid doing something.

DOWNSTAIRS

Downstairs in a dream can represent your physical body while upstairs represents mental activity.

Going downstairs is about moving your consciousness down from your head to your heart, to get in touch with your feelings. You are rationalizing too much with regard to the subject matter of the dream. Involve your heart in the decision making process. Ask yourself if you heart was fully in charge of the decision or the direction of your life, what would you be doing now?

Going downstairs can also be about your birth symbolizing your arrival on the ground.

DR. PHIL

Dr. Phil in a dream, indicates you can use your enlightened intellect to demonstrate new thinking to others. It is as if you are putting your hands inside their head and rearranging their thought process so that they absolutely connect with what you are saying. Of significance with Dr. Phil, is that he works with one person at a time even when dealing with groups, so you must address each client individually. The effects can be achieved very quickly and are lasting. See *flying* for more.

DRACULA

Dracula symbolizes absent healing, strong intellect. *Vampires* have the power of flight and as such they signify the same thing as *flying* in a dream. Since your physical body can not fly it symbolizes being able to project your mind onto others. This is quite useful if you work in marketing or sales but it also has a spiritual dimension. You can use your strong mind to influence how others think and to influence their health. It works along the lines of thinking yourself healthy, but in this case you can think somebody else healthy. This ability is best known from the bible when Jesus heals the centurion's servant without ever seeing him. You are probably wondering why the vampire though. The reason is that while you can heal someone by thinking well of them, you can also negatively affect someone by harboring negative thoughts about them. For those of us without this ability, it is not a problem as our thoughts do not affect others that way. In your case, however, dreaming of a vampire is reminding you that you have a special ability, and right now you are using it in a way that is sucking the life force out of somebody. You should know who it is already, and if you do not, then check how you think in general. Do you see everyone as a jerk and wish bad luck on them? The dream is reminding you of your power and that it is your responsibility to control it, or accept the karmic consequence. Oh yes, and please don't think badly of me for telling you what it means!

DRAIN

A *drain* or *drain pipe* is about your elimination system. It can be the colon, particularly if it connects to a sewer. It can also represent your bladder.

An *overflow drain pipe* connected to a heating or water system is about the immune system. Here the drain pipe kicks in when required. This is how the immune system works. It is connected to the circulatory system and drains infection from it. You will notice this if you get a cut on your shin. A swelling bellow the knee at the back of your leg is where the immune system drains the infection.

DRAINPIPE

A *drainpipe* indicates your colon or bladder.

DRESS

How you *dress* in dreams indicates your attitude towards the subject matter of the dream as we dress to suit our mood or to suit the role we feel obliged to play (e.g. career). In the dream context, we are free to wear anything we want or to even wear nothing. How we dress, particularly the colors worn, can be very revealing. *Old fashioned dress* would indicate that you have adopted an old fashioned attitude towards the subject matter. This is most likely handed down to you by one or both parents. Being given *hand me downs* belonging to your father would be clearly showing you have adopted your fathers attitude.

DRIVER

The *driver* of a vehicle in a dream can indicate influences in your life, guidance or spiritual abilities you have. Whether in a car or not, a *taxi driver* indicates you have a counseling ability that works well one on one. It means this because taxi drivers take you from where you are to where you need to be on a one on one basis. In the same way, a *bus driver* indicates you are a group leader / teacher.

If the *driver* is a successful family member the dream tells you to listen to their guidance – let them sit in the

driving seat for a while. If it is a member with difficulties, a parent or partner, it means you are not following your own direction in life and are letting others push you around either consciously or subconsciously.

DRIVING

Driving along a road is about striving towards your ideals or goals as we use cars to take us from where we are to where we need to be. The dream can indicate movement forward mentally or spiritually.

Driving towards a crossroads indicates you are heading for trouble or suffering.

Driving alongside a river indicates our spiritual path, as water here represents our spiritual side. It is common in these dreams for the river to have flooded the road at some point. It is usually not dangerous in the dream. This is a request to let your spiritual development become part of your quest, or more precisely to use your spirituality in the pursuit of your goals.

Driving with family means you are carrying family influences which could be blocking you in the pursuit of your goals. For example, are you in the back seat or not in the driver's seat? Not being in the driving seat symbolizes not being in charge of the direction of your own life. In this case the family member in the car, is there to represent the issue or trait that is holding you back. Although very unusual it is not always a negative influence. For example, if you dream of driving with a sibling who broke free from something that has affected both of you, the dream can be showing you that you too have to do what they did. *Driving with someone* can indicate you are carrying the influence of that person or a parent of the same gender.

To dream of *driving over the line* at a traffic signal or stop sign, when your intention in the dream was to stop, is a pun on overstepping your bounds in waking life. Whatever it is you have been doing recently, take a step back. It's not good.

Driving on a highway, motorway is about your heart and circulatory system, as these are main arterial roads. The artery network of the body is part of the circulatory system.

To receive penalty points for speeding or other *driving violation* signifies that something you are doing is incurring karma. Since driving has to do with pursuit of goals, are you pushing your responsibilities onto someone else or blocking them from pursuing their own goals?

DROWNING

Drowning in a dream signifies that life (water) is threatening or overwhelming (coming in on top of you).

To *save someone from drowning* indicates that you do spirit rescue. Spirit rescue can be done consciously or when you have left your body during sleep.

DRUG

Drugs indicate you suppress your feelings.

DRUNK

To be *drunk* indicates you suppress your feelings.

DUCT

A *duct* for a ventilation system symbolizes your respiratory system and lungs.

DUSTBIN

A *dustbin*, a receptacle for waste, symbolizes your elimination system and colon.

DUSTPAN

A *dustpan* indicates your elimination system, the need to eliminate something from your diet, or the need to eliminate conditioning. For example, to dream of a silver dustpan tells you that keeping your system clean is directly linked to your ability to intuit things. It also means that you can use your intuition to help you overcome issues.

EAGLE

In mythology an *eagle* is said to fly so high that it can see the past present and future from its high vantage point. Due to this an eagle in a dream indicates that you have the gift of prophecy. However, it is unlikely that this is the only symbol indicating prophecy in the same dream. Look for more to indicate the same things in this or other dreams.

EAR

To dream of *ears* indicates that you are a clairaudient channel. Clairaudience is a gift where you literally hear messages from the spirit world. Mostly the messages are heard as lines from songs popping into your head. The segment of the song will repeat over and over making you wonder why you can't get it out of your head. Once you accept it is a message, it immediately changes to a line from another song or stops if it is the end of the message. It can also work through hearing lines from movies.

EARRINGS

Earrings indicate you have a channeling ability where you can communicate with spirits. This is not as frightening as it sounds. There are many TV shows now where the host does this and from these you can see how natural the ability is.

EGGS

Eggs indicate your ovaries or reproductive cycle. This is particularly the case if the eggs are in a box as a box, through English slang usage, can also indicate the womb

Running out of eggs indicates the approaching end of your fertile period for having children.

Crows laying eggs would indicates a serious health warning as in this case the crow represents cancer and the eggs show the cancer multiplying. Before becoming alarmed, realize that dreams warn of health conditions many years in advance of a physical problem manifesting. If these dreams persist over a period of months, consult your doctor. Where the eggs are being laid or where the crows are getting into a house in a dream, symbolically indicates where the physical threat is.

ELEPHANT

To dream of an *elephant* symbolizes that while you portray yourself as being thick skinned, you are in reality a very sensitive person. It means this because elephants are called pachyderms, which means thick-skinned animals. However, though tough, an elephant's skin is very sensitive.

ELEVATOR

An *elevator* can indicate a number of things. Due to its small space, lack of windows and claustrophobic atmosphere, it can indicate your womb or being in your mother's womb.

A *descending elevator* indicates being in your mother's womb and your birth by symbolizing your move down onto the planet. Here the movement down indicates movement from a higher vibration to the dense physical environment. In these dreams the people you meet in the lift or just after you exit it, usually represent the reaction of your parents to your birth.

A *descending elevator* can also symbolize movement of your centre of consciousness from your head (logic) to your heart. Here the dream is asking you to get in touch with your feelings – move down out of your head.

An *ascending elevator* indicates movement to the spirit world – movement to a higher vibration. This in itself can mean that you are a channel.

An *ascending elevator* can also symbolize activating your intellect. This is required when you become too emotional about the subject matter of the dream or need to overcome an irrational fear.

An *ascending and descending elevator* indicates you are a channel – you can communicate with spirits. The elevator shows that you have the ability to move between the physical and spirit worlds. In these dreams you will often find yourself delivering letters or other mail to people in the building.

ENGINE

An *engine* represents your heart and circulatory system as an engine is the heart of a vehicle.

Engine trouble is a health warning for your heart.

To *switch off an engine* indicates that you suppress your feelings. The dream is showing you this so that you will switch your feelings back on (get in touch with them).

A *very powerful engine* indicates you have a hands-on healing ability. You are a source of power.

ENGLAND
England, due to Oxford and Cambridge universities, represents education. This meaning does not hold if you are from England.

ENTITLED
To be *entitled* to something in a dream means you need to accept your entitlement with regard to the subject matter of the dream.

ETHERNET
The internet is a communications medium that mostly works through *Ethernet* connections. As such it indicates you are a medium – you can communicate with spirits through the ether.

EXAM
Sitting an *exam* indicates you are ready to move from one state of consciousness to another. Usually you find that you have not studied or the exam is on a subject you are not prepared for in these dreams. Authorities, however, do not allow you to sit an exam unless you have put in the required classes. So despite your feelings or fears – you are ready for this transition.

EXIT
To *exit* a building indicates your birth. For example, to exit a cinema with an apostle indicates you purpose in life is to teach spiritual awareness to others.

EXPELAIR
An *Expelair* ventilation system symbolizes your lungs.

EXTRACTOR FAN
An *extractor fan* symbolizes your respiratory system.

EYE
Eyes symbolize you are clairvoyant – can see spirits or get communication from spirits through images.

References to your *third eye* indicate you are intuitive / psychic. The third eye, the brow chakra, is located in the middle of your forehead. It is commonly depicted on business cards advertising psychics.

FARMHOUSE
A *farmhouse* symbolizes your emotions. Farmhouses are typically isolated (another symbol for the emotions) and in the open country side.

FAST FOOD RESTAURANT
To dream of any *fast food restaurant* is about the need to speed up your digestive system. It is a symbolic antidote to a sluggish digestive system with *fast food*. To emphasize the healing the dream will often place you in the drive through which provides *faster* fast food and is usually very brightly lit in the dream.

FATHER
A dream including your *father* is likely a comment on your relationship with him and how it is holding you back in some area of your life now. Dreams only focus on problems in your life. Although you may have had a wonder-

ful relationship, there are still often traits or attitudes you copied that you could do without.

To dream of your *father dying* is not a warning about his death. Rather it asks you to let some negative aspect of yourself die so that a more positive one can find expression. The negative aspect is connected with your father that you either copied or developed, as a result of your relationship. It does not matter if your father is already dead or you have not seen him in many years. It is the effect you are carrying today that is the target of the dream. Male energy is affected by your relationship with your father and gives you confidence, belief in yourself, creativity, individuality, various spiritual gifts and more. The dream can be about any of these.

FECES
To dream of *feces* indicates there are problems with your colon.

FENCE
A *fence* is used to mark your personal space. In dreams this is a symbol of sharing and indicates suppression of feelings. You do not share your feelings with others and more importantly you do not acknowledge your feelings yourself. Feelings come from your heart and persistent suppression can lead to health problems in this area. Also look for symbols to do with your head such as roofs or being up a height, as these dreams are often asking you to move your centre of consciousness down from your head and into your heart.

FERRIS WHEEL
Wheels represent your heart due to their circular shape. Here circular is a pun on circulation system where the wheels circular movement symbolizes your blood circulating around your body.

A *Ferris wheel* or *big wheel* is likely to be about being caught on a karmic cycle. This is where you miss the opportunities in life to repay the karmic debts you owe. The result of this is the need to plan another life to pay the debts you had planned to pay this time around. A Ferris wheel journey symbolizes this perfectly as it just does a complete cycle and you end up back where you started.

FIAT
Since *Fiat* cars are made in Italy they symbolize passion and your heart in dreams.

FIELD
A *Field* symbolizes your heart and feelings, as green is the color of the heart chakra. Fields are generally open and expansive so the dream is also asking you to be more open with your feelings. Green also symbolizes harmony. See *Green*.

A *harvest field* symbolizes your reproductive cycle.

FIGHTER AIRPLANE
A *fighter plane* indicates you are an angry person – ready with a verbal arsenal to win arguments and defend your space. The dream will likely say how this came about and will be encouraging you to soften up.

FIGHTING
Fighting symbolizes conflict within yourself or between you and the subject matter of the dream.

FIRE

Any symbol of *fire* in a dream indicates your emotions. For example, to dream of a fireplace with no fire lit is asking you to add passion to your heart.

FIREPLACE

A *fireplace* symbolizes your heart and circulatory system. Another word for fireplace is hearth which is a pun on heart.

FISH

Fish symbolize spirituality as they live in water.

FLAMES

Flames like any symbol of fire represent your heart. If something is in *flames* it can indicate a health warning.

FLOATING

Intellectual, absent healer, projector, hypnotist.

Floating indicates that you have the ability to project your mind onto others. You can use this to good and bad effect. It is very useful in marketing, sales and teaching. Be careful not to think badly of others as your negative thoughts can have a negative effect on them. Whether you believe in karma or not you will bring it on yourself for doing this.

Floating also indicates you have the ability to hypnotize others. Hypnosis is achieved by the practitioner projecting their mind onto their subject. This is regardless of other tools the hypnotist may use or believe is doing the hypnosis for them. It is their mental projection onto the mind of the subject that makes it work.

FLOOR

Floors symbolize something you must overcome. For example, to dream of black and white floor tiles means you are being asked to over come extremism (seeing things as black and white).

Floors in kitchens, bathrooms or when the state of the floor is the focus, can also symbolize your elimination system. This is particularly the case if the floor is dirty or something has spilled onto it. For example, if milk boils over on the cooker and spills onto the floor it means you have an intolerance to milk and your system cannot eliminate it properly from your body.

Sitting on a floor in a dream brings you back to your childhood as that is when you used to sit on the floor.

FLOWER

Flowers symbolize love just as they do when you receive them in reality.

A *potted flower* symbolizes reproduction, the uterus, new growth and the possible heralding of a child.

A *rose* symbolizes virginity – giving someone your flower.

FLYING

Since you cannot physically fly, to dream of *flying* symbolizes that you have a strong intellect which you can use to mentally rise above a problem. In the dream, when flying you are looking at things from a higher perspective. This is a very practical ability and you are most likely aware you have it. When you've had enough of a particular problem you can step back and consciously decide to see the bigger picture. You will almost always feel exhilarated upon waking from a flying dream. This is because all your problems have become smaller through your dream.

Flying is symbolic of projecting your mind and this means three abilities are part of your nature. The first is absent healing – which is healing from afar. This is what Jesus performs on the centurion's servant in the bible.

The second is that you have the ability to project your mind onto others. You can use this to good and bad effect. It is very useful in marketing, sales and teaching. Be careful not to think badly of others, as your negative thoughts can have a negative effect on them. Whether you believe in karma or not you will bring it on yourself for doing this.

The third is the ability to hypnotize others. Hypnosis is achieved by the practitioner projecting their mind onto their subject. This is regardless of other tools the hypnotist may use or believe is doing the hypnosis for them. It is their mental projection onto the mind of the subject that makes it work.

Flying with a guide in a dream indicates you are a channel. You can travel to the spirit world to communicate with spirits and bring back the messages you receive. A guide is anyone with a title, anyone who speaks with authority or anyone who offers you a gift in a dream.

Flying down and landing symbolizes your birth (arrival onto the planet).

FLYING SAUCER

A *flying saucer* symbolizes angels / guides. Anything circular can symbolize ideals / God and in this case the divine nature of your angels. Since they are depicted in your dream as extra terrestrials, it means that you have not come to terms with the fact that you have angels looking after you or

that you are equal to them.

FOOD

Food symbolizes your digestive system. *Food items* shown in a negative way, for example exploding or spilled on the floor, indicate food you need to cut down on or cut out of your diet. For example, removing soggy milk cartons that are clogging the toilet indicates that your body cannot properly eliminate dairy products.

Food also indicates you are a spiritual healer (hands-on healer) as food is the energy source that sustains us throughout our lives.

FOOTBALL

A *football* symbolizes ideals and goals. In dreams anything circular or spherical symbolizes the same. A circle, like God, has no beginning and no end.

A *football game* symbolizes how you pursue your goals in life.

FORECOURT

A *forecourt* is a pun on court and symbolizes that you are judgmental with regard to the subject matter of the dream.

FOREIGN COUNTRY

A *foreign country* symbolizes expansion of yourself when the country in question is larger than the country you are moving from in the dream.

Some countries have specific meanings and indicate what is required for this expansion. These symbols only hold if you are not from the country in question. If one of your parents is from that country it may also change the meaning of the symbol. It all depends on how you view the place in question. The meaning ascribed to foreign countries comes mostly from the predominant view held by historians writing about them.

The reader from a particular country listed here may find the meaning ridiculous or offensive. On my courses where I teach dream analysis, nobody from Ireland has ever gotten that it symbolizes conflict although every non Irish person sees it immediately. It will be the same for the country you are from which is why, for you, the symbolism does not hold.

Moving to another country signifies a change in consciousness. Generally you want to be moving to a country that is larger than the one you are leaving as this would indicate an expanded consciousness.

Africa, being the origin of the human species, is about getting to the root of an issue.

Canada indicates an expansion of consciousness through dharma. This is often referred to as living in a state of grace and is the way Jesus proposed we live. On this path you choose what you know will be spiritually beneficial to you and not necessarily what is logical.

England, due to Oxford and Cambridge universities, represents education.

France represents sexuality. The sexual revolution started in France.

Germany, due to the rise of Nazism and their belief that the Aryan race was the purest and noblest, also due to two world wars, symbolizes arrogance and a regimented way of thinking. As in all cases this does not hold if you are German. To the German reader this may seem offensive but ask any child in the developed world to tell you one thing they know about Germany and they will invariably bring up World War II.

India indicates karma, as karma has been referred to as an Indian disease. Anyone who has ever been there will testify to the general attitude of the affluent towards those with nothing. Beggars are stepped over on the street with a general view that they must not be helped as it would interfere with their karma.

Ireland, due to the conflict in Northern Ireland, represents conflict with the potential for peace.

Italy, due to the passion of its citizens symbolizes your heart and circulatory system.

Spain and any other hot country indicate the need for healing. This is because the Sun in dreams symbolizes healing.

Due to the current peace process going on in ***Northern Ireland,*** to dream of it or ***Belfast*** can symbolize the need to resolve conflict. It can also mean that you and whoever you are in conflict with are polar opposites, like the Catholics and Protestants in Northern Ireland.

The ***United States of America*** indicates an expansion of consciousness. Much of the Western 'New Age' movement has its origins in America. However, America is viewed by many non Americans as a very male oriented society and as such would also indicate being on the karmic path.

FOREST
Forests in a dream nearly always have to do with your colon. This is because paths through forests are typically brown, muddy or dirt trails and difficult to follow. Your colon is the dirt trail in your body.

FORK

A T-junction, a Y-Junction or *fork* in the road symbolizes a choice you have to make, but in this case the choice is not too dramatic. You only have to change your direction slightly and might not even have to slow down to do so. Therefore the choice should not be too difficult

Road junctions symbolize choices ahead. A *fork* also indicates change but does not require you to change direction as much. The new direction will only be subtly different from your current course.

FORTUNE TELLER

To dream of a *fortune teller* means that you have the gift of prophecy. Anyone with a title in a dream is a guide and whatever ability they have, you have too. Therefore you have the ability to predict the future. This is not a very common gift even though public perception is that everyone who is psychic in any way can tell the future. The fortune teller may offer you a gift in the dream to highlight that this is indeed your gift.

FOUNTAIN PEN

To dream of a *fountain pen* indicates you have a special writing ability. A fountain is a source so a fountain pen implies that you have a creative writing source that you can tap into.

FOX

A *fox* symbolizes a threat of cancer in your colon. Do not be immediately alarmed. We all develop cancer cells from time to time and our immune system deals with it. Health warnings become an issue when you persistently have them in your dreams night after night.

FRANCE

France represents sexuality and sexual liberation. The sexual revolution started in France. This meaning does not hold if you are from France.

FRENCH

Sexuality. See *France.*

FRIDGE

A *fridge* symbolizes your stomach as it is located in the kitchen (digestive system) and is used to temporarily hold food. For example, to dream of moldy bacon in a fridge shows that your digestive system cannot digest bacon properly. See *Kitchen.*

FRONT DOOR

The *front door* represents your vagina – the front door to the body by which someone can exit.

FRUIT

Fruit symbolizes your reproductive system. Fruit is the ripened ovary, together with seeds, of a flowering plant. There is also the expression that your children are the fruit of your loins.

FUNERAL

Attending a *funeral* in a dream is about letting go of the negative influence of either the person whose funeral you are attending, a parent or other significant person of the same gender. This influence is holding you back from doing something that will help you develop in a positive way.

FURNACE

A *furnace* indicates your heart and circulatory system. Symbols of fire are always linked with the heart. A furnace uses fire and also pumps water out to the extremities of a building and back. The pump and circulation are symbolic of your heart and circulation system.

FURNITURE

Furniture is used to decorate rooms and as such indicates how you feel with regard to something else identified in the dream. For example, if the furniture belongs to a parent it indicates that the parent in question is the one influencing you negatively. The room being decorated can also qualify what the subject is. A bedroom is about your sexuality or sex, the kitchen is about digestion including what you eat and eating habits, a bathroom is about elimination, living room can be about the heart, and office is about the mind or career. The type of furniture can also qualify the meaning in the same way. Is it office furniture, bedroom furniture, etc?

Antique furniture indicates ideals. It is always good to have ideals and goals. However, if the ideals are not part of your life purpose and are hindering you in any way, your dreams will show this. Moving your parent's furniture or furniture that looks like theirs into your house is a common theme here. A clash of ideals is indicated if you find yourself having to be careful not to hit against the furniture in the dream or find yourself moving it around looking for space for it.

GAP

Going through a *gap* indicates your birth. The birth imprint is so indelibly marked in your psyche it shows up in many guises in dreams.

GARAGE

Garage: attached to a house symbolizes your heart, circulatory system and emotions.

Garage: refueling point is healing for your heart. Fuel drives the engine and the engine is the heart of the car. Also fuel is pumped and your heart is your body's pump. Lastly fuel, being an energy source, symbolizes healing.

Garage: car repair center is healing for your body.

GARBAGE

Garbage symbolizes your elimination system.

Garbage disposal indicates your colon and rectum. Anything in a waste bin needs to be eliminated from your diet.

GARDEN

A *garden* with flowers symbolizes love.

A *back garden* symbolizes influences from your past. It can also symbolize your colon.

A *front garden* symbolizes facing life or the future.

A *basement garden* indicates the womb.

A *garden path* symbolizes your colon. A *garden shed* also symbolizes your colon.

Garden trees indicate your reproductive system – family tree.

Garden gnomes due to their shape indicate your kidneys.

GARDEN PATH

A back *garden path* is about your colon or elimination system. If it is a cement path, the dream is saying that food is caked onto the walls of your colon and you need to do something to eliminate it.

GARDEN TREES

A *garden tree*, especially in the front garden, is indicative of the family tree and your reproductive system. As a symbol it may often appear along with flowers which symbolize love.

GAS PUMP

A *gas pump* symbolizes your heart, circulatory system and emotions. It is a healing symbol for your heart. The connection to your heart is made because the heart is the body's pump. Healing is implied as gas is a power source and as such indicates you have a power within that can be projected into others through hands-on healing. In this dream, however, you are symbolically using your own healing ability to help your heart.

GAS TANK

A *gas tank* is a power source and indicates that you have a power within you that can be channeled into others in a hands-on healing fashion. This is the healing attributed to Jesus in the bible.

GATE LODGE

A *gate lodge*, being a small house within the grounds of a large house is a perfect symbol for your womb. The womb is a place within your body where another person lives.

GATE LODGE

A *gate lodge* is a good symbol of the womb. It is a small lodge in the grounds of a larger house where both lodgings represent a physical body. The larger house indicates yours or mother's body and the gate lodge indicates the womb (a smaller place where

a soul can live). You were once a lodger in your mother's body.

GENERATOR

A *generator* indicates you are a hands-on / spiritual healer. Generators produce power and symbolize you having a power within your body that can be channeled into others through your hands.

GERMANY

Due to the rise Nazism and their belief that the Aryan race was the purest and noblest, and due to two world wars, *Germany* symbolizes arrogance and a regimented way of thinking. As in all cases, this meaning does not hold if you are German. To the German reader this may seem offensive but ask any child in the developed world to tell you one thing they know about Germany and they will invariably bring up World War II.

GIFT

Gifts in dreams are normally given by guides. Being given a gift symbolizes you were bestowed with a special gift at birth. The specific ability may or may not be indicated by the gift itself but it will be shown by other symbols in the same dream.

GIRAFFE

A *giraffe* represents an ability to see things from a higher perspective. From this higher perspective you can see the obstacles in other people's paths very clearly and indeed the obstacles, if any, in your own path are diminished, as the path around them is clearly visible from this high vantage point.

GIRL

A *girl* can indicate you at the age of the girl in the dream. This is true regardless of your gender. If you are male it means that there are issues with your mother / female side that were triggered at the age of the girl in the dream. If you are a woman it can be any event at that age around either parent.

A *girl* can also symbolize your female side needs development to maturity.

We each have both male and female aspects to ourselves. Dreams always encourage you to restore balance to this energy mix. In fact that is one of the main purposes of your life.

GLASS

Glass often indicates a strong psychic or intuitive ability. Quite often these dreams show glass walls, sometimes where only the top half of the wall is made of glass.

Glass walls represent a strong psychic or intuitive ability. Literally you have the ability to see when all others can see is the wall. We don't all see it as glass.

To refuse a *glass of milk* in a dream means you had major issues with your mother.

GOLD

To dream of *gold* or anything that is gold in color indicates that you are a hands-on healer. This is the same ability Jesus uses in the bible to heal others. Hands-on healing involves channeling energy through your body and projecting that life energy into your client. *Gold* in your dream is also healing for your current illness. For example a hands-on healer with a throat problem

dreamed of being given a *gold neck chain*. In ways like this, a hands-on healer symbolically uses their gift to heal themselves in their dreams.

Gold and brown as a combination is a request to view hands-on healing as practical.

GOLDFISH

A *goldfish* indicates that you are a hands-on healer. Fish represent spirituality in dreams and hands-on healing is a spiritual gift which is also known as spiritual healing. A problem being pointed out here is that you have no outlet for your work as goldfish are generally held captive in a fish bowl. Hands-on healing involves channeling energy through your body and projecting that life energy into your client.

GOVERNMENT

Government in dreams represents your guides / guardian angels.

GPO

A *General post office* indicates you have an ability to communicate with spirits. The older term for this is you are a medium but it is now referred to as being a channel. A channel receives message from spirits and Angels in the spirit world and passes them on to their intended recipients. A post office is the perfect symbol for this as its purpose is to receive messages and pass them on to the intended recipient.

GRACELAND

Graceland symbolizes the Dharmic path. This is where you live in a state of grace - living your life in accordance with your spiritual path. Depending on your age you may dream of the album Graceland by Paul Simon or

Elvis Presley's mansion. In both cases your Dharmic path includes channeling as this is what music indicates in dreams.

GRANDFATHER
Your *grandfather* symbolizes your father in a dream. Here the dream is telling you something about the nature of your relationship with him. Most likely it is something negative for which that influence needs to be eliminated.

GRANDMOTHER
Your *grandmother* symbolizes your mother and female side in a dream. For example, her dying in a dream asks you to let the negative influence of your mother die.

To dream of your sick or deceased grandmother receiving a transfusion and coming back to life, asks you to rediscover and nurture your female side.

To dream of your *grandmother* may also be telling you that you will make a fine parent – you will be a *grand* mother.

GRASS
Grass, being green – the color of your heart chakra, is healing for the heart and circulatory system in dreams. In addition to being healing it links the dream to your heart and feelings. See *Green* for more.

Weedy grass or *water logged grass* symbolizes your blood stream is not being cleansed by your lymph system. This could be linked to toxins getting into your blood stream from your colon.

GRAVE
A *grave* in dreams can represent your digestive and elimination system. The color brown and the earthiness of the burial place are sufficient to indicate the digestive system. However, a morbid symbolic link exists because both the digestive system and a grave are used to receive dead meat.

Attending a funeral in a dream is about letting go of the negative influence of either the person whose funeral you are attending, a parent or other significant person of the same gender. This influence is holding you back from doing something that will help you develop in a positive way.

GREEN
Green is the color of the heart chakra so dreaming about it is healing for your heart. For example, dreams in the countryside where you are surrounded by green are particularly healing and are asking you to open your heart and share your feelings.

Green also indicates a need for adaptability or reconciliation with regard to the subject matter of the dream. Something is out of harmony and needs healing through balance. This can be aspects of yourself or could be between you and others such as your partner.

Dark green or green and black indicates difficulties with sharing such as jealousy, rivalry and envy - the green eyed monster. This indicates you need to balance male and female energies within, to avoid health problems with your heart. By becoming more giving, generous and emotionally open, you restore balance and provide healing for your heart, circulatory system and emotions.

Green attempts to harmonize opposites. Dreaming of green pork meat, for example, means your body cannot digest pork. The dream tries to put the food in harmony with your body by making it green. In these cases always remove the food in question from your diet. Your body can't handle it.

Green can sometimes indicate you have a counseling ability. This is particularly true if a guide or guardian angel is wearing green in the dream.

GREY

Grey indicates being uncommitted, uncertain, having a 'grey area', depression and the mental denial of emotion. It is a common color in relationship dreams where you suppress your feelings. For example, dreaming of your fiancé wearing a ***grey wedding dress*** shows that you suppress your feelings. The problem here is that when you are not in touch with your feelings, you are unlikely to be aware of it. Only when you do a therapy to restore that connection will you have a frame of reference to know what the difference *feels* like.

Grey clouds can indicate depression, either present or imminent.

A ***grey fog*** indicates you cannot see your way from where you are now to where you need to go with regard to the subject matter of the dream.

GROCERY CART

A ***grocery cart / trolley*** symbolizes your stomach. This is where you first place food that will end up in your body.

GROUP

To dream of ***groups*** can indicate you are to work with groups as a spiritual

leader / teacher. Spiritual teachers empower others rather than taking their problems away from them. Look for other symbols in the dream that indicate leadership such as a leader, instructor or someone talking with authority.

Groups can also be indicative of your body being packed with waste food. In this case look for other symbols that indicate the dream is about your digestive system such as references to eating, food, tables, kitchens or bathrooms.

Lastly ***groups crowded*** in large rooms can be indicative of breathing problems.

GUARD

In dreams a ***guard*** or ***guarding*** something, indicates you are protective in some way, and the dream is asking you to let go of this security. The specific security mechanism is usually referred to in the same dream – for example if a security guard is trying to impress a group, it means that your security blanket is to aim to impress with your gift. This is not the way to approach the subject matter of the dream – be comfortable within yourself regardless of how others perceive you.

GUIDE

A ***guide*** symbolizes one of your guardian angels. They are often silent in dreams and indicate their message by what they are doing, wearing, or have with them. For example, if he or she is ignoring you it means you are ignoring your guide in reality. When a guide speaks in a dream they are infallible. Always take their message as it is.

GUINNESS

Guinness being black and white indicates you have a tendency to see the subject matter of the dream in black and white terms. This comes across as being intolerant or extremist. You see others as either being with you or against you. There is no neutral position allowed. You need to be more tolerant.

Holding a Guinness in your hand means you are holding onto a black and white attitude. Read the description for Guinness above and ask yourself: "are you aware that you are doing this but refusing to change?"

GUITAR

A *guitar*, like any musical instrument, symbolizes that you are a channel / medium. You can communicate with spirits.

A *6 string guitar* shows that channeling is your way onto the path of dharma.

A *12 string guitar* signifies guilt or a critical nature (12 people on a jury) is causing you to suppress your ability.

GUN

A *gun* is a sexual symbol in dreams indicating a penis. There is the obvious connection with the shape and size of a gun but also the pun in having to cock a gun. It also shoots projectiles which symbolize ejaculation. For example, playing *Russian roulette* with your friends in a dream could indicate engaging in promiscuous sexual activity without a condom. In such cases you are not only having sex with your partner, but each of the partners he / she has slept with before you. Just like the Russian roulette in the dream, the more people that go before you, the greater the risk to your life when it is your turn.

HAILSTONES

Hailstones, due to their milky color, represent a milk or dairy produce allergy.

HAIR

Hair comes from our heads so in dreams can symbolize thoughts or how you think with regards to the subject matter of the dream.

Having your hair done or a *haircut* is a request to change how you think with regard to the subject matter of the dream.

Hair tied up or in a bun means your way of thinking is restricted. The restriction can be due to conditioning or it can simply be your refusal to look at things with an open mind.

Hair loss can indicate a refusal to think about something. Being bald in a dream indicates the same thing. Hair loss is also a symptom of an under active thyroid so can also indicate that.

Blonde hair indicates a guide. Whatever they say in the dream is infallible.

Hair on fire is a threat of stroke. Look for other symbols in the dream to do with expression of feelings.

HAIRDRESSER

A *hairdresser* is a request to change the way you think with regard to the subject matter of the dream.

HALL

A *hall* or *hallway*, being a location you walk through to get to where you are going, indicates transition.

HALLWAY

The front door represents your vagina

– the front door to the body by which someone can exit. The *hallway*, being just behind the front door, represents the womb. For example, being chased down a hallway by a woman with a scissors indicates your mother considered abortion while pregnant with you.

HANDBAG
A *handbag* indicates responsibility. When you take it with you attention is given to holding it, keeping an eye on it or knowing where it is at all times.

HANDS
To dream of *hands* indicates you have a hands-on healing ability. With this healing you channel energy through your hands into your client.

If it is a *skeleton hand* in the dream it means that you need to breathe life into your healing ability. You are literally letting it die.

HARBOR
A *harbor* symbolizes your birth as this is where ships berth with berth being a pun on birth. Dreams about birth will invariably show the spiritual abilities you have, as you have these from day one.

HARVEST FIELD
A *harvest field* symbolizes your reproductive system. The plants that were sown have now produced the next generation.

HAY
Hay, due to its brown color and use as bedding for animals, symbolizes your elimination system.

Moldy hay or *steaming hay* indicates you have mold growing in your colon – check for candida albicans.

HEAD
To dream of a *head* indicates that you are intellectual – your head rules your heart. The dream is showing you this in an attempt to get you to move your center of consciousness down from your head to you heart.

A *bald head* indicates that you are not thinking with regard to the subject matter of the dream.

Darkness around a head indicates depression.

HEALER
A healer indicates that you too are a healer. In your case you have a hands-on healing ability like Jesus had. Healing energy is channeled through your body and into your client from your hands.

HEARTH
Hearth is a pun and symbolizes your heart and circulatory system.

HEAT
Heat in dreams can be healing if it refers to a sunny day, the heat of the sun or a hot country in a positive way.

Heat is also indicative of your heart and feelings. For example, if the dream is saying *there is no heat from the fire* you are being asked to add warmth / passion to your heart with regard to the subject matter of the dream.

Heat can also be about negative emotions from others. To feel heat from someone would indicate they are angry at you. To direct heat at yourself, e.g. sun melting your car, would indicate you are frustrated over something.

243

HEDGEHOG

A *hedgehog* symbolizes your digestive system is slow moving. The dream is pointing it out so that you do something to speed it up.

HELP

To *help others* in a dream is indicative that you are a spiritual teacher / leader. Spiritual leaders empower others to be able deal with their challenges themselves.

HEN HOUSE

A *hen house*, being a place for egg production, is about your ovaries.

HIGHWAY

A *highway*, being a main arterial road, symbolizes your heart, circulatory system and emotions.

HILL

Hills can symbolize a number of things but are usually about the difficulty of your journey in life. *Climbing a steep hill*, especially if it is rocky, indicates that you feel life is an uphill struggle. It also means you are on the karmic path.

HOLE

A *hole* in the earth can symbolize your colon and elimination system.

HOLIDAY

A *holiday* or *holiday scene* is a request to relax or take a rest. It can be triggered by overworking or getting stressed over an issue. For example, to dream of holidaying in Spain would indicate you need to rest and allow your body to rejuvenate (sunny country).

HOME

Dreaming of your *home* when the room is not specified indicates a family influence. In dreams about your physical body specific rooms represent specific parts of your body. See *house* or lookup the specific room for more.

HOMETOWN

To dream of your *hometown* symbolizes influences from the past. Dreams mix the past, present and future. To symbolize the past they frequently physically locate you in a place from your past.

HORSE

A *horse* symbolizes balance. This can be validated by anyone who has ever tried to ride one!

A *powerful horse* or many horses indicate that you are a hands-on / spiritual healer. Horses are powerful animals and power output is still measured in horse power. The horses in your dream symbolize the power that can be channeled through your hands into your client.

HOSIERY

Hosiery symbolizes your intestines.

HOSPITAL

Dreams of *hospitals* are about your state of mind and how it influences your health or healing.

A *private ward* in hospital asks you to develop your individuality.

HOT

Hot symbolizes healing if it refers to a sunny day, the heat of the sun or a hot country in a positive way.

Hot or heat is also indicative of your heart and feelings. For example, if the dream is saying *there is no heat from the fire* you are being asked to add warmth / passion to your heart with regard to the subject matter of the dream.

Hot or heat can also be about negative emotions from others. To feel heat from someone would indicate they are angry at you. To direct heat at yourself, e.g. sun melting your car, would indicate you are frustrated over something.

HOTEL

The most significant place in a *hotel* is the reception and in dreams they symbolize your reception at birth, and due to the normally receptive welcome in a hotel is healing for your reception at birth. This is the most significant reception of your life, and how you were welcomed on your arrival can subconsciously control a lot of your actions and philosophy of life. The birth imprint is so indelible it comes up time and again in your dreams. As with many dreams bringing you back to birth, it is likely to also show the spiritual gifts you brought with you for this journey.

HOUSE

A *house* represents your physical body in dreams with specific rooms representing different parts of your body.

Attic: Mind, brain.

Basement: Subconscious.

Bathroom: Elimination, elimination system.

Bedroom: reproductive system, sexuality, rest, meditation, astral activities.

Dining room: Communication, interaction, digestive system.

Hallway: Transition, uterus.

Kitchen: Digestive and elimination system.

Landing: Transition.

Stairs: Spine.

Wiring: Central nervous system.

HURT

To be *hurt* in a dream indicates emotional trauma. While the trauma is likely to be in the past you are dreaming about it because it is still affecting your actions today.

HYPNOTIST

To dream of a *hypnotist* means that you too have that ability. This ability comes as a set which includes absent healing and projection.

Projection is the ability to project your mind onto others. You can use this to good and bad effect. It is very useful in marketing, sales and teaching. Be careful not to think badly of others, as your negative thoughts can have a negative effect on them. Whether you believe in karma or not you will bring it on yourself for doing this.

Hypnosis is achieved by the practitioner projecting their mind onto their subject. This is regardless of other tools the hypnotist may use or believe is doing the hypnosis for them. It is their mental projection onto the mind of the subject that makes it work.

INDIA

India indicates karma as karma has been referred to as an Indian disease. Anyone who has ever been there will testify to the general attitude of the affluent towards those with nothing. Beggars are stepped over on the street with a general view that they must not be helped as it would interfere with

245

their karma. This meaning does not hold if you are from India.

INDIGO
Indigo is the color associated with your third eye and to dream of it means you are psychic / intuitive.

INSECT
Insects or bugs represent things that are bugging you in reality.

INSPECTOR
An *inspector* symbolizes you are good at uncovering the underlying cause of problems, for example, through regression.

INSTRUCTOR
To dream of an *instructor* means that you are a leader / spiritual teacher. Spirituality is expression of the soul so you will teach others to express what is in their core, either by example or through instruction. If the instructor in the dream is working with groups, it means you are to use your gift with groups.

INTERCOURSE
Intercourse in a dream is asking you to get intimately in touch with your male side if you are having sex with a man, your female side if with a woman. We all have male and female aspects to ourselves which have their own unique traits. For example, compassion, listening, leadership and your philosophy of life work through your female side. Confidence, belief in yourself, feeling worthy of the space you occupy, career and spiritual healing work through your male side. The dream may be triggered due to an imbalance which is affecting your ability

to develop or move forward in an aspect of your life related to a particular energy. The dream tries to heal this by representing their male or female side as something desirable.

The dream wants both male and female sides of yourself to share closeness in an uninhibited way. This sharing restores balance to the dreamer so they can draw on the strength inherent in the aspect of their nature they were repressing. Many people are shocked to find themselves having sex in a dream with a person of the same sex. This still has the same meaning. A woman having sex with another woman in a dream is still a healing device intended to put the dreamer in close contact with her heart / feelings.

Dreams can also include members of the family in sexual roles with the dreamer. Here the intent is to use an existing loving relationship as a pull to seduce the dreamer into have sex and therefore accept the healing the dream is offering.

Where you are able to be honest to themselves in private but puts on 'an air' or represses their feelings in public they can dream about having sex in public. Again the purpose of the dream is the same but here it is also asking the dreamer to not be afraid of being honest with themselves in front of others.

The second reason for dreaming about *having intercourse* is to heal the dreamer of the fact that they are currently not having sex with their partner. In this case the dream attempts to heal stress or whatever impact abstinence is having on the relationship.

INTERNET
The *internet* is a communications me-

dium that mostly works through Ethernet connections. As such it indicates you are a medium – you can communicate with spirits through the ether.

INTRANET
See internet.

IRELAND
Ireland, due to the conflict in Northern Ireland, represents conflict with the potential for peace. This meaning does not hold if you are from Ireland.

ISLAND
Islands symbolize your heart, circulatory system and emotions. In dreams it means that you are an island – you keep yourself isolated from others when it comes to sharing your feelings.

ISLE
Names that include the word *Isle*, for example, the Isle of Man, indicate that you are a channel. You can communicate with spirits.

ITALY
Italy, due to the passion of its citizens symbolizes your heart and circulatory system. This meaning does not hold if you are from Italy.

JAIL
Jail symbolizes your heart and emotions. Specifically it means that you suppress your feelings (keep them captive) and do not share them with others. The logic behind the action is that if people cannot get close they cannot hurt your feelings. Over time you can become so good at suppressing your feelings that you do not even acknowledge them to yourself. For example, a dream where a woman reluctantly re-

leases you from jail means that you are reluctant to open up or share your feelings with others.

JAPAN
If you have never lived in *Japan,* to dream of it symbolizes an extremist attitude towards the subject matter of the dream. This comes from the Japanese ritual suicide, hara-kiri. A tradition of being expected to fall on your sword to atone for shame and dishonor.

JEANS
Jeans are a pun on genes and are indicative of concern over picking up a genetic trait from either parent. It could be non life threatening like a tendency to put on weight, or serious like celiac disease.

JESUS
Jesus symbolizes your spiritual level in a dream. You are either at an enlightened level of awareness or have the potential to reach that stage in this life time. Jesus is also particularly known for his hands-on healing and spiritual leadership so it also means that you have these abilities.

JET
A *Jet* being lofty, can indicate being up in your head or too logical with regard to how you go through life or with regard to the subject matter of the dream. Come down out of your head and let your heart have a say in decisions too.

A *jet arrival* or *landing* signifies your birth - your arrival onto the planet.

A *jet crash* signifies a difficult birth - one that was either traumatic emotionally and possibly a life and death situation.

A *Jet departure* signifies the beginning of a new project or phase of your life. Often these dreams show what is holding you back from the new project. For example, to dream of your partner forgetting your passports for the flight signifies there are problems in your relationship and you are blaming these for not taking the jump.

JEWELRY

Jewelry is often used in dreams to highlight your spiritual gifts and that they are the most precious part of your nature. You use them to repay your karmic debts and achieve your life purpose.

Silver indicates a psychic / intuitive ability.

Gold indicates a spiritual healing ability in your hands.

Earrings indicate a channeling ability where you can communicate with spirits.

A *chain* indicates something you are obliged to develop.

JEWELRY SHOP

A *jewelry shop* indicates your spiritual values. Pay attention to what the shop keeper directs you to, as this will reveal your spiritual gifts to you. If the shop keeper does not want to sell you something it means you do not have that ability and you are being politely asked not to develop it.

JUDGE

To dream of a *judge* means that you are judgmental with regard to the subject matter of the dream.

JUG KETTLE

Jug kettles symbolize your heart due to their heart shape and the fact that they are used when sharing tea and coffee with visitors. Anything to do with sharing implies your heart.

JUMP

To watch others *jump into water* is a request for you to get into life or to develop your spiritual side.

To see others *jump a dangerous crevice* is a request for you to take a leap of faith with regard to the subject matter of the dream.

JUNCTION

Road *junctions* in dreams symbolize choices or conflict ahead.

A *T-junction* means you face a difficult choice that requires you to change the direction you are currently taking with regard to the subject matter of the dream.

A *Y-Junction* also indicates change but does not require you to change direction as much. The new direction will only be subtly different from your current course.

A *crossroads* indicates difficulty ahead on your path. You have to take care at a crossroads to ensure your movements do not collide with others.

KETTLE

Kettles symbolize your heart, circulatory system and emotions due to the fact that they are used when sharing tea and coffee with visitors. Jug kettles are a particularly strong symbol because of their heart shape. Anything to do with sharing implies your heart.

KEY

Keys symbolize solutions to a problem

and knowledge.

KITCHEN

A *kitchen* symbolizes your digestive system as it is a place where we prepare and eat food. It is probably the most common symbol used in dreams to indicate the digestive system. Many appliances and items in the kitchen indicate various parts of the digestive system. The state of the kitchen shows the state of your digestive system. If the room is moldy, it indicates that mould is growing inside the colon. If plaster or wall paper is falling off the walls, it indicates that the lining of the intestines is damaged.

A *kitchen table* is also about your digestive system.

Kitchen walls indicate the walls of your intestines. If the paper or plaster is falling off the walls it indicates the lining of your intestines is damaged.

Since most days start in your *kitchen* they can also symbolize facing the day or your outlook on the day.

KNIFE

A *knife* in dreams symbolizes anger. An angry person is said to be cutting. The expression, "I felt like she stuck a knife in me," sums it up.

LAKE

A *lake* indicates that you have a deep spiritual reservoir for which you need to find an outlet. It means this because water represents spirituality, and lakes develop where an outlet for water flow is not present. Spirituality is expression of your soul, and in dreams is not connected with religion. Other symbols in the dream will tell you what spiritual aspect is being focused on. You are being asked to create an outlet for this in your life.

A *polluted lake* is about pollutants in your blood stream. You need to discover what is triggering these dreams and cut it down or cut it out.

Diving into a lake asks you to get into life.

LAMB

A *lamb* indicates a timid nature with regard to the subject matter of the dream.

LAMP

A *lamp* indicates that you are psychic. You have the ability to shine light into aspects of yours and other people's lives. Being psychic is the same as being intuitive.

LANDING

A *landing* is a location you walk briefly over to get to where you are going. In dreams it symbolizes transition – you are not yet where you are going to end.

LATE

Being *late* in a dream is a reminder that you are on the karmic path, and have not developed yourself to the degree you agreed and had planned before being born. For example, have you developed your spiritual abilities or created an outlet for them in your life?

LAWN

A *lawn* symbolizes you blood and circulatory system. The connection is through the green color of the grass, as green is the color of your heart chakra.

A *weedy* or *water logged lawn* indicates problems with your lymph system when it comes to draining your bloodstream.

LAWYER

Lawyers give counsel in the legal profession and in dreams symbolize you have a counseling ability which you can use to help others.

LEADER

To dream of a *leader* means that you are a leader / spiritual teacher. Spirituality is expression of the soul so you will teach others to express what is in their core, either by example or through instruction. If the leader in the dream is working with groups, it means you are to use your gift with groups. A spiritual leader empowers others to deal with their problems.

LEFT

Left in dreams can symbolize your female side, emotions or the past. For example, if an angry woman is standing to your left you are asked to let go of the negative effects of your mother's anger – leave it in the past (left).

LETTER

Letters indicate that you are a medium / channel – you can communicate with spirits. Letters are messages from someone remote. As a channel you can pick up messages from someone remote.

LIBRARY

To dream of a *library* means you have a counseling ability. In this case the books represent a depth of knowledge or inner wisdom that you have. This depth of knowledge can be used to help others deepen their knowledge of themselves. You have this counseling ability regardless of whether you have

had formal training. Note that many countries require you to have a formal qualification before practicing counseling officially under the counselor banner.

LIFT

A *lift* can indicate a number of things. Due to its small space, lack of windows and claustrophobic atmosphere, it can indicate your womb or being in your mother's womb.

A *descending lift* indicates being in your mother's womb and your birth by symbolizing your move down onto the planet. Here the movement down indicates movement from a higher vibration to the dense physical environment. In these dreams the people you meet in the lift or just after you exit it, usually represent the reaction of your parents to your birth.

A *descending lift* can also symbolize movement of your centre of consciousness from your head (logic) to your heart. Here the dream is asking you to get in touch with your feelings – move down out of your head.

An *ascending lift* indicates movement to the spirit world – movement to a higher vibration. This in itself can mean that you are a channel.

An *ascending lift* can also symbolize activating your intellect. This is required when you become too emotional about the subject matter of the dream or need to overcome an irrational fear.

An *ascending and descending lift* indicates you are a channel – you can communicate with spirits. The lift shows that you have the ability to move between the physical and spirit worlds. In these dreams you will often find yourself delivering letters or other mail to people in the building.

LIGHT

A *light* in a dream indicates that you have a psychic / intuitive gift. You have the ability to shine light into aspects of yours and other people's lives.

Turning on a light indicates you are doing something in waking life that is illuminating what you need to be doing now. *Turning off a light* is saying the opposite. You are avoiding the steps you need to take in reality.

Lights off upstairs in a house indicate you are depressed or heading towards depression. The rest of the dream will explain what is triggering this. For example, if you see an old woman with her hair in a bun walking upstairs towards where the lights are off says that your depression is linked with issues around your mother (old woman), and how she restricts how you are thinking (hair tied up).

LIGHT SWITCH

A *light switch* indicates that you have a psychic / intuitive gift and you are being asked to switch it on.

LIGHTHOUSE

A *lighthouse* symbolizes you have an intuitive / psychic ability. The dream asks you to use this to help others find their path in life.

LIGHTNING

Lightning in dreams, like any symbol of fire, symbolizes your heart, circulatory system and emotions. Lightning is generally negative with the potential to cause damage, so the dream is likely focusing on a negative emotion you project.

LILAC

Lilac indicates responsibility. For example, to dream of women exercising in lilac leotards tells you it is your responsibility (lilac) to develop your emotional expression (women exercising).

LIME

Balance, heart, reconciliation. See *Green*.

LINE

To dream of *a line of people* symbolizes a sluggish digestive system in which food is literally queued or delayed waiting to move through your system. The dream is asking you to do something to speed it up. For example, remove the foods from your diet that slow it down. The foods in question are often indicated in the same dream. See *Digest This* for a complete description.

LION

The *lion* is the king of the jungle and as such in dreams indicates that you are a spiritual leader. If the lion is threatening, it means that someone abused their authority over you and this is now distorting your view of authority. In turn it affects your view of leaders and causes you to restrict your leadership ability. Spiritual leadership is where you empower others to deal with their own challenges.

A *lion behind you* means you used your spiritual leadership in a former life. As such it is very natural to you this time around.

A *pride of lions* can indicate pride is limiting your animal nature.

LOCKER

A *locker* represents keeping things hidden or locked away. *Opening a locker* indicates dealing with something hidden.

LOCKET

A *locket* represents your heart due to it's familiar heart shape.

LOUDSPEAKER

A *loudspeaker* in a dream can indicate you are guide. In spiritual terms you have reached the level of awareness required to effectively help others achieve their life purpose. You most likely attained this level before this lifetime.

LP

A *LP record* indicates you are on the karmic path. The karmic path is far longer than the dharmic path when it comes to increasing your awareness. Playing a 45 or single release indicates the dharmic path.

LUG NUTS

Lug nuts indicate your lymph system. Lug nuts keep a wheel safely on a vehicle and wheels indicate your circulatory system. In a symbolic way your lymph system does the same for your circulatory system.

LUGGAGE

Luggage indicates karma – baggage you are carrying from something in your past. This can be something from as far back as childhood or it could be baggage from a previous relationship or other venture. The dream will nearly always indicate how this baggage is affecting something you need to do in the present.

Losing your luggage or items from your luggage is actually a good symbol in a dream. It is a request to let go of baggage or past issues that you are carrying around. It doesn't matter in the dream what is in the bags. The bags represent issues that are holding you back.

Losing clothing from your luggage or clothing being stolen, specifically indicates that you need to let go of an attitude or role that you picked up from past conditioning.

Throwing away your luggage, throwing away items from your bags or leaving them behind in a dream is even more positive as it means that you are consciously going through a process that is successfully resulting in the elimination of past baggage.

Your *luggage being stolen* is the same as losing your luggage.

MAGAZINES

Magazines indicate you have a counseling ability. You have a depth of knowledge which can be used to help others see where they are in their life, and what they need to do, to get to where they need to be.

MAGICIAN

A *magician* is a guide in a dream and as such his or her advice is infallible. Whatever he or she is trying to get you to do is something you need to do in reality. Magicians are masters of illusion and show you that nothing is impossible.

MAID

A *maid* is a healing agent because she cleans and puts things back into order. Healing agents appear in dreams to heal issues with the parent of the same gender – in this case your mother. Other symbols in the dream may detail the specific issue.

MALL
A *mall*, being a place where we go to pick up things we need, indicates what you need or think you need. It can also indicate accountability with regard to the subject matter of the dream.

MAN
A *man* in your dreams can represent a number of things. He can represent the man himself, your father, an idea or logic, a guide, a healing agent or an aspect of yourself. If the man is helpful and supportive he is a healing agent. He is called a healing agent because his purpose is to heal issues with the parent of the same gender - dad. He heals this symbolically, by acting the opposite way to how dad was in reality.

If the *man has a title*, speaks with authority or offers a gift he is a guide. Guides often take up a position just to your right or slightly elevated. A guide is the only infallible character in a dream. They commonly demonstrate their purpose by action, rather than speaking. However, if they do speak always heed their advice.

If the *man is someone you know* but do not have a direct relationship with, it is often to show you that you have the same trait that they are either displaying in the dream, or that they have in reality. For example, if the trait is confidence, the dream is attempting to boost your confidence with regard to the subject matter of the dream. It could also be a negative trait. If the person is always angry, it shows that you too have this trait and you are be-

ing asked to acknowledge it and eliminate it.

If the *man is your partner*, the dream is about your relationship and it is likely that all other events and symbols in the dream are a comment on it.

It is very common for a *man* to stand in for your father. In this case, like earlier, he is likely to be either healing an issue with your father or to demonstrate a trait that you adopted as a result of the way he was. Usually the dream is asking you to eliminate this trait as it is affecting you negatively with regard to the subject matter of the dream. For example, a *man in black* could indicate that you picked up fears (black) from your father. This is only the case if the black color of the man stands out in the dream.

Man, often accused by women of being too logical, can also represent logic, an idea or a mode of thought. For example, if in reality you have an idea you want to put money into, and have a dream where your view of a man working is obstructed, it means that you cannot see the idea (the man) working.

A *man* can also represent your male side. If you are *having sex with a man* in your dream you are being asked to get intimately in touch with your male side. This is regardless of your gender. Your male side gives you confidence, belief in yourself, creativity, individuality and various spiritual gifts. If any of these are lacking, your dreams will encourage you to discover that aspect of yourself.

MAP
Maps indicate the need to find out where you are with regard to the subject matter of the dream. We use maps

to find out how to get to places but first we must locate our current position on the map.

MARKET

A *market*, being a place where we go to pick up things we need, indicates what you need or think you need. It can also indicate accountability with regard to the subject matter of the dream.

MAROON

Maroon, being a dark red, indicates frigidity. Red is the color of the base chakra and indicates sexuality in dream. Dark shades indicate fear so the combination shows fear linked to sexuality.

MATHEMATICAL EQUATIONS

In dreams *mathematical equations* indicate expanded awareness.

To dream of a *teacher explaining mathematical equations,* indicates that you have the ability to help others to expand their consciousness.

To dream of *writing mathematical equations,* means that you have a creative writing ability which you can use to expand your awareness of yourself, and in doing so can also pass this on to help others. It is the deduction process engaged in while you write that helps you expand your awareness of yourself.

MAUVE

Mauve symbolizes endurance.

McDONALDS

To dream of *McDonalds* or any fast food restaurant, is about the need to speed up your digestive system. Fast food is a symbolic antidote to a slug-gish digestive system. To emphasize the healing, the dream will often place you in the drive through which provides *faster* fast food, and is usually very brightly lit in the dream.

MEADOW

A *meadow* asks you to open up and allow others to get close to you. See *Grass* and *Field*.

MEAT

To dream of *meat presented nicely* in a butcher's window is a request for you to see yourself, literally your flesh, in a positive way. The dream is saying you are beautiful and your body is good enough to be on display! Don't see the flesh as being weak.

To dream of *meat at a buffet* is a request to be selective of the food you eat and eat what is required to keep your body healthy. Don't starve yourself.

MEDIUM

To dream of a *medium* means that you too are a medium / channel. You have the ability to communicate with spirits.

MEETING

Meetings in dreams symbolize preparation you made for birth. It may seem crazy that your memory could go back to before you were born, but in the grand spiritual scheme of things it makes sense. We prepare for the life we have planned with our guides – rehearsing use of our spiritual gifts and more.

MEN

Men represent your male side, father, ideas, logic, positive traits, negative traits, healing agents, guides. See *man*.

MICE

Mice symbolize a threat of cancer. If the mice are eating a particular food or it is shown in the same dream, it is likely you are being told your body has a very low tolerance for this food

MICROWAVE OVEN

A *microwave oven* is almost always about your reproductive system. Think of the phrase, "she has a bun in the oven."

MIRROR

Mirrors are one of the most common symbols to indicate your reproductive system in dreams. Mirrors reproduce an image of whoever is looking into them. Quite often there are other symbols of the reproductive system such as teeth or bedrooms in the same dream.

A *black mirror* indicates karma. Karma is in effect negativity reflecting back on itself.

MIXING BOWL

A *mixing bowl* symbolizes your bowel. In general whatever is being mixed into the bowl is causing you health problems. This could be a general food ingredient or a specific food.

MOBILE PHONE

A *mobile phone* indicates you are clairaudient. Clairaudience is a gift where you literally hear messages from the spirit world. Mostly the messages are heard as lines from songs popping into your head. The segment of the song will repeat over and over making you wonder why you can't get it out of your head. Once you accept it is a message it immediately changes to a line from another song or stops if it is the end of the message. It can also work through hearing lines from movies.

MOLD

Mold in a room, on hay or in a barn indicates you have mold growing in your colon. Most likely symbolizing candida albicans.

MOM

This is likely a comment on your relationship with your *Mom*. See *Mother*.

MONEY

Money in dreams is about your heart and circulatory system. Money circulates in the economy and thus symbolizes your circulation. Sharing is symbolized through the constant receiving and giving of money. For example, an inability to share is symbolized by your wallet being stolen in a dream.

If the *money* is a price tag, it is a request to put energy into something. Lookup numbers to see what the price means. For example, to be asked for $3 means you are being asked to make a commitment about the subject matter in the dream.

MONK

A *monk* symbolizes your spiritual side. It indicates that although you may be operating in the secular world, you still have spiritual aspects to your nature. The rest of the dream is likely to tell you what ability you have that will allow you to deepen your spiritual understanding.

MOON

The *moon* has long been associated with psychic activity and in dreams means you are psychic / intuitive. It is a light in the dark of night and symbolizes your unique ability to shine your light in the dark. The silver color of the moon alone would also indicate this.

MOSQUE

To dream of a *mosque*, *synagogue*, *church* or other *place of worship* means that the dream is about your spiritual side / idealism. Look for other symbols in the dream to indicate what you are being specifically asked to develop.

MOTHER

A dream including your *mother* is likely a comment on your relationship with her and how it is holding you back in some area of your life now. Dreams only focus on problems in your life. Although you may have had a wonderful relationship, there are still often traits or attitudes you copied that you could do without.

To dream of your *mother dying* is not a warning about her death. Rather it asks you to let some negative aspect of yourself die, so that a more positive one can find expression. The negative aspect is connected with your mother, and is one that you either copied or developed as a result of your relationship. It does not matter if your mother is already dead or you have not seen her in many years. It is the effect you are carrying today that is the target of the dream. Female energy is affected by your relationship with mother and allows you to forgive, listen, lead, have two-way communication, shapes your philosophy of life, and more. The dream can be about any of these.

MOTORBIKE

A *powerful motorbike* symbolizes that you are a hands-on / spiritual healer.

The power of the motorbike is symbolic of the healing power you can channel through your body.

MOTORWAY

Motorways are the arterial roads of the road network and as such represent your heart and circulatory system.

Motorway exit or off ramp, indicates a warning that something you are doing has the potential to end your life journey. The rest of the dream will comment on what it is and what counter measures you need to take. Death itself is inevitable, so it is therefore inevitable that you will have dreams like this. There is no need to panic about such dreams. Just take their advice and wait for your dreams to change.

MOUNTAIN

Mountains can symbolize a number of things but are usually about the difficulty of your journey in life. *Climbing a steep mountain*, especially if it is rocky, indicates that your life is an uphill struggle and always indicates you are on the karmic path.

Being *at the top of a very high mountain* can indicate that you have reached a point in your life where you feel you can see where you are going. If this is not the case, in reality the dream is predicting that you will get there. This type of dream can also indicate you have the gift of prophecy, as you have such a clear view of everything around you from your high vantage point.

MOUSE

A mouse or mice symbolize a serious health threat, such as cancer. If the mice are eating a particular food or it is shown in the same dream, it is likely you are being told your body has a very low tolerance for this food.

MOVEMENT

Movement upwards in a dream indicates striving toward ideals or activating your spiritual side. It can also indicate mentally rising above a problem by activating your intellect.

Movement downwards indicates activating your emotions – moving your center of consciousness from your head to your heart. It can also symbolize moving into your body and birth.

MOVIE STAR

A *movie star* indicates that you are a channel / medium. The words a movie star says in a movie are given to them. In a similar way the words a channel passes on are also given to them. The star asks you to set a goal of developing your channeling ability.

MOVIE THEATER

A *movie theater* indicates expansion of life and is present in dreams where you are being shown how to make your life into the bigger picture that is meant for you. Long before television, the movie theater was the means for news dispersal and letting the masses know what existed in the world.

MUD

Mud symbolizes your colon in dreams.

MUDDY WATER

Muddy water or a *muddy river* indicate that toxins from your colon are getting into you blood stream.

MUM

This is likely a comment on your rela-

tionship with your **Mum**. See *Mother*.

MUSIC

Music or a *musician* in your dream indicates you have the ability to channel. You can communicate with discarnate spirits. If you accept that you are a body with a soul then communication with spirit is not so alien. It is merely one soul communicating with another.

MUSIC ALBUM

A *music album*, when full length, indicates you are on the karmic path. The karmic path is far longer than the dharmic path when it comes to increasing your awareness.

MUSICIAN

You are a channel / medium. See *Music*.

MUTATION

A *mutation*, particularly a *mutated animal* is a health warning about cancer. Everyone dreams of cancer from time to time. It does not mean that you have already developed the condition. Your immune system is designed to spot it and kill cancer mutations. The same dream is likely to also show what is triggering this warning and what needs to be done to prevent it. Culling mutated animals in such a dream is positive as it indicates you immune system is doing its job.

NAKED

Being *naked* in a dream is a very good symbol and shows that you are being asked to be yourself when it comes to the subject matter of the dream - literally show your true self. The disturbing feeling usually associated with this type of dream, indicates the level of discomfort you would have in being yourself in the given situation. If you are currently undergoing therapy in reality, this type of dream shows it is working well and restoring your sense of identity.

NAMES

Place names and people's names in dreams are quite often a pun. Here are listed names and their likely interpretation.

Arizona, once you are not from there and have never lived there, is a pun being in the zone. Whatever you are doing right now is correct. Don't question it.

Auliffe see Olive

Chernobyl is a pun on Share Noble meaning to Share is Noble. This dream is about your heart.

Croke Park is Ireland's national games pitch. Due to the pun on 'croak' to dream of it indicates that something you are doing has the potential to shorten your life.

Fairbanks, since it contains the word bank is about your heart. The theme is reinforced by the fact that Fairbanks, being in Alaska, is cold for 6 months of the year. A cold heart is anything but fair!

John, being the name of one of the apostles and bible writers, can indicate a spiritual leadership ability. Look for other apostle names in your dreams to confirm this.

Mary being the mother of Jesus and almost always being referred to as mother Mary, indicates your own mother.

Olive is a pun on, "Oh Live" and is a request to accept your life and live it fully.

Peter, see John.
Simon, see John.

NAVY

Navy indicates you have a negative philosophy of life or are at least negative with regard to the subject matter of the dream. See *Blue*.

NEWS COMMENTATOR

A *news commentator* in a dream represents a counselor and to dream of one means two things. You have a counseling ability that you should develop. You also should take note of what the commentator is pointing out to you in the dream. They are likely indicating something you did in the past that is holding you back in the present day. Their function in the dream is to bring it to conscious awareness.

NEWSPAPER

Newspaper can symbolize you have a counseling ability – you have the ability to uncover detailed information about people.

Soggy newspaper indicates you have the condition candida albicans.

Shredded newspaper can indicate damage to the lining of your intestines.

NIGHT

Night generally indicates that you are in the dark with regard to the subject matter of the dream. Other symbols in the same dream will tell you how to move forward. For example, lights, candles or the moon tell you to use your intuition / psychic ability to get insight into what you need to do.

Night can also indicate depression.

NORTH

North symbolizes your head – the top of your body. For example, going north in a dream asks you to get into your head / think rationally about the subject matter of the dream.

NORTHERN IRELAND

Due to the current peace process going on in *Northern Ireland,* to dream of it or *Belfast* can symbolize the need to resolve conflict. It can also mean that you and whoever you are in conflict with are polar opposites, like the Catholics and Protestants in Northern Ireland. This meaning does not hold if you are from there.

NOSTRADAMUS

To dream of *Nostradamus* or any other prophet means you have the gift of prophecy and can foretell the future.

NUCLEAR POWER PLANT

A *nuclear power plant* means you are a hands-on healer. This is one of the types of healing attributed to Jesus in the bible. Like the power plant you have a source of power within you. This power can be channeled into others by placing your hands on them and letting the energy flow.

NUMBERS

A common use of *numbers* is to indicate you at a particular age. This may be obvious if the dream has, for example, a 3 year old child in it. A less obvious symbol is the use of a number of people. For example, a dream with 2 women behind you is introducing an issue with mother when you were 2 years old. A dream with 7 children playing together brings you back to the age 7, and so on.

Numbers can also indicate the need to put energy into developing an aspect of yourself when they are part of a price tag. For example, $3 for a pen asks you to commit (3) to developing your writing ability. Price tags can also indicate reward for development. Being offered $600,000 to work in the music industry tells you there will be great reward from developing your channeling ability (music).

For the meaning of specific numbers lookup the individual numbers that form it in this reference.

NYLONS

Nylons symbolize your intestines.

OCEAN

The *ocean* symbolizes spirituality and life. Life is a spiritual journey so expect to see other symbols in the dream indicating your spiritual gifts or giving advice on your life journey.

OFFICE

An *office* symbolizes your mind as in general non-physical work is performed in an office. An office can also symbolize your work.

OIL

Oil symbolizes your blood and circulatory system. Oil circulates around the engine of a car just like blood circulates around your body. For example, to dream of a car engine leaking oil would indicate you are anemic (losing red blood cells).

OIL TANKER

An *oil rig*, *oil well* or *oil tanker* symbolizes that you are a hands-on healer. The huge quantity of oil within an oil tanker is a great source of power. Like the oil tanker you have a source of power within you. This power can be channeled into others by placing your hands on the person and letting the energy flow.

OLD FOLKS HOME

An *old folks' home* represents your childhood home. More specifically the dream is about your relationship with your parents and possibly some limiting influence over you that is affecting you today.

OLD WORLD SETTING

An *old world setting* symbolizes a past life influence.

OLIVE

An *olive*, whether it is the food or a person's name in a dream, is a pun on "Oh Live" and is a request for you to do a mental check on your philosophy of life. The dream is asking you to accept life and drop any attitude such as, "Well if this is all life has to give I don't really care if I live or die."

An *olive branch* symbolizes resolution of conflict and peaceful living.

OPEN AREAS

Open areas in dreams are healing for your heart, circulatory system and emotions. These dreams ask you to openly share your feelings.

OPEN PLAN

An *open plan* in a house or building asks you to open up – remove the walls you have erected to keep others from getting close to you.

OPEN TOP BUS

The *top of a bus* represents the top of your body – your head / mind. An *open top bus* is asking you to open your mind to something new in your life. If you have recently 'made up your mind' about something, you are being asked to think again. If something has come your way and you are dismissing it, you are being asked to think differently. The rain coming into an open top bus asks you to open your mind to letting life in while on your journey.

OPENING

An *opening* is exactly what it sounds like – you are being asked to create an opening in your life for the subject matter of the dream.

OPERA

Opera symbolizes emotional expression and is healing for your lack of emotional expression in reality. The dream is asking you to openly share your feelings from this point forward.

ORANGE

Orange symbolizes drive, ambition. It is an energizing color often prominent in career dreams.

Orange also has to do with assimilation of new ideas and can indicate a profound change in perspective is being attempted or required. The sacral chakra, which is located close to the stomach, is energized by this color and helps with assimilation. When given good news, we can feel it here as butterflies in our stomach. When given overwhelmingly bad news, we feel it as if our stomach is in knots.

Orange is used in dreams to indicate digestive system trouble and to help heal it (The sacral chakra is orange and feeds energy to the stomach and digestive system). A common theme is to dream of standing in line for an orange drink. The slow moving line indicates that your digestive system is slow moving and the orange drink symbolically heals this.

Black and orange as a color combination in dreams, indicates ambition driven out of fear and always indicates career. Tigers have this color combination so often symbolize career in dreams.

ORCA

Orca is a whale and a *whale* symbolizes channeling in a dream. A channel is someone who can communicate directly with spirits and Angels. Whales mean this because they are mammals that live in the ocean. In dreams the ocean represents spirituality, so here we have an air breathing mammal that has adapted enough to travel into the spirit world. The type of whale involved is not important, although *Orca is a* killer whale. In this context, the killer portion of the name shows the fear the dreamer has with regard to talking with *the dead*. Also their strong black and white color would indicate a difficulty the dreamer has with regard to accepting spiritual communication. In essence they must overcome their black and white attitude that tells them things are either good or evil. When you have this attitude it is difficult to open your mind to something new. This could be due to religious doctrine.

ORGY

An *orgy* in a dream asks you to get in touch with your male / female side and be uninhibited about expressing yours feelings in public. See *Sex*.

OUT OF ORDER

To dream of something *out of order* is usually about your physical body and something not functioning correctly within it. The focus is the subject matter of the dream. For example, a toilet out of order would indicate problems with your elimination system.

OVEN

Ovens usually indicate your reproductive system. The expression to have a bun in the oven is synonymous with being pregnant.

On occasion, an *oven* can also symbolize your stomach as both are places we put food.

OVERCROWDED ROOM

An *overcrowded room* signifies difficulty with breathing as it is hard to breathe in such locations.

OVERFLOW DRAIN PIPE

An *overflow drain pipe* connected to a heating or water system is about the immune system. Here the drain pipe kicks in when required. This is how the immune system works. Always alert to prevent a problem.

OWL

An *owl* signifies inner wisdom and that you have a counseling ability.

Like other birds an *owl* can also signify an ideal (something to look up to).

Owl can also be a pun on old.

PAINTING

Paintings represent ideals. For example, a painting of a man up high on a wall would indicate your ideal man.

PARADE

Parades are a celebration of identify and in dreams signify you need to establish your identity.

PARENT

To dream of your *parent* signifies that you are carrying the influence of that parent. While your parents may influence you in many positive ways – dreams only focus on changes you need to make. The likelihood is that the parent in the dream is influencing you in a negative way with regard to the subject matter of the dream. This may not be obvious to you.

PARK

A *park* symbolizes your heart, circulatory system and emotions. Green is the color of the heart chakra.

An *amusement park* is healing for depression or a request to enjoy yourself. It symbolically tries to put a sense of fun and amusement back into your heart.

PARNELL

Charles Stewart Parnell, the uncrowned king of Ireland, symbolizes conflict between love and career. In the last years of his life, Parnell could not chose between the two and trying to keep both became his last struggle.

PARTNER

To dream of your *partner* means the dream is primarily about the nature of your relationship. The rest of the symbols in the dream will expand on the theme. Walking or driving down a *dead end street*, for instance, shows that the relationship is going nowhere.

Sitting in a *parked car* can mean the same thing.

Sleeping at opposite ends of the bed indicates that you and your partner are polar opposites – your heads are pointing in different directions. Consequently, there will be a lot of conflict in your relationship. A dream of moving to Belfast would indicate the same thing unless you are from there or have reason to move there.

Dreaming of your *partner driving while you are in the back seat,* shows that you are not treated equally in the relationship – your place is in the back.

To dream of your *partner dying,* is indicative of being in a relationship that you do not want to lose. While it seems dramatic, the dream is trying to get you to face your fear of losing your partner in order to get over it. This is a common dream when you find yourself in a relationship that feels like true love, particularly when it follows a bad relationship. The most common theme is your partner dying in a car crash.

To dream of your *partner dying* or *leaving you stranded* can also be about a previous relationship, including the foundation of all male relationships, the one with your father. If your father has died recently or his death is still heavy in your heart, then it natural enough to have dreams where you face this happening again with another man you love.

PARTY

Any *party* in a dream symbolizes your birth – the event to be most celebrated in your life. It does not matter if it is someone else's party in the dream.

PASSING

Passing is sometimes a pun on death,

as in my mother passed away. In dreams it will usually refer to the passing of someone close to you in the past. It normally shows up in dreams with words such as, "the heating pipe burst and a woman passed." Note the missing preposition from the dreamer's words. We would normally say, "passed by". This is the most common way it is recorded when passing refers to a person passing into spirit. In the example given, the dream was reminding the dreamer of their mother's death due to a heart / circulatory condition. The rest of the dream explained why it was important to look at.

PEACH

Peach symbolizes Empathy. Empathy is the trademark of a skilled counselor. If a ***guide wears or brings peach*** it means that you have the potential to be a counselor. It is common to have other gifts that complement your counseling ability. For example, to dream of peach lamp shades means that your intuition (lamp) helps you when counseling.

PEARL

Pearls are synonymous with wisdom and as such signify that you have an inner wisdom and a counseling ability.

The color ***pearl white*** also signifies this in a dream.

PEN

To dream of a ***writing pen*** symbolizes that you have a gift for writing. This dream is asking you to create space in your life for writing.

A ***fountain pen*** indicates the same thing. In this case a fountain is a source, so a fountain pen implies that you are a creative writing source – an

inspired writer.

A ***pen enclosure*** indicates suppression of feelings. You do not let your feelings out.

A ***play pen*** indicates the uterus – a place for a child to develop.

PEN SHOP

To dream of a ***pen shop*** or any shop that specializes in writing implements means you are obliged to develop your writing ability. This is particularly the case if the shop owner is trying to sell you a pen. If the owner is telling you not to buy a pen or taking a pen back at his request it means you are being told writing is not the path for you.

PENALTY POINTS

To receive ***penalty points*** for speeding or other driving violation signifies that something you are doing is incurring karma. Since driving has to do with pursuit of goals, are you pushing your responsibilities onto someone else or blocking them from pursuing their own goals?

PETROL PUMP

A ***petrol pump*** symbolizes your heart, circulatory system and emotions. Gas pumps are particularly healing for your heart as they also symbolize a source of energy / power. See *Pumps*.

PHONE

A ***phone*** can symbolize communication. For example, if you dream about your partner, and there is a telephone in the dream, it is about communication with your partner. The location of the phone can also be significant. For example, a dream of a broken phone in the bedroom means you need to work on sexual communication with your partner.

A *phone* can also indicate you are telepathic. Telepathy is where you can read other peoples' minds. If you have this ability you already know it.

PHOTOCOPIER

A *photocopier* reproduces copies of an original and as such symbolizes your reproductive system. Commonly to reinforce its symbolism, the copier is located in the bedroom.

PHOTOGRAPH

A *photograph* asks you to be objective about the subject matter of the dream. Step back and look at the present moment rather than everything that lead up to it.

PIANO

A *piano*, like any musical instrument, symbolizes that you are a channel / medium. You can communicate with spirits.

PIER

A *pier* in a dream usually has to do with your spiritual side as it is beside water. Pier is also a pun on peer so can indicate that you need to see yourself as the equal of another figure. This figure may appear in the dream as themselves or symbolically. Lastly, if ships or boats can dock at the pier it can also be about your birth. Another word for dock is berth so this is a pun on birth. Dreams about birth will invariably show your spiritual abilities which you have had from day one.

PIG

A *pig* can indicate overeating or that you are not comfortable with your body. This can be to do with your

looks or it can be that you suppress animal desires in favor of spiritual pursuits. Animal desires in this context also include essentials like eating and sleeping. The pink color of the pig asks you to love yourself unconditionally.

A *pig head* can indicate you are being pig headed about the subject matter of the dream.

PILOT

Having a title a *pilot* is a guide. It indicates you have a strong intellect and can project your mind onto others. It also indicates you have a counseling / teaching ability where you can work with large groups of people.

PINK

Pink, a mix of red (passion) and white (perfection), indicates love. To dream of this color is enough to show that you did not bond well with your mother or that she did not love unconditionally. The most significant bond is at birth, so it is likely the dream brings you right back to the start of childhood. A poor bond affects the flow of female energy within and negatively impacts on spiritual gifts that require a female energy flow such as intuition, counseling, and teaching.

PIPE

A *pipe* that is part of a central heating system symbolizes your circulatory system. For example, if a steam pipe in an office bursts, it means that pressure (steam) in work (office) is putting a strain on your heart that could lead to a serious health problem (pipe bursting).

A *drain pipe* symbolizes your colon or bladder.

PLACE OF ORIGIN

To dream of your *place of origin* shows you are carrying influences form your past. This is a common theme in dreams.

PLACE OF WORSHIP

To dream of a *place of worship* means that the dream is about your spiritual side / idealism. Look for other symbols in the dream to indicate what you are being specifically asked to develop.

PLANE

Planes being lofty, can indicate being up in your head or too logical with regard to how you go through life or with regard to the subject matter of the dream. Come down out of your head and let your heart have a say in decisions too.

A *plane arrival* or *landing* signifies your birth - your arrival onto the planet.

A *plane crash* signifies a difficult birth - one that was either traumatic emotionally and possibly a life and death situation.

A *plane departure* signifies the beginning of a new project or phase of your life. Often these dreams show what is holding you back from the new project. For example, to dream of your partner forgetting your passports for the flight signifies there are problems in your relationship and you are blaming these for not taking the jump.

A *fighter plane* indicates you are an angry person – ready with a verbal arsenal to win arguments and defend your space. The dream will likely say how this came about and will be encouraging you to soften up.

PLASTER

To dream of *plaster* falling off the walls indicates you have the condition candida albicans or another condition that is affecting the walls of your digestive system or colon.

PLASTIC

Plastic is man made and indicates something unnatural.

Plastic wrapping often indicates a man made obstacle to spiritual understanding. Literally the spiritual goal you are trying to reach is obscured by conventional views Discarding plastic wrapping indicates you are clearing through this.

PLATE

A *plate* can symbolize an ideal or goal. Any circle in a dream can indicate this, as circles have no beginning and no end so are symbolic of the divine. For example, to dream of hitting someone on the head with a plate in a shopping mall, warns you of the need to be responsible (shopping mall) when it comes to pushing your ideals (plate) onto others.

A *dirty plate* indicates you need to cleanse your colon.

A *plate of food* shown in a negative way, indicates food items you need to cut down or cut out of your diet.

PLAY PEN

A *play pen* indicates the uterus – a place for a child to develop.

POET

To dream of a *poet or writer* means you have a creative writing ability and you are being asked to use this in your life, as a means of connecting with your inner core. Through writing, you

265

will find your distinctive style of expression, and expand your understanding of yourself. For example, to dream of writing mathematical equations would mean that through the deduction process engaged in while you write, you will expand your awareness of yourself.

POLICE

Police are guides / angels in a dream. Their presence is a reminder that your guides are aware of everything you do and are there waiting to be asked to help.

If a police officer is giving you a *ticket* it means you are failing in your obligations or life purpose in some way. For instance a ticket for drink driving means you are being told that your drinking is affecting the pursuit of your goals. A parking ticket is telling you that now is the time for action – set goals and pursue them.

POLITICIAN

Politicians represent your guides / guardian angels in a dream. Quite often guides demonstrate to you in dreams the way you are in reality. Guides are infallible and incorruptible. So if you dream of a *corrupt politician* it does not mean one of your guides had gone renegade – rather you have corrupted your life purpose. Your guides are aware of it and asking you to correct the situation.

POND

A *pond* often indicates your bladder. Particularly a small back garden pond with a water feature. Sludge at the bottom of the pond indicates the state of your colon and that toxins are seeping from your colon into your blood stream.

POOL

A *pool* is about your spiritual side. These dreams normally focus on specific spiritual abilities which are indicated by other symbols in the dream. The significance of the pool is that it is a contained body of water with no outlet. The dream is asking you to remove any tendency you have to contain or limit your ability, and to create an outlet for it in your life.

Diving into a pool, whether it is you or others in the dream, this is a request to dive into life and / or your spiritual side.

The *game of pool* is about pursuit of goals in the game of life. Anything spherical in a dream represents goals.

POST OFFICE

A *post office* indicates you have an ability to communicate with spirits. The older term for this is that you are a medium but it is now referred to as being a channel. A channel receives messages from spirits and Angels in the spirit world, and passes them on to their intended recipients. A post office is the perfect symbol for this as its purpose is to receive messages and pass them on to the intended recipient.

POSTER

A *poster* signifies strong intellect, absent healer, projector and hypnotist. See *flying*.

Projecting your mind onto others can be used to good and bad effect. It is very useful in marketing, sales and teaching. Be careful not to think badly of others, as your negative thoughts can have a negative effect on them. Whether you believe in karma or not you will bring it on yourself for doing this.

Hypnosis is achieved by the practitioner projecting their mind onto their subject. This is regardless of other tools the hypnotist may use or believe is doing the hypnosis for them. It is their mental projection onto the mind of the subject that makes it work.

POSTMAN

A *postman* is a guide in a dream and whatever ability a guide has you have too. A postman's job is to deliver messages to people and so symbolizes channeling. You have the ability to receive messages from the spirit world and pass them on to people.

POTTED PLANT

A *potted plant* symbolizes your reproductive system as this is where new life is sown, cared for, loved and nourished to maturity. As such they symbolize children and pregnancy in dreams. For example, to dream of a potted sunflower on the table tells you that there is likely a son (sun flower) in your future (on the table).

POWER LINE

A *power line* symbolizes you are a hands-on healer. See power plant.

POWER PLANT

A *power plant* means you are a hands-on healer. This is one of the types of healing attributed to Jesus in the bible. Like the power plant you have a source of power within you. This power can be channeled into others by placing your hands on them and letting the energy flow.

POWER SOURCE
See *Power plant*.

PREGNANCY

Pregnancy in a dream, whether yours or someone else's, does not foretell you will become pregnant. It indicates that a new and positive aspect of you is developing. Other symbols in the dream will indicate what it is. However, these dreams normally happen when you are consciously trying to change or opening your mind to something new.

PRESIDENT

To dream of the *president* or leader of a country means you are a spiritual leader. Spiritual leaders lead through empowering others to tackle their own challenges. This gift works through our female side so quite often, either the leader is a woman or the leader's wife is introduced in the dream.

PRICE

The *price* you are asked to pay for something in a dream is indicative of the energy you are being asked to commit to the subject matter of the dream. The tag can also indicate the direction in which this will take your life. For example a six in the price indicates a move towards dharma. Seven indicates it is part of your spiritual path. Refer to the chapter on numbers for more information.

PRINCE

To dream of the *musician Prince* means you are a channel / medium as music comes from the spirit world.

To dream of a *royal prince* means you are a spiritual leader and teacher. This works through empowering others to deal with their own challenges and is a female energy gift. Since a prince is male it means you lack confidence at this time with regard to being a leader.

PRINCESS

To dream of a *royal princess* means you are a spiritual leader and teacher. This works through empowering others to deal with their own challenges and is a female energy gift. It requires compassion and listening.

PRISON

Prison symbolizes your heart and emotions. Specifically it means that you suppress your feelings. You keep your heart in a cage so that others cannot get close to you. The logic behind the action is that if people cannot get close they cannot hurt your feelings. Over time you can become so good at suppressing your feelings that you do not even acknowledge them to yourself. For example, a dream where a woman reluctantly releases you from prison means that you are reluctant to open up or share your feelings with others.

PROJECTOR

A *projector* symbolizes that you have a strong intellect which brings with it the gifts of absent healing, projection and hypnosis.

Projecting your mind onto others can be used to good and bad effect. It is very useful in marketing, sales and teaching. Be careful not to think badly of others, as your negative thoughts can have a negative effect on them. Whether you believe in karma or not you will bring it on yourself for doing this.

Hypnosis is achieved by the practi-

tioner projecting their mind onto their subject. This is regardless of other tools the hypnotist may use or believe is doing the hypnosis for them. It is their mental projection onto the mind of the subject that makes it work.

PROPELLER

A *propeller* is part of an engine and as such symbolizes you heart and in particular means that you are too analytical or logical - a propeller head. Come down from your head and get in touch with your feelings.

PROPHET

To dream of a *prophet* means you have the gift of prophecy and can foretell the future. This does not mean you will foretell the next messiah – rather you can predict the future for yourself and others.

PROPHETIC DREAMS

If you have *prophetic dreams* it means that you are prophetic in reality. You can predict the future for yourself and others. Prophetic dreams predict exactly what will happen. Dreaming of an uncle dying just before your aunt dies in reality is not a prophetic dream. Prophetic dreams can be vague but not inaccurate. Most importantly, prophetic dreams have a strong feeling associated with them that pervades the whole of the dream. If you have prophetic dreams you will already be aware of this feeling.

Segments of your dream can be prophetic. For instance, if you know what is going to happen next in a dream, that indicates you have the prophetic gift. You are using your ability in your dream.

PROTECTING

Protecting yourself in a dream is pointing out that the effect of some negative situation is causing you to protect yourself in some way. This protection comes at a price, and the dream is asking you to deal with whatever caused you to be this way. For example, a dream where you are crouching down protecting your three year old son, says that you are protecting your inner child from an event that happened at age 3. Now is the time to look back at this time, and do whatever it takes to eliminate the negative effects that you still carry with you today.

PROTECTIVE ARMOR

Protective armor indicates that you do not allow others to get close to you. This is always about your heart and emotions. The idea is that by keeping people at a distance you cannot get hurt. The dream shows you this, to ask you to open up and allow others to get close. It is not healthy for your heart if you suppress your feelings over a long period of time. Ideally you are open and honest about your feelings both to yourself and to others.

PSYCHIC

To dream of a *psychic* means that you are a psychic in reality.

PUB

Pubs symbolize social contact as going to one is a social occasion.

Getting drunk in a pub indicates repression of feelings, as drinking alcohol inhibits your sensitivity.

PULLING PINTS

Pulling pints symbolizes your heart, circulatory system and emotions. Your heart is the pump in your body and pints are pulled at a pump.

PUMP

Pumps symbolize you heart, circulatory system and emotions. Your heart is your body's pump. For example *pumping air* into the wheels of your car is healing for your heart, as both the pump and wheel symbolize your heart and pumping the wheel restores it to best functioning order.

PURPLE

Purple symbolizes nobility of purpose, spiritual leadership, spiritual teaching, regal, power and authority in spiritual matters. It signifies you are a spiritual leader / teacher. Spiritual leadership works through empowering others to be able to face their own challenges and works through female energy.

Purple is the color of the crown chakra which is associated with spiritual understanding. It has long been associated with leadership, royalty and religious dress. In Roman times only leaders and boys under 17 years old (potential future leaders) were allowed wear the color purple.

Mauve indicates endurance.

Lilac indicates responsibility. For example, to dream of women exercising in lilac leotards tells you it is your responsibility (lilac) to develop your emotional expression (women exercising).

Indigo is the color of the brow chakra. This chakra is often depicted as the third eye and in dreams indicates you are psychic.

PURSE

A *purse* symbolizes your heart, circulatory system and emotions. Money symbolizes the same and is held in your purse. Also purses are constantly opened to accept money and again to give money. This symbolizes sharing of feelings in your heart. To dream of someone *stealing your purse* indicates an inability to share.

PYRAMID

A *pyramid*, like a triangle, symbolizes mediation in dreams. Focus your mind, body and soul on the subject matter of the dream.

QUEEN

To dream of the *queen* means you have a teaching / spiritual leadership ability. Each of us has both male and female aspects. Leadership uses the female aspect. This is why the Queen is commonly used to indicate this gift.

QUEUE

To dream of *a queue of people* can symbolizes a sluggish digestive system in which food is literally queued or delayed waiting to move through your system. The dream is asking you to do something to speed it up. For example, remove the foods from your diet that slow it down. The foods in question are often indicated in the same dream.

To be at the *top of the queue* means you are further along than you think with regard to the subject matter of the dream.

RABBIT

Rabbits are often associated with re-production so symbolize your repro-duction. This is particularly the case if the rabbits have young.

RADIATOR

A *radiator* symbolizes your heart and circulatory system and asks you to share your warmth with others (radiate it).

RADIO

To dream of *radio receiving sets* indi-cates that you are a clairaudient chan-nel. Clairaudience is a gift where you literally hear messages from the spirit world. Mostly the messages are heard as lines from songs popping into your head. The segment of the song will repeat over and over making you won-der why you can't get it out of your head. Once you accept it is a message, it immediately changes to a line from another song or stops if it is the end of the message. It can also work through hearing lines from movies.

RADIO STATION

A *radio station* symbolizes a strong intellect, absent healer, projector and hypnotist.

Projecting your mind onto others can be used to good and bad effect. It is very useful in marketing, sales and teaching. Be careful not to think badly of others, as your negative thoughts can have a negative effect on them. Whether you believe in karma or not you will bring it on yourself for doing this.

Hypnosis is achieved by the practition-er projecting their mind onto their sub-ject. This is regardless of other tools the hypnotist may use or believe is doing the hypnosis for them. It is their mental projection onto the mind of the subject that makes it work.

RADIOACTIVE

To dream of something *radioactive,*

indicates that you are a clairaudient channel. Clairaudience is a gift where you literally hear messages from the spirit world. Mostly the messages are heard as lines from songs popping into your head. The segment of the song will repeat over and over making you wonder why you can't get it out of your head. Once you accept it is a message, it immediately changes to a line from another song or stops if it is the end of the message. It can also work through hearing lines from movies. Radio active is a pun, meaning that your clairaudient channeling is active.

RAILWAY STATION

A *railway station* symbolizes the start of your life journey or a phase of your life journey. For example, stepping off a train onto the platform symbolizes your birth.

RAIN

Rain, like any symbol of water, represents life or your spiritual nature. Getting *caught in the rain* in a dream is very positive as it means letting life in. *Sheltering from rain* is about avoiding life or some specific aspect that you need to include in your life. For example, *rain falling onto a car engine* asks you to let life into your heart. Rushing out to close the bonnet / hood when the rain starts would mean that you do not want to let that happen.

RAT

Rats indicate a threat of cancer. For example, rats under the cooker in the kitchen are a warning of cancer of your stomach (cooker).

A *rat* can also symbolize betrayal as in being ratted on.

REAR

While *rear* can be about the past (what is behind you), it is also a pun on rearing. This can either be about your childhood and events back then or about you raising children. Other symbols in the dream will be specific about the issues.

RED

Red symbolizes joy, sexuality, aggression, animal passion and fun. It is the color associated with your base chakra which is responsible for keeping you grounded.

Red in dreams often indicates passion and joy. In a negative context it symbolizes anger. For example, to dream of your fiancé in a dress with a *red border* would indicate that your passion is border line in the relationship.

Red is an energizing color and is often used in dreams to give you the energy to be passionate about life. This is especially true when dreaming of *red and white*. For example, to dream of your deceased son greeting you wearing a red and white shirt attempts to restore your lost joy and hope in life after his death. It is common after such dreams to wake up feeling like you can once again get on with your life.

Red and black indicates anger. For example, to dream of following a woman wearing a black and red dress would indicate that you copied (followed) your mother's anger (black and red). The dream is identifying the source of your anger so you can do something to eliminate it.

Dark red, maroon and auburn can indicate frigidity – fear linked to sexuality.

REFRIGERATOR

A *refrigerator* symbolizes your stomach as it is located in the kitchen (digestive system) and is used to temporarily hold food. See *Kitchen*.

RELIEVED

To feel *relieved* in a dream asks you to relax with regard to the subject matter of the dream.

RESIST

To *resist* in a dream means that in waking life you are resisting or stubborn with regard to the subject matter of the dream. The dream is asking you to change this behaviour.

RESTAURANT

Restaurants signify social contact and your digestive system.

RESTROOM

Restrooms have to do with elimination. The elimination being asked for can be a negative trait, the effects of a trauma or the negative influence of someone in your life.

When dreams focus on the *physical toilet* it is about your physical elimination system. For example, if the toilet is blocked with milk cartons is means your body cannot eliminate milk or dairy products properly so you need to cut down on dairy products or cut them out.

A *toilet bowl* symbolizes your bowel.

REVOLUTION

Revolution indicates a progressive health illness, such as cancer. To dream of resistance to a revolution shows your immune system is working fine.

RIB

A *rib* in a dream is usually a pun on something that is upsetting you – something is ribbing you.

RIGHT

Right in dreams can symbolize your male side, intellect or the future. When positive characters are to your right in a dream you are being asked to adopt their positive traits.

RING

A *ring* symbolizes ideals or goals. For example, to dream of a gold ring asks you to set development of spiritual healing (gold) as a goal.

RIVER

To dream of a *river* is a request to develop a natural flow to whatever spiritual aspect is the subject of the dream. It means this because water represents spirituality and rivers carve their own course to the sea. Spirituality is expression of your soul and in dreams is not connected with religion. The specific aspect is given by other symbols in the dream, however, you may already know what it is. If you are already practicing the aspect in question, it may be that you are blindly following someone else's instruction when you need to put your unique stamp on it.

A *dirty* or *polluted river* is about your blood stream. Most likely something you are eating is causing toxins to get into your blood stream. Look for food symbols in the same dream. Dreams often show the color of the food rather than the food itself. For example, brown could indicate chocolate and white could indicate milk or dairy products. However, you will know what you have eaten in the last few days so look for something in common each time you have a similar dream.

A *river bank* is about your heart if the bank is green. This is for two reasons. The first is that banks represent the heart and circulatory system and the second is that the color green is associated with the heart chakra.

More often the *river bank* is muddy in dreams and this is about your colon. If the river is also polluted the dream is making a direct link between your colon / digestive system and your blood stream. If you are looking at something in the water such as baby crabs it is a warning of cancer of the colon. In these dreams it is more important to determine the trigger food and eliminate it or cut it down in your diet. Dreams of cancer are only serious if you have them consistently night after night.

ROAD

A *road* can symbolize where you are currently going in life. This does not necessarily tie in with where you think you are going!

Driving along a road indicates striving toward ideals / goals – getting closer to where you need to be. It can also symbolize moving forward mentally or spiritually.

A *road alongside a river* or the shore line is about your spiritual path. It is common in these dreams for the road to flood in places. In this way the dream is encouraging you to get even deeper into your spiritual quest.

A *narrow road* indicates a narrow state of consciousness with regard to the subject matter of the dream.

A *dirt road* symbolizes your colon –

the dirt road in your body.

A *main arterial road* symbolizes you heart and circulatory system.

A *dark road* means you cannot see where you are going. This invariably means that you are unaware of the direction your actions are taking you. Other symbols in the dream will show why this is the case.

An *endless road* normally indicates the karmic path and more particularly being caught on a karmic cycle. Spiritually this is where you live a life with the intention of repaying all your karmic debts. However, something does not work out right for you and when you review your life on your return to the spirit world, you discover that you either have not paid all your debts or that you have incurred others. The result is that you plan another life to repay your new debts! Your dream is showing this has happened you at least once. The big question is how many times? The purpose of pointing this out is so that you ensure that you do not make similar mistakes this time.

ROAD JUNCTION

Road *junctions* in dreams symbolize choices or conflict ahead.

A *T-junction* means you face a difficult choice that requires you to change the direction you are currently taking with regard to the subject matter of the dream.

A *Y-Junction* also indicates change but does not require you to change direction as much. The new direction will only be subtly different from your current course.

A *crossroads* indicates difficulty ahead on your path. You have to take care at a crossroads to ensure your movements do not collide with others.

RODENT

Rodents indicate a threat of cancer. For example, rats under the cooker in the kitchen are a warning of cancer of your stomach (cooker).

A *rodent* or *rat* can also symbolize betrayal as in being ratted on.

ROLLER COASTER

A *roller coaster*, and indeed any system of wheels, symbolizes you heart, circulatory system and emotions. Wheels are circular so are a pun on circulatory system.

ROOF

A *roof* symbolizes your brain – the top of your body. For example, a roof on fire warns of a threat of stroke. Fire symbolizes your circulatory system so this dream warns of damage to your brain (roof) caused by your circulatory system (fire).

ROOM

Rooms in houses and buildings signify specific things.

Attic: Mind, brain.

Basement: Subconscious.

Bathroom: Elimination, liver, kidneys, colon.

Bedroom: Reproductive system, sexuality, rest, meditation, astral activities.

Dining room: Communication, interaction, digestive system.

Hallway: Transition, uterus.

Kitchen: Digestive and elimination system.

Landing: Transition.

Stairs: Spine.

Wiring: Central nervous system.

An *overcrowded room* signifies your lungs as it is hard to breathe in such locations.

ROSE

A *rose* symbolizes virginity and love. It is common to choose roses as the flower to give your lover, while losing your virginity is known as giving your flower to someone.

ROTTEN

Something *rotten* indicates a threat of cancer. For example, rotten wood threatens cancer of the colon while a rotten tooth threatens cancer of the uterus.

ROUNDABOUT

Roundabouts represent your heart due to their circular shape. Here circular is a pun on circulation. Blood travels from your heart through your arteries until it reaches your body's roundabouts, where it begins its return journey through your veins.

ROYALTY

To dream of *royalty* signifies that you are a spiritual leader. Spiritual leaders empower others to deal with their own problems.

RUBBISH

Rubbish symbolizes your elimination system. Anything in a waste bin needs to be eliminated from your diet.

RUBBISH DISPOSAL

Garbage disposal indicates your colon and rectum. Anything in a waste bin needs to be eliminated from your diet.

RUBY

Naturally occurring rubies are rare and very precious. In dreams they are used to highlight the uniqueness of your special spiritual ability and to ask you to value and respect it. The red color of rubies also asks you to be passionate about your gift.

RUSSIA

Russia used to symbolize repression of feelings due to the repressive regime there. More recently it symbolizes openly expression your feelings. If Russia can open up – so can you!

RUSSIAN ROULETTE

Playing *Russian roulette* with your friends in a dream could indicate engaging in promiscuous sexual activity without a condom. In such cases you are not only having sex with your partner, but each of the partners he / she has slept with before you. Just like the Russian roulette in the dream, the more people that go before you, the greater the risk to your life when it is your turn.

RUST

Rust indicates a progressive illness, such as cancer. Where the rust is warns of where the threat could manifest. For example, rust on the fridge warns of cancer of the stomach.

SALESMAN

A *salesman* is a guide in a dream. Guides are often silent in dreams and indicate their message by what they are doing, wearing, or have with them. For example, if the salesman is ignoring you it means you are ignoring your guides in reality. When a guide speaks in a dream they are infallible. Always take their message as it is.

SAND

Sand is on a *beach* and so represents your spiritual approach or your approach to life itself. The sea represents life since that is where life on earth began. The beach is the approach to the sea so symbolically represents your approach to life. Any unpolluted water in a dream can also indicate your spiritual side.

SANDCASTLE

A *sandcastle* asks you to be more creative with your approach to life / spirituality. It means this because a beach is the approach to the sea (spirituality) so indicates spiritual approach.

SATELITE

A *satellite*, being used for communication, symbolizes that you have an ability to communicate with spirits.

SCAFFOLDING

Scaffolding, when high up, indicates the dream is about your spiritual side (higher side). Other symbols in the dream will give the specific subject matter. This will most likely be given by the building in question. Scaffolding around the education centre of a church is about your spiritual education. . Scaffolding at a post office is about channeling and so on.

To be afraid when *up high on scaffolding* indicates a fear of persecution with regard to the spiritual issues you are delving into. This is common when getting into channeling, for instance.

SCHOOL

School, being a place of learning, symbolizes learning about yourself with a view to improving yourself.

A *medical school* symbolizes learning about yourself with a view to improving your health.

A *school bus* symbolizes your life journey. Indeed life is all about learning about yourself while living your journey.

SCIENCE ROOM

Being in a *science room* indicates your approach to life is restricted to what science has already proven.

SCREEN

A *projection screen* indicates a strong intellect and the ability to project your mind onto others. Along with that comes the ability to perform absent healing and hypnosis – both of which work through mind projection.

A *screen* can also indicate medical screening for health problems.

SCROLL

A *scroll* is associated with ancient writing and wisdom and in dreams indicates that you have a creative writing ability. As with any other spiritual ability you are being shown you have to encourage you to develop and use it.

SEA

The *sea* symbolizes life and spirituality in dreams, except when dirty or polluted, in which case it symbolizes your circulatory system.

Drowning at sea indicates that you feel completely overwhelmed with life right now. There is so much going on that you feel like you are going under. The rest of the dream will have symbols for why this is how you feel, and this should give clues as to what you need to do to overcome it.

Rescuing someone lost at sea indicates you have a special spiritual ability. When people die, we often assume that the transition to the spirit world is a straight forward process that happens automatically. This is not always the

case. Souls have to traverse the astral plane to get to where they need to be. However, the astral plane is vast and souls often get lost in a state of confusion there. When you sleep, and your soul leaves your body, you also visit the astral plane. Your special ability is to find souls lost on this plane and help them to the other side. How you have this ability is irrelevant. It is important that you do not refuse to rescue people in your dreams as this indicates reluctance on your part to using your gift. While you are not immediately rewarded physically for doing this, your actions do lead to positive karma.

SEASIDE

The *seaside* symbolizes your approach to life or spirituality. The sea represents life since that is where life on earth began. The beach is the approach to the sea so symbolically represents your approach to life. Any unpolluted water in a dream can also indicate your spiritual side.

SECURITY

In dreams *security* is always negative and indicates you are protective in someway and the dream is asking you to let go of this security. The specific security mechanism is usually referred to in the same dream – for example if a security guard is trying to impress a group, it means that your security blanket is to impress others with your gift. This is not the way to approach the subject matter of the dream – be comfortable within yourself regardless of how others perceive you.

SEEDLINGS

Seedlings represent new growth and your reproductive system, children and pregnancy. A seedling in a plant pot always indicates your reproductive system.

SEWER

Sewers always indicate your colon. In particular it indicates that toxins are building up in your colon and from there they get into your blood stream.

SEX

Sexual activity in a dream is asking you to get intimately in touch with your male side if you are having sex with a man, your female side if with a woman. We all have male and female aspects to ourselves which have their own unique traits. For example, compassion, listening, leadership and your philosophy of life work through your female side. Confidence, belief in yourself, feeling worthy of the space you occupy, career and spiritual healing work through your male side. The dream may be triggered due to an imbalance which is affecting your ability to develop or move forward in an aspect of your life related to a particular energy. The dream tries to heal this by representing your male or female side as something desirable.

The dream wants both male and female sides of yourself to share closeness in an uninhibited way. This sharing restores balance to the dreamer, so they can draw on the strength inherent in the aspect of their nature that they were repressing. Many people are shocked to find themselves having sex in a dream with a person of the same sex. This still has the same meaning. A woman having sex with another woman in a dream is still a healing device intended to put the dreamer in close contact with her heart / feelings.

Dreams can also include members of the family in sexual roles with the dreamer. Here the intent is to use an existing loving relationship as a pull to seduce the dreamer into have sex, and therefore accept the healing the dream is offering.

Where you are able to be honest to yourself in private but put on 'an air' or repress your feelings in public, you can dream about having sex in public. Again the purpose of the dream is the same, but here it is also asking the dreamer to not be afraid of being honest with themselves in front of others.

The second reason for dreaming about *having sex* is to heal the dreamer of the fact that they are currently not having sex with their partner. In this case the dream attempts to heal stress or whatever impact abstinence is having on the relationship.

SHARING

References to *sharing* in dreams always indicate your heart, circulatory system and sharing of feelings.

SHEEP

A *sheep* indicates that you are timid with a tendency to follow others rather than do your own thing. Exactly who you are taking leadership from is likely to be indicated in the dream by the person in question or by something belonging to them. If this is the case the dream is asking you to ignore their negative influence and to get the resolve to set and follow your own goals instead.

SHELL

A *shell* indicates that you do not allow others to get close to you. This is always about your heart and emotions.

277

The idea is that by keeping people at a distance you cannot get hurt. The dream shows you this to ask you to open up and allow others to get close. It is not healthy for your heart to suppress your feelings over a long period of time. Ideally you are open and honest about your feelings both to yourself and to others.

SHELTER

A *shelter* is a safe place in times of trouble. The purpose of dreams is to deal with your problems, so if you find yourself in a shelter, the dream is about how you protect yourself from having to face your problems.

SHEPHERD

A *shepherd* indicates you have a spiritual teaching or leadership ability as a church leader is referred to as a Sheppard. This does not mean you should be teaching religious doctrine or necessarily preaching to others. Rather you have an innate ability to teach and you should be engaging it in whatever you do. Spiritual teaching / leadership is often just leading by example rather than instructing others. This can certainly be employed in almost any situation. This is a female energy gift and works through the heart. The best leaders are compassionate.

SHIELD

A *shield* indicates that you do not allow others to get close to you. This is always about your heart and emotions. The idea is that by keeping people at a distance you cannot get hurt. The dream shows you this to ask you to open up and allow others to get close. It is not healthy for your heart to suppress your feelings over a long period

of time. Ideally you are open and honest about your feelings both to yourself and to others.

SHIP

A *ship* represents your life journey.

SHOES

Shoes symbolize your approach to the subject matter of the dream. This is because it is best to wear the right shoes for the occasion whether it be work, jogging, dancing, etc.

SHOP

A *shop* indicates your needs or responsibilities. In the western world we supply our needs through purchases in shops. This too is linked with responsibilities as obligations to yourself and others often dictate your needs, and what you must purchase such as food and clothing for you and your children.

A *jewelry shop* indicates your spiritual gifts as they are the most precious part of your nature. You can use them to repay your karmic debts. These dreams show you what gifts you have and need to develop.

A *shop owner* is a guide in a dream. Listen to what he is saying or what he is encouraging you to do. In reality this is what your guides are saying you have a responsibility to do.

A *shop window* is often used in dreams to encourage you to adopt a better outlook towards the subject matter of the dream. Shop windows usually have bright and inviting displays that make everything look attractive.

SHOPPING MALL

A *shopping mall* indicates needs and responsibilities. For example, to dream of hitting someone on the head with a plate in a shopping mall, warns you of the need to be responsible (shopping mall) when it comes to pushing your ideals (plate) onto others.

SHOPPING CART
A *shopping cart / trolley* symbolizes your stomach. This is where you first place food that will end up in your body.

SHOULDER
To *shoulder* something symbolizes a burden. For example, a dark cat on your shoulder indicates a burden of guilt.

SHOWER
Being a place of cleansing a *shower* indicates the need to eliminate a negative influence in your life. For example, to dream of urinating in the shower while your partner enters and leaves the shower or bathroom is a request to eliminate the negative influence of your partner leaving you. It can also mean you need to (deal with) eliminate the aspects of the relationship that invade your personal space.

SIGNPOST
A *signpost* can indicate you are guide. In spiritual terms you have reached the level of awareness required to effectively help others achieve their life purpose. You most likely attained this level before this lifetime.

SILVER
The color *silver* always indicates that you have a strong intuition / psychic ability and you are being encouraged by the dream to use it. The encouragement to use it does not have to show up in the dream, but it can in any

number of ways. Firstly by showing a problem you have in your life. In this case, the dream is asking you to use your intuition to guide your own path through the difficulty.

A *silver chain* is a very strong symbol and means that you are obliged to develop your psychic ability – you are chained to it. Most likely you are to use this to help yourself and to repay your karmic debts to others.

A *silver tap* would be simply asking you to tap into your own psychic ability.

SINGER
A *singer* indicates you are a channel – you can communicate with spirits. Music is inspired by the spirit world.

SINK
A *sink* represents your elimination system. The taps symbolize your kidneys and the basin and drain symbolize your liver and bladder.

SITTING ON THE FLOOR
Sitting on the floor in a dream brings you back to your childhood as that is when you used to sit on the floor.

SKELETON
Skeletons indicate the unusual ability of psychic surgery. Psychic surgery has two forms. One is where you place your hands physically inside a client you are working on, and remove cancers, growths and blockages. In the second form you place your hands on the client just as you would for hands-on healing. In this form in addition to healing energy flowing into the client, it will also feel like spirit hands are working inside the client's body directly under your hands. It literally feels

like the clients skin under your hands is being massaged from underneath.

SKINNY

Dreaming of someone *skinny* is most likely a request for you to eat properly. Are you skipping meals or dieting to lose weight?

SKY

The *sky* is something you always have to look up to and in dreams asks you to adopt a better view of the subject matter – look up to it rather than looking down on it.

The sky is often used in dreams to introduce the color blue. A *blue sky* represents your philosophy of life with regard to the subject matter of the dream and attempts to get you to lighten up. White fluffy clouds in a blue sky also heal a negative philosophy of life by restoring confidence (white) for the future. When the sun is prominent in the dream, it is also very healing and encourages creativity (sun) in dealing with your current challenges. See *blue* for more.

SKY SCRAPER

Sky scrapers either symbolize that you are intellectual or the dream is about your spiritual (higher) development.

SLAUGHTERHOUSE

A *slaughterhouse* indicates self destruction.

SLEEP

Sleep in dreams is often about being asleep to the spiritual reality of your life. Do what it takes to learn what your individual life purpose is and take steps to achieve it.

SLOW MOVING ANIMAL

Slow moving animals indicate you have a sluggish or slow moving colon and need to do something to speed it up.

SLUDGE

Sludge indicates the state of your colon. Take steps to cleanse it through diet and other means. When your colon gets to this state, your energy levels quite often drop as your liver expends much energy detoxifying your blood stream.

SLUGS

Slugs indicate you have a sluggish or slow moving colon and need to do something to speed it up.

SMOKE ALARM

A *smoke alarm* symbolizes your immune system.

SNAIL

A *snail* always indicates your elimination system and specifically that you have a slow moving or sluggish colon.

SNAKE

Snakes in their most common usage in dreams, assuming you don't work with snakes in reality, represent a threat of cancer. This is because snakes eat living organisms, camouflaging or hiding themselves and striking unawares. A single dream or two or three in a row are nothing to worry about. If, however, you consistently dream of snakes go to your doctor for a check-up. Where the snakes are located and other symbols in the dream give a clue to where the cancer will manifest if left to its own devices. The kitchen represents the digestive system. The fridge or cooker indicates the stomach. The bathroom or waste pipe indicates the colon or bowel. A frying pan indicates the pancreas. Vacuum cleaner, air ducts, ventilation system or coffee table indicates the lungs.

Snakes can also indicate that you have a counseling ability. In these dreams the snake is non-threatening. The snake is also a Chinese astrological sign and snakes tend to sit back and analyze a situation. They don't just jump right in.

A *snake* can also indicate that you are in a bad relationship and this is how you now view your partner.

SNOOPING

To dream of someone *snooping* shows a level of mistrust with regard to that person or to the subject matter of the dream.

SNOW

Snow, being cold, indicates that you suppress your feelings. Being white, it also signifies being critical or judgmental – being a perfectionist you set the bar too high for others and even yourself to achieve.

SOCCER

A *soccer game* symbolizes how you pursue your goals in life. In dreams anything circular or spherical symbolizes a goal. A circle, like God, has no beginning and no end.

SOCKS

Socks often indicate the intestines and colon in particular.

Since *socks* cover your feet they can also indicate your ability to move forward with regard to the subject matter of the dream. For example, in her dream, a woman was about to put away laundered clothes when she noticed a trail of *black socks*, all in pairs, leading out into the back garden. Through this the dreamer is asked to adopt a new attitude (put away clothes) with regard to relationships (in pairs) as she goes forward in life (socks). In particular she needs to eliminate (back garden) the ongoing effects (trail leads to where she is) of negative relationships (black pairs) in the past (back garden).

SOFTWARE

Software symbolizes programming of the mind or conditioning. This always happens in the past so something in your past has conditioned you to think in a certain way. The dream is asking you to address this.

Changing a software program or fixing it is a direct request to change how you think with regard to the subject matter of the dream.

SOGGY PAPER

To dream of *soggy paper* indicates mold is growing in your colon – often indicative of candida albicans.

SOLAR PANEL

To dream of a *solar panel* means you are a hands-on healer. To dream of the sun alone would indicate this but a solar panel harnesses the invisible rays of the sun to power other devices. Like the solar panel you can channel invisible energy that is around all of us. This energy can be channeled into others by placing your hands on them and letting the energy flow.

SON

Your *son* can indicate your male side

or that you had issues with your father when you were the age of your son in the dream. We each have both male and female aspects to ourselves. Dreams always encourage you to restore balance to this energy mix. In fact that is one of the main purposes of your life.

To dream of your **son dying** asks you to eliminate the negative conditioning you picked up around the age of your son in the dream.

To dream of **rescuing your son** asks you to rescue a male aspect of yourself that was lost at the age of your son in the dream.

SOUTH

South symbolizes your emotions – down from your head and away from logic. For example, going south in a dream asks you to get in touch with your feelings with regard to the subject matter of the dream.

SPACESHIP

A **spaceship** represents your guides or guardian angels. Even if you believe in them, if the concept is any way strange or feels alien to you, they can show up in your dreams like this. The dream is asking you to let them make contact.

SPAIN

Spain and any other hot country indicate the need for healing. This is because the Sun in dreams symbolizes healing. This meaning does not hold if you are from Spain.

SPEEDING

To receive **penalty points** for speeding or other driving violation, signifies that something you are doing is incurring karma. Since driving has to do with

pursuit of goals, are you pushing your responsibilities onto someone else or blocking them from pursuing their own goals?

SPIDER

A **spider** indicates childhood fears. If you have a fear of spiders or have witnessed anyone with it, you can understand that the fear is irrational. There is no way you are under any threat from the spider. The dream is pointing out that you have an irrational fear when it comes to the subject matter of the dream. You need to overcome this fear.

SPINE

The **spine** of a book represents the spine in your body. Threads in the spine indicate nerves within your spine.

SPIRIT

A **spirit** in a dream is exactly that – a spirit. If you can see them in your dream you have the ability to see spirits while awake. While this may sound scary, with a little education, it becomes a blessing. Since you can see them you do not have to take it on blind faith that there is more to life than what we can physically see. Seeing spirits in dreams is sometimes, but not always, indicative of being clairvoyant. It is highly indicative of being a channel but your connection for dialogue may be something other than clairvoyance.

To see the **spirit of a loved one** who has passed, or indeed a relative whom you never met in real life but is in spirit now, will indicate the same thing. Here, however, they will usually dialogue with you with an important message that needs no symbolic translation. It is, unfortunately, common for many people to forget the dialogue but the message that you can dialogue with spirits (channel) is clear, so why not start developing it today so you do not have to wait until you are asleep to talk to them!

SPIRITUAL LEADER

To dream of a *spiritual leader* indicates that you too are a spiritual leader. Spiritual leadership works through empowering others to deal with their own problems. Should they find themselves in a similar situation they can deal with the problem on their own.

SPLIT LEVEL

A *split level* floor in a dream is often used to indicate what you should step up to. You are being asked to aspire to what is symbolically represented on the raised part of the floor. For example, if a movie star is on the raised part of the floor, you are being asked to develop your channeling ability.

SPORTS CAR

A *sports car* indicates you have a great power in your body (cars represent your body) and this manifests as a spiritual healing ability in your hands. Spiritual healing is what Jesus uses in the bible when he places his hands on people to cure them.

A sports car or motorbike on the roof of a building also indicates you have a strong mind which gives you the ability to perform absent healing, projection and hypnosis. See *Flying*.

SPORTS MOTORBIKE

A *sports motorbike* indicates you have a spiritual healing ability. See *Sports Car*.

SQUARE

A *square* indicates limitation and restriction. A square has four sides and just like the number indicates being boxed in.

STAIN

A *stain* indicates guilt – a stain on your soul. In spiritual terms guilt has no positive function whatsoever and just eats away at you.

STAIRCASE

Spine. See Stairs.

STAIRS

Stairs represent your spine in dreams about the physical body. If the dream shows a problem with a step on the stairs it is about a physical problem with the vertebra that matches the step number.

Going upstairs in a dream is about activating your intellect or your spiritual side. To tell which it is, look for other symbols in the dream about spirituality, the heart or intellect.

Going downstairs is about moving your consciousness down from your head to your heart to get in touch with your feelings. You are rationalizing too much with regard to the subject matter of the dream. Involve your heart in the decision making process. Ask yourself if you heart was fully in charge of the decision or the direction of your life what would you be doing now?

Going downstairs can also be about your birth symbolizing your arrival on the ground.

STARFISH

A *starfish* symbolizes spiritual ideals

or goals. Stars symbolize ideals and water symbolizes spirituality.

STARS
Stars represent goals and ideals. We set our goals by wishing on a star. When pursuing something new we are often encouraged to reach for the stars to put our very best into it. Like stars our goals and ideals are something we always look up to.

Colliding stars represent a clash of ideals – often leading to depression. This is usually with one or both parents. The parent in question is given by the gender of someone else in the dream playing a negative role. It can also be with someone close to you whose opinion or authority matters to you.

Falling stars indicate depression – your goals and ideals are falling down around you.

STATION
A *railway station* symbolizes the start of your life journey or a phase of your life journey. For example, stepping off a train onto the platform symbolizes your birth.

A *railway station master* is responsible for the movement of people so indicates you are a spiritual teacher / leader.

A *TV station* or *radio station* indicates a strong intellect, absent healer, projector and hypnotist.

Projecting your mind onto others can be used to good and bad effect. It is very useful in marketing, sales and teaching. Be careful not to think badly of others, as your negative thoughts can have a negative effect on them. Whether you believe in karma or not you will bring it on yourself for doing

this.

Hypnosis is achieved by the practitioner projecting their mind onto their subject. This is regardless of other tools the hypnotist may use or believe is doing the hypnosis for them. It is their mental projection onto the mind of the subject that makes it work.

STATUE
A *statue* is a work of art and as such symbolizes ideals in a dream.

STICKY DRINK ON STAIRS OR FLOOR
This dream asks you to eliminate this drink from your diet or to at least cut down on your consumption.

STOMACH
The *stomach* is the location for digestion and in dreams indications your assimilation or digestion of new ideas. Normally it means that you are having difficulty assimilating a new concept that affects your philosophy of life. Although it seems horrific, a dream may even go so far as to open you up to digesting a new idea that you have your *stomach cut open* to assist you in opening up!

STORM
Air indicates state of mind so a *storm* indicates depression or conflict.

SUN
The *sun* is the life giver for planet earth. Without it life here would not exist and if it were to stop shining tomorrow life on this planet would disappear almost instantly. In dreams the sun represents healing energy and it means you have a hands-on healing ability just like Jesus uses in the bible.

Hands-on healing involves channeling energy through your body and projecting that life energy into your client.

SUNDIAL
A *sundial* is a healing symbol for your heart. The connection to your heart is made through the sundial being a timepiece (see *clock*) and the connection to healing is made through the symbol of the sun (see *sun*). Together they imply healing for your heart.

SUNFLOWER
To dream of a *sunflower* indicates that you have a hands-on healing ability, as the sun is the life force energy of our planet.

A *sunflower* can also foretell that you will have a son. This is particularly the case if the sunflower is in a pot.

SUPERMARKET
A *market*, being a place where we go to pick up things we need, indicates what you need or think you need. It can also indicate accountability with regard to the subject matter of the dream.

SURGERY
Dreams of *a doctor's surgery* are about your state of mind and how it influences your health or healing.

SWAMP
A *swamp* indicates your colon and elimination system.

SWAN
A *swan* signifies ideals and goals. See *Bird*.

SWIMMING
Swimming indicates getting in touch with your spiritual nature. Other symbols in the dream will indicate exactly what your spiritual abilities are.

SWIMMING POOL
A *swimming pool* is about your spiritual side. These dreams normally focus on specific spiritual abilities which are indicated by other symbols in the dream. The significance of the swimming pool is that it is a contained body of water with no outlet. The dream is asking you to remove any tendency you have to contain or limit your ability, and to create an outlet for it in your life.

Diving into a swimming pool, whether it is you or others in the dream, this is a request to dive into life and / or your spiritual side.

SYNAGOGUE
To dream of a *synagogue* or other *place of worship* means that the dream is about your spiritual side / idealism. Look for other symbols in the dream to indicate what you are being specifically asked to develop.

TABLE
A *kitchen table*, *wooden table* or *table for eating at* is about your digestive system. A dining room table indicates the same thing but can also indicate social interaction.

A *coffee table* can be about your lungs because of the pun on cough.

Tables can also be about something you are accountable for or are being asked to take on board. For example, to dream of magazines on a table, asks you to develop your counseling ability – counseling is what's on the table for you.

A *table in the bedroom* is about your menstrual cycle. The pun being in the Latin name for table – mensa.

TAP

A *tap* usually represents the kidneys. This is particularly the case when there are two taps to indicate the left and right kidneys.

To dream of a *tap* can also be a pun on asking you to tap into some creative resource you possess. For example, a *silver tap* would be clearly saying that you are to tap into your innate intuition / psychic ability.

TAXI

A *taxi* indicates you have a counseling ability that works well on a one on one basis. It means this because taxis take you from where you are to where you need to be on a one on one basis.

TAXI DRIVER

Whether in a car or not, a *taxi driver* indicates you have a counseling ability that works well one on one. It means this because taxi drivers take you from where you are to where you need to be on a one on one basis.

TEA CHEST

A *tea chest*, like any large cavity in a dream symbolizes your lungs, respiratory system and chest as they are the spatial cavity within your body. This is especially true if the chest is described as at chest level.

TEACHER

To dream of a *teacher* means that you are a leader / spiritual teacher. Spirituality is expression of the soul so you will teach others to express what is in their core, either by example or through instruction. If the teacher in the dream is working with groups, it means you are to use your gift with groups. A spiritual teacher empowers others to deal with their problems.

TEAPOT

Teapots symbolize your heart due to the custom of drinking tea with visitors and sharing your news since you last saw them. They also tend to have a half heart shaped handle. Anything to do with sharing implies your heart.

TEETH

Teeth in dreams indicate your reproductive system or raising children. Animals carry their young around with their teeth. To lose their teeth would mean they cannot raise their young. We often forget that we too are animals in the animal kingdom.

Teeth can also indicate that you need to be more assertive or less assertive. If a dentist is repairing your teeth, it means that you need to be more assertive and stand up for yourself. To dream of an animal with a lot of teeth, such as a crocodile, means the same thing. This type of dream can be triggered through being in a situation where you feel you cannot stand up for yourself or have lost your grip. For example, a relationship with an over powering partner or a work situation where you feel you would get fired if you speak up. The dream is healing with the intention of giving you renewed vigor to get a grip on the situation.

If a dentist is *filing down your teeth* it means you need to be less aggressive or assertive when it comes to the subject matter of the dream. Take a step back and stop sinking your teeth in.

Loosing teeth indicates losing the ability to have or raise children, because of a physical condition or through the onset of menopause.

Dreams of *loosing teeth* can also be triggered due to a number of non physical conditions such as; **1)** If your child is leaving home to go to college or to live on their own, and you are concerned for their ability to cope on their own. **2)** If you are losing a grip on a situation or life in general. This can be to do with your children but does not have to be. An example involving your children would be if your child is on drugs or hanging out with the wrong crowd, and all your attempts at helping them to get their life back on track have failed. **3)** If you feel completely helpless in a situation and you can't do anything to get out of it.

A *rotten tooth* in a dream is a threat of cancer of the uterus.

TELEPHONE
A *telephone* can symbolize communication. For example, if you dream about your partner, and there is a telephone in the dream, it is about communication with your partner. The location of the phone can also be significant. For example, a dream of a *broken telephone* in the bedroom means you need to work on sexual communication with your partner.

A *telephone* can also symbolize clairaudience. This is communication with your angels through hearing them.

A *telephone* can also indicate you are telepathic. Telepathy is where you can read other peoples' minds. If you have this ability you already know it.

TELESCOPE
A *telescope* indicates you are prophetic as it allows you to see what's up ahead on the horizon.

TELEVISION
A *television* indicates you are clairvoyant – you can see things from a distance.

A *television station* indicates you are intellectual, an absent healer, projector and Hypnotist. Projecting your mind onto others can be used to good and bad effect. It is very useful in marketing, sales and teaching. Be careful not to think badly of others as your negative thoughts can have a negative effect on them. Whether you believe in karma or not you will bring it on yourself for doing this.

Hypnosis is achieved by the practitioner projecting their mind onto their subject. This is regardless of other tools the hypnotist may use or believe is doing the hypnosis for them. It is their mental projection onto the mind of the subject that makes it work.

TEMPLE
A *temple* indicates spirituality. It is a location you go to, to get closer to God.

TERROR
Strong emotions such as *terror* appear in dreams as a result of your subconscious rejecting the message of the dream. You need to be more accepting of the change your dream is asking you to make.

THEATRE
A *movie theatre* indicates expansion of life and is present in dreams where you are being shown how to make your life

into the bigger picture that is meant for you.

In the audience of a theatre symbolizes looking at life.

On a theatre stage indicates performance anxiety with regard to the subject matter of the dream.

Backstage in a theatre indicates preparation for life.

THERMOSTAT

Since it is connected with a central heating system a *thermostat* is about your heart. Are you cold or warm to others?

THIRD EYE

References to your *third eye* indicate you are intuitive / psychic. The third eye, the brow chakra, is located in the middle of your forehead. It is commonly depicted on business cards advertising psychics.

THUNDER

Thunder indicates emotions as it includes lightning. Any symbol of fire represents your heart, circulatory system and emotions in a dream.

TICKET

A *ticket* indicates a karmic debt to be paid. If the ticket is already paid for in your dream you are being asked to realise that your karma is paid already.

A *speeding ticket* indicates you incurred a karmic debt with regard to striving towards your goals (driving). Are you pursuing your life purpose?

TIDAL WAVE

A tidal wave indicates emotional turmoil – life (water) is threatening.

If you nearly drowned as a child you can also dream of tidal waves. For ex-

ample, to dream of a *100 foot tidal wave* approaching your house can indicate you nearly drowned at age 10. Dreams tend to exaggerate and here the age is exaggerated.

TIGER

A *tiger* indicates career due to the color combination of orange and black. Traffic also indicates career and it is common to dream of tigers walking in traffic.

TIGHTS

Tights symbolize your intestines.

TILE

Tiles are generally square and indicate you limit yourself in some way. For example, *black and white tiles* in a bathroom ask you to eliminate (bathroom) your black and white attitude as this can affect your health (colon) and your openness to new ideas.

White tiles show that you are too much of a perfectionist. You set the bar so high that you rarely achieve your own standard. The result is to criticize yourself for this failing, rather than to accept what you did achieve. Cream is the antidote to this and indicates acceptance of yourself.

T-JUNCTION

Road junctions symbolize choices ahead A *T-junction* symbolizes a choice you have to make – literally in reality you are faced with having to change direction with regard to pursuit of a goal. When you consider that driving in dreams indicates the pursuit of a goal, when you reach a T-junction you have a choice in which direction you will continue to drive. You will not continue on in the same direction you are currently going, and even more to the point, the choices are mutually exclusive in that you cannot continue on both paths. The choice you have to make and the reason for it does not always appear, even symbolically, in these dreams. This is because you are usually consciously aware of it, and have been mulling it over for some time.

TODDLER
A *toddler* can indicate influences you picked up around the age of the toddler in the dream.

TOILET
Toilets have to do with elimination. The elimination being asked for can be a negative trait, the effects of a trauma or the negative influence of someone in your life.

When dreams focus on the *physical toilet* it is about your physical elimination system. For example, if the toilet is blocked with milk cartons is means your body cannot eliminate milk or dairy products properly so you need to cut down on dairy products or cut them out.

A *toilet bowl* symbolizes your bowel.

TOMATOES
Tomatoes are about passion. They are referred to as passion fruit due to the red color. Red on its own in dreams is also indicative of passion.

TOMB
A *tomb* indicates your digestive and elimination system. A morbid symbolic link exists because both the digestive system and a tomb are used to receive dead meat.

TOOTH
Reproductive system. See *Teeth*.

TORNADO
A *tornado* indicates mental stress.

TRACTOR
A *tractor* or any tracked vehicle symbolizes your digestive tract. This is because of the pun on tract but also because these vehicles are associated with working with dirt or dirt tracks.

TRAFFIC
Traffic in dreams symbolizes career. Being caught in traffic means that your career is slowing you down from achieving your life purpose. It is also indicative of being on the karmic path.

Two way flow of traffic is about your heart and the two way flow of feelings (sharing with others) required to keep your heart emotionally and physically healthy.

TRAIN
A *train* can symbolize a number of things. It commonly symbolizes your digestive system. Here the train moving along the track is symbolic of food moving along your digestive tract. In fact any track, especially a *train track* is going to be about your digestive tract.

A *train journey* symbolizes your life journey or the current phase of your life journey. In this case a train station indicates the beginning or end of the phase. If you meet your parents on the train station platform, it is clearly about the beginning of your life. Other symbols in the dream will indicate what you need to include on your journey. For example, if the train is silver you are being reminded that you are to develop and use your psychic ability / intuition as you travel your journey.

A *train set* also symbolizes your life journey.

A *train carriage* is a common symbol for the womb and is bringing you right back to before your birth and early childhood. The train is still about your life journey but the very start is being emphasized as being important. Carriage is a common term referring to babies - for example, baby carriage and miscarriage. It is common in these dreams to show the conditions of the womb by their being no windows in the carriage. While it may seem ridiculous that you could have any memory or lasting effect from that time in your life, look at the message in the dream to see why it is important enough for you to be getting a message about it.

TRAIN STATION

A *train station* symbolizes the start of your life journey or a phase of your life journey. For example, stepping off a train onto the platform symbolizes your birth.

TREASURE CHEST

A *treasure chest* symbolizes your spiritual nature and spiritual gifts. Your spiritual gifts are the most precious part of your nature.

TREAT

The symbol *treat* most likely means you have a hands-on healing ability, which you can use to treat others. This is the same ability Jesus uses in the bible to heal others. Hands-on healing involves channeling energy through your body and projecting that life energy into your client. If it shows up

in a Halloween trick or treat setting, it means that you do not believe this is a real ability – it's a trick. Given the society we grew up in, having that view is understandable but you need to do something to open your mind to it.

TREE

A *garden tree*, especially in the front garden, is indicative of the family tree and your reproductive system.

A *forest tree* is usually about your elimination system / colon due to the strong brown color of a forest.

A *rotting tree* represents your colon.

A *tree without leaves* also indicates your colon.

TRIAL

A *trial* indicates you are judgmental / critical in nature. You put yourself and others on trial.

TRIANGLE

A *triangle* symbolizes mediation and commitment in dreams. Focus your mind, body and soul on the subject matter of the dream.

TRICK

To dream of a *trick* indicates a level of mistrust or lack of belief in the subject matter of the dream.

TRICYCLE

Tricycles are a balanced bicycle and symbolize your heart. It also symbolizes commitment due to the connection with the number 3.

TRUCK

A *truck* can symbolize your father or career. To dream of *urinating in the back of a pick up truck* is a request to eliminate the negative influence you picked up from your father (truck) in the past (back of truck).

TRUNK

A *car trunk* indicates your elimination system. Trunks are used to carry groceries and they are the back door to the car.

A *car trunk* can indicate the uterus, yours or your mothers, in some dreams.

A *tree trunk* is usually brown so can indicate the colon.

A *telephone trunk* line is about communication and channeling with spirits.

T-SHIRT

A *T-shirt* indicates that you have a somewhat difficult choice to make that you are already most likely aware of. It means the hard choice in the same way a T-Junction does (see *T-Junction*) and the fact that you wear a t-shirt means you are carrying the decision around rather than making the choice.

TUBE

A *tube* can also indicate you are a channel – you can communicate with spirits. The symbolism here is that a tube, like a channel, is open at both ends.

TUBING

Tubing is commonly about your intestines – particularly your colon if it is about six feet long.

TURF

Turf symbolizes your colon due to its brown color.

TURKEY

Turkey symbolizes a blending of vary-

ing traditions. Turkey is a bridge between two continents, Europe and Asia. It is bordered by eight countries and has a unique blend of Islamic and Western traditions.

TV

A *TV* indicates you are clairvoyant – you can see things from a distance.

TV PERSONALITY

A *TV Personality* in your dream indicates you have a powerful intellect which brings with it the gifts of absent healing, projection and hypnosis.

Projecting your mind onto others can be used to good and bad effect. It is very useful in marketing, sales and teaching. Be careful not to think badly of others as your negative thoughts can have a negative effect on them. Whether you believe in karma or not you will bring it on yourself for doing this.

Hypnosis is achieved by the practitioner projecting their mind onto their subject. This is regardless of other tools the hypnotist may use or believe is doing the hypnosis for them. It is their mental projection onto the mind of the subject that makes it work.

TV STATION

A *TV station* indicates a strong intellect, absent healer, projector and hypnotist. See TV Personality

TWINS

Twins indicate you are a channel / medium – you can communicate with spirits.

TWISTER

A *twister* indicates you state of mind / stress.

TYPEWRITER

To dream of a *typewriter* indicates you have a special writing ability. You may already know this because you are drawn to it. If you have not already written something give it a try. It is you.

UMBRELLA

An *umbrella* shelters you from the rain. In dreams the rain represents life, so being sheltered from it indicates you protect yourself from life. If the umbrella is given to you by someone it will tell you who you picked this protective mechanism up from – a man would means it is from your father while a woman says it is from your mother.

UNDERGROUND

Underground symbolizes your subconscious – something that is below conscious awareness (ground level).

UNIFORM

Uniforms are a pun on a uniform or unchanging way of thinking. The dream is asking you to change how you think with regard to the subject matter of the dream.

UNIVERSITY

University indicates spirituality and learning about yourself with a view to improving yourself. See school.

UPHILL

Uphill indicates that you feel life is an uphill struggle. It also means you are on the karmic path.

UPSET

Dreaming of you or someone else *upset* shows that you are hurting with regard to the subject matter of the dream.

UPSTAIRS

Upstairs can indicate either your spiritual side or your intellect. Look for other symbols that indicate Spirituality in the same dream. When a dream has a lot of symbols for the heart, the upstairs is often about the intellect. It is very common for dreams to show the cost on your heart because you rationalize all the time (operating from your head).

Walking upstairs can be about activating your spiritual side or your intellect. Again to tell which, you need to look at the other symbols in the same dream.

URINATE

Urinating eliminates waste that would harm the body if kept any longer. In dreams it symbolizes the need to eliminate an issue from the past or a negative influence in the present. For example, to dream of *urinating in the shower* while your partner enters and leaves the shower or bathroom is a request to eliminate the negative influence of your partner leaving you. It can also mean you need to (deal with) eliminate the aspects of the relationship that invade your personal space. To *urinate in the back of a pick up truck* is a request to eliminate the negative influence you picked up from your father (truck) in the past (back of truck).

URINATE

To *urinate* in a dream symbolize elimination. For example, to dream of urinating in the back of a truck asks you to eliminate (urinate) the negative past (back of truck) influence of your father / career (truck)

USA

The *United States of America* indicates an expansion of consciousness. Much of the Western 'New Age' movement has its origins in America. However, America is viewed by many non Americans as a very male oriented society and as such would also indicate being on the karmic path to awareness. This meaning does not hold if you are from the USA.

VACATION

A *vacation* or holiday scene is a request to relax or take a rest. It can be triggered by overworking or getting stressed over an issue. For example, to dream of a vacation in a hot country would indicate you need to rest and allow your body to rejuvenate (sunny country).

VACUUM CLEANER

A *vacuum cleaner* symbolizes your lungs as it is a device that works with air.

A *vacuum cleaner hose* can symbolize your intestines.

VAMPIRE

Vampires have the power of flight and as such they signify the same thing as *flying* in a dream. Since your physical body can not fly it symbolizes being able to project your mind onto others. This is quite useful if you work in marketing or sales but it also has a spiritual dimension. You can use your strong mind to influence how others think and to influence their health. It works along the lines of thinking yourself healthy, but in this case you can think somebody else healthy. This ability is best known from the bible when Jesus heals the centurion's servant without ever seeing him. You are probably wondering why the vampire though. The reason is that while you can heal someone by thinking well of them, you can also negatively affect someone by harboring negative thoughts about them. For those of us without this ability, it is not a problem as our thoughts do not affect others that way. In your case, however, dreaming of a vampire is reminding you that you have a special ability, and right now you are using it in a way that is sucking the life force out of somebody. You should know who it is already, and if you do not, then check how you think in general. Do you see everyone as a jerk and wish bad luck on them? The dream is reminding you of your power and that it is your responsibility to control it, or accept the karmic consequence. Oh yes, and please don't think badly of me for telling you what it means!

VAULT

Vaults, being connected with banks, are about the circulatory system and the heart. In this case the dream is saying you should be less protective of your heart. Do not lock your feelings inside. Share them openly and honestly with yourself and others.

VENTILATION

A *ventilation system* symbolizes your lungs.

VESSEL

Any *vessel* for holding water can symbolize your womb as water represents life.

293

An **unclean vessel** means you do not respect your feminity. Often the cause is being conditioned at a young age to view sex as dirty. This leads to viewing any part of your body that distinguishes gender as unclean or dirty. For example, dirty bottles, a dirty bath tub and a dirty barrel all indicate this.

VINE
Reference to a **vine** in a dream is a pun on something being divine. For example, if you dream of turning on a light that is in the shape of a vine you are being told that your gift of intuition is divine.

VIOLET
.**Violet** is the color of the crown chakra which is associated with spiritual understanding. As such, in dreams it symbolizes spiritual leadership, spiritual teaching and authority in spiritual matters. You are a spiritual teacher. Spiritual teaching works through empowering others to be able to face their own challenges and works through female energy.

VIOLIN
A **violin**, like any musical instrument, symbolizes that you are a channel / medium. You can communicate with spirits.

VOLCANO
A **volcano** symbolizes your lungs as it is a great cavity in the earth. A **smoking volcano** can indicate damage to your lungs due to smoking, or being in a smoky environment.

WAITER
A **waiter serving food or drink** indicates you are a hands-on / spiritual healer. Food is the energy source for the human body and the dream is pointing out that you are a supplier of life-sustaining energy.

WAKE
Attending a **wake** asks you to eliminate the negative influences of either the person whose wake you are attending, a parent or other significant person of the same gender. This influence is holding you back from doing something that will help you develop in a positive way .

To **wake up** in a dream is very positive and symbolizes having your eyes opened to the reality of your life. This is invariably associated with reaching a level of spiritual awareness that puts you on track for achieving your life purpose. To be **woken up** is a request for you to wake yourself up to the spiritual reality of your life.

WALKIE TALKIE
A **walkie talkie** indicates you are clairaudient. Clairaudience is a gift where you literally hear messages from the spirit world. Mostly the messages are heard as lines from songs popping into your head. The segment of the song will repeat over and over making you wonder why you can't get it out of your head. Once you accept it is a message it immediately changes to a line from another song or stops if it is the end of the message. It can also work through hearing lines from movies.

WALL
Walls represent keeping people out of your heart. This is usually due to some early childhood conditioning. In regression I have noticed that this wall is

usually fully built by the age three. As a child we cannot reason and live through expressing our feelings as we experience them. We are also highly tuned to the feelings of those charged with our care. Being in a position where you feel in the way or unloved starts this process off. The first two years are spent in emotional confusion and then the wall building starts.

To *bang your head off a wall* is a warning of stroke. It signifies this as walls are a common symbol for the heart and circulatory system and the dream is coupling it with damage to the head. Stroke is a circulatory problem that damages your head.

A *dividing wall* is also about your heart with the emphasis being on how you separate yourself from others. You have erected a dividing wall between you and your neighbor – literally you and others who are close to you.

Glass walls represent a strong psychic or intuitive ability. Literally you have the ability to see when all others can see is the wall. We don't all see it as glass.

Kitchen or bathroom walls indicate the lining of your intestines. If the paper or plaster is falling off the walls it indicates the lining of your intestines is damaged.

Dirty walls indicate that your colon needs cleansing. Toxins from your colon are getting into your blood stream.

WALLET

A *wallet*, because it usually contains money, represents sharing and therefore your heart. When you take out your wallet to pay for something you give money and get something in return. This give and take represents sharing of feelings.

To dream of a *wallet stolen* means that you don't normally share your feelings and your sense is that it is pointless. Your thinking is along the lines of it doesn't matter what I give I'll get nothing back in return. This is almost certainly due to some past conditioning where you feel this happened .Do people know the real you or only what you choose to show on the surface?

WALLPAPER

Wallpaper indicates the lining of your stomach or intestines particularly if in a kitchen, bathroom or dining room.

Wallpaper falling off a wall indicates damage to the lining of your intestines caused by a condition such as candida albicans.

Anyone *wallpapering* in a dream is a healing agent. They have the same gender as the parent with whom you have issues regarding the subject matter of the dream.

WANDERING

Wandering in a dream signifies you currently have not focus in life with regard to the subject matter of the dream. Set a goal to work through the issues that are holding you in this space.

WAR SCENE

A *war scene* symbolizes conflict either within you or between you and others. It can also symbolize an infection your body is fighting, such as the flu. Quite often the army is German as a pun on germs.

An *underground movement* symbolizes a threat of cancer – a threat that attempts to overthrow the normal order (of your body).

WARD

A *private ward* in hospital asks you to develop your individuality.

WASH BASIN

A wash basin represents your elimination system. The taps symbolize your kidneys and the basin and drain symbolize your liver and bladder.

WASHING MACHINE

In countries where *washing machines* are located in the kitchen they symbolize your stomach. The churning motion of the washing machine is symbolic of the churning nature of your stomach. For other countries the washing machine can represent anxieties – the need to cleanse attitudes (clothes).

WASTE

A *waste pipe* indicates your colon – the waste pipe of your body.

A *waste bin* indicates your elimination system. If full of a food item the dream is asking you to eliminate it from your diet or to seriously cut it down.

WATCH

A *watch* is a symbol of the heart and circulatory system. You are literally being asked to watch yourself. If the watch is worn in an unusual place, such as your leg, it indicates that you have the potential to develop a circulatory problem there. A watch symbolizes this as it is a miniature clock. The connection is between ticking and the English slang usage of *ticker* to mean the heart.

WATER

Water can symbolize your spiritual side or life itself. It has no shape of its own and can assume the shape of anything into which it is placed. How the water is depicted in the dream says something about your spiritual side. Our spiritual side is quite often the most neglected aspect of our nature. Spirituality is expression of the soul and not to be confused with religion. Expression of the soul connects you with life and is your true essence. What gives you expression? Is it writing, poetry, playing musical instruments, dancing, teaching, helping others, etc? Do you know what it is and if you do have you created space for it in your life?

Rain is about letting life in, and being caught in the rain in a dream is very positive. What the rain is hitting can be significant. For example, rain falling onto a car engine asks you to let life into your heart.

A *river* has a natural flow and has carved out its own path over time. This dream is asking you to be like a river and allow your spirituality to flow freely in the direction it must take.

A *lake* is a large body of water with no outlet. You are being asked to create an outlet for your spirituality. It is deeper than you think.

A *canal* is a flow of water whose path is controlled by manmade structures. This indicates that your spirituality is limited by conventional or manmade ideals.

The *sea* is the ultimate body of water. This dream can be about life or your spiritual life. Other symbols in the dream will refine the subject matter.

Shallow water indicates that despite what you may think you still have room to deepen your spiritual side.

Watching others *jump into water* is a

request to jump into life or develop your spiritual gifts.

A *swimming pool* is a body of water contained by four sides. This indicates that you completely limit your spiritual expression or flow of life.

Polluted water symbolizes toxins in your blood stream. These dreams will usually indicate what foods or drinks are causing the toxins to get there. You are being asked to cut them down or cut them out altogether.

Water running down the walls or from the ceiling of a house or building is indicative of your body being dehydrated. This is common particularly if you were drinking alcohol the night before.

Soapy water hitting your back is a request to cleanse something from your past. Deal with it and let it go.

WAVE
Waves usually indicate difficulties in life. For example, sailing a boat that is getting knocked by waves. The boat trip represents your life journey and the waves are symbolic of events or emotions that are causing ups and downs in your life. If a boat with two men in it is getting knocked into a cliff by the waves, it means that an event involving your father (men) when you were age two (two men) in your past (behind you), knocked you to the extent that you began rationalizing (cliff) everything in life (water).

WEDDING
Weddings represent uniting male and female aspects of yourself and also commonly indicate you are a channel – you can communicate with spirits.

WEEDS
Weeds indicate a progressive health illness, such as cancer.

WHALE
A *whale* symbolizes channeling in a dream. A channel is someone who can communicate directly with spirits and Angels. Whales mean this because they are mammals, as are humans, but they live in the ocean. In dreams the ocean represents spirituality, so here we have an air breathing mammal that has adapted enough to travel into the spirit world. The type of whale involved is not important, although it is almost always *killer whales* that show up in dreams. In this context, the killer portion of the name shows the fear the dreamer has with regard to talking with *the dead*. Also their strong black and white color would indicate a difficulty the dreamer has with regard to accepting spiritual communication. In essence they must overcome their black and white attitude that tells them things are either good or evil. When you have this attitude it is difficult to open your mind to something new. This could be due to religious doctrine.

WHEEL
Wheels represent your heart due to their circular shape. Here circular is a pun on circulation system where the wheel's circular movement symbolizes your blood circulating around your body.

Wheel lug nuts indicate your lymph system. Lug nuts keep the wheel safely on the car. The lymph system drains the bloodstream.

A *big wheel* or *Ferris wheel* can also symbolize your heart but is also likely to be about being caught on a karmic cycle. This is where you have failed to repay your karmic debts in a previous life and have the potential to miss the opportunities presented to you in this life also.

WHEELCHAIR

A *wheelchair* indicates you repress your feelings. Literally when it comes to expression of feelings (wheel) you are handicapped.

WHITE

White symbolizes hope, faith, purity, perfection, confidence and enlightenment.

To dream of *white alone* can indicate you strive for perfection to such an extent that you are rarely impressed with your own efforts as it is almost impossible to reach the exceptionally high standard you set for yourself. For example, if you were to begin painting you would be overly critical of your first attempts because they are not good enough to hang in a museum. White in this context indicates a proud, rigid, judgmental immaturity - a 'should be', controlling attitude. While you are hard on yourself you are also hard on others as it is unlikely they will reach your standard either. Dreams point this out in an effort to get you to realize your controlling nature so that you be easier on yourself. Do not start by trying to be easier on others, as when you slip at this, you will be even more critical of yourself because you did not reach that goal on your first attempt either. When you ease up on yourself and become more tolerant, that will eventually spill over onto others and they will benefit. The dream invariably shows you where this part of your nature began.

White mixed or associated with other colors purifies and refines their meaning. To dream of navy with white is an attempt to heal your negative philosophy of life (navy) by giving you faith and confidence in the future.

The *soft white* or *pearl white* associated with a crystal ball indicates the gift of prophesy. This is not a very common gift so look for other symbols to confirm this.

WIELDING

Wielding indicates a strong male approach to life or the subject matter of the dream. You act without listening to your heart. You need to restore the balance between male and female aspects of yourself. Female energy allows you to forgive, listen, have two-way communication, lead and more.

WIG

A *wig* indicates someone is pretending about how they think with regard to the subject matter of the dream.

A *blonde wig* indicates a sham. Someone who pretends to have purity of thought but in reality has ulterior motives.

WINDOW

Windows give you a view from a house and as such can represent your eyes, your viewpoint or your outlook in a dream.

The room the window is in, or where it looks out to is significant. For example a *bedroom window* can represent outlook on your sexual identity. A *kitchen window* can represent your general outlook, if that is the room you normally sit in with a close friend when they visit, and you share a cup of tea or coffee. A *window looking out to the front* of the house can be about your outlook on the future. A *window looking out to the back* of the house or back garden can be your outlook on the past. A *narrow window* looking onto the back garden indicates you have a restrictive view on the past or a restricted outlook due to your past. These dreams ask you to improve your view as a way of dealing with the other issues in the dream. Don't just choose to see what you want. Life will be better if you can let go of this.

Unusually large windows on a house indicate you are psychic / intuitive.

A *bay window*, particularly if it is in your mother's house, represents the womb. Houses represent the body and here you are symbolically in a location in your mother's body (her house) which extends out to the front – the womb. The dream is showing you how you are still affected today by something from way back in the past. Because these dreams are about being born they often include symbols that indicate something precious you brought with you on this life journey. It is something that for you gives expression of your soul and connects you to life.

If a dream refers to a room or vehicle with *no windows* it is again about being in the womb. The smallest place you have every been with no view of the world.

WIRING
Wiring indicates your nervous system.

WOMAN
A *woman* in your dreams can represent a number of things. She can represent the woman herself, your mother, your female side - emotions, a guide, a heal-

ing agent or an aspect of yourself. If the woman is helpful and supportive she is a healing agent. She is called a healing agent because her purpose is to heal issues with the parent of the same gender - mother. She heals this symbolically by acting the opposite way to how mother was in reality. To indicate an issue at a specific age you may dream of a number of women behind you. For example, to dream of three women behind you indicates you picked up issues from your mother at age 3.

If the *woman* has a title, speaks with authority or offers a gift she is a guide / angel. Guides often take up a position just to your right or slightly elevated. A guide is the only infallible character in a dream. They commonly demonstrate their purpose by action rather than speaking. However, if they do speak always heed their advice.

If the *woman* is someone you know but do not have a direct relationship with, it is often to show you that you have the same trait that they are displaying in the dream or that they have in reality. For example, if the trait is confidence, the dream is attempting to boost your confidence with regard to the subject matter of the dream. It could also be a negative trait. If the person is always angry, it shows that you too have this trait and you are being asked to acknowledge it and eliminate it.

If the *woman* is your partner the dream is about your relationship and it is likely that all other events and symbols in the dream are a comment on it.

It is very common for a *woman* to stand in for your mother. In this case, like earlier, she is likely to be either healing an issue with your mother, or to demonstrate a trait that you picked up from her. Usually the dream is asking you to eliminate this trait, as it is affecting you negatively with regard to the subject matter of the dream.

Women can also represent expression of feelings, as your heart is governed by female energy. In fact difficulty with emotional expression is often connected to issues with your mother, as it is through her unconditional love that we learn to love ourselves and stay in touch with our hearts. If this was lacking from your mother it will show up in your dreams. If mother put a price on her love you may dream of a *woman sitting at a cash register*.

A *dead woman* indicates that you are emotionally dead or cold. The dream is showing you this so that you may work on the issue and breathe new life into your heart.

A *woman* can also represent your female side. If you are *having sex with a woman* in your dream you are being asked to get intimately in touch with your female side. This is regardless of your gender. Your female side governs your philosophy of life, inner world, feelings, compassion and various spiritual gifts. If any of these are lacking, your dreams will encourage you to discover that aspect of yourself.

WOOD

Wood, and anything made from it, symbolizes your colon due to the brown color. Most often a wooden table is the feature of these dreams.

Rotting wood indicates the threat of cancer of your colon.

A *wood* or forest also symbolizes your colon due to dirt trails through it.

WOODEN
See Wood.

WOODLOUSE
A *woodlouse* symbolizes problems with your digestive system. The blend of what you are putting into your body is allowing harmful bacteria and toxins (bugs) to develop in your colon. It is common in these dreams for the woodlouse to be crawling across a wooden floor.

WORKPLACE
A *workplace* symbolizes your work in a dream.

WORMS
Worms indicate cancer or a threat of cancer.

WRITER
To dream of a *writer* or *poet* means you have a creative writing ability and you are being asked to use this in your life, as a means of connecting with your inner core. Through writing, you will find your distinctive style of expression, and expand your understanding of yourself. For example, to dream of writing mathematical equations would mean that through the deduction process engaged in while you write, you will expand your awareness of yourself.

WRITING
You have a creative *writing* ability. See *writer*.

X-RAY
An *X-Ray* indicates that you have the gift of psychic surgery. This is an unusual gift, so look for it in more than one dream to be sure. Psychic surgery

is practiced a lot in the Philippines. It has two forms. One is where you place your hands physically inside a client you are working on and remove cancers, growths and blockages. In the second form you place your hands on the client just as you would for hands-on healing. In this form, in addition to healing energy flowing into the client, it will also feel like spirit hands are working inside the client's body directly under your hands. It literally feels like the clients skin under your hands is being massaged from underneath.

XYLOPHONE

A *xylophone*, like any musical instrument, symbolizes that you are a channel / medium. You can communicate with spirits. The pun on *phone* reinforces your communication ability.

YELLOW

Normal Yellow represents your usual reaction to the subject matter of the dream showing that you rationalize at the expense of your feelings.

If *yellow* is brought by a healing agent, a supportive, helpful character in the dream, it means you have difficulty rationalizing or are timid with regard to the subject matter of the dream. The healing agent brings yellow to help you rationalize your fears. An irrational fear, like a fear of spiders, has no basis and never helps you in life.

Muddy or mustard yellow also indicates that you have a difficulty rationa-

lizing with regard to the subject matter of the dream.

If a guide wears or brings *pure bright yellow* then you have an intuitive or enlightened intellect - yellow (intellect) plus white (enlightenment). You are being asked to use this to gain an enlightened perspective on the subject matter of the dream. To dream of pure bright yellow on its own is also sufficient to indicate you have this ability.

Y-JUNCTION

Like a T-junction a *Y-Junction* or *fork* in the road symbolizes a choice you have to make, but in this case the choice is not too dramatic. You only have to change your direction slightly and might not even have to slow down to do so. Therefore the choice should not be too difficult

Road junctions symbolize choices ahead. A *Y-Junction* also indicates change but does not require you to change direction as much. The new direction will only be subtly different from your current course.

ZEBRA

A *zebra* being black and white indicates that you have a tendency to see the subject matter of the dream in black and white terms. This comes across as being intolerant or extremist. You see others are either with you or against you. There is no neutral position allowed. You need to be more tolerant.

Symbol Index

U

V

W

X

Y

Z

Further Reading

Dreams Secret Language of the Soul
by
George Rhatigan
(Currently out of print, but try to get your hands on it!)

The Grand Design
by
Patrick Francis (Paddy McMahon)

A Free Spirit
by
Patrick Francis (Paddy McMahon)

Cutting The Ties That Bind
by
Phyllis Krystal

What You Will Find on the Website

www.HowToInterpretYourDreams.com

- ▶ Hundreds of pages on dream interpretation
- ▶ An automated program to help you interpret your dreams
- ▶ An extensive dream symbol reference
- ▶ An integrated journal to let your record and index your dreams
- ▶ Suggested therapies to help you deal with issues you discover from your dreams
- ▶ Podcasts of interviews with Michael Sheridan
- ▶ Schedules of courses and talks by Michael
- ▶ Updates / errata on this book

Log on today!

www.HowToInterpretYourDreams.com

Notes

Notes

Notes

Notes

Notes

Notes